CONSUMER BEHAVIOUR

CONSUMER BEHAVIOUR

Vishwajeet Prasad

genNEXT Publication

Consumer Behaviour

Rs. 890

ISBN: 978-81-908675-7-3

Published in 2009 in India by
Gennext Publication
23 Main Ansari Road, Darya Ganj,
New Delhi-110002
E-Mail:GenNextpublication@hotmail.com
Phone: 23282060

Printed at: Singhal Print Media, Delhi

Contents

Preface *ix*

1. **Consumer Behaviour and Marketing Action** **1**
Consumer Behaviour, Customers Versus Consumers, Consumer Motives, Motives Influencing Purchase Decision, Nature of Motive Purchase Decision, Need for Study of Consumer Behaviour, Importance in Day to Day Life, Pertinence to Decision Making, Organizational Buyer versus Individual Buyer

2. **Consumer Involvement** **7**
Causes of Consumer Involvement, Personal Factors, Product Factors, Situational Factors, Types of Involvement, Situational Involvement, Enduring Involvement, Effects of Consumer Involvement, Stages in Processing of Information, Models regarding Consumer Involvement, Low Involvement Learning Model, Learn-Feel-Do Hierarchy Model, High Involvement/High Thinking, High Involvement/High Feeling, Low Involvement/Low Feeling, Low Involvement/Low Thinking, Level of Message Processing Model, Product versus Brand Involvement Model

3. **Consumer Decision Making Process** **15**
Stages in Decision Making Process, Rules Regarding Consumer Decision, Levels of Consumer Decision Making

4. **Consumer Behaviour and Marketing Implications** **19**
Consumer Behaviour and Marketing Strategies, Consumer Behaviour and Marketing Segmentation, Consumer Behaviour and Product Positioning, Consumer Behaviour and Marketing Research, Consumer Behaviour and Non-Profit and Societal Marketing, Consumer Behaviour and Governmental Decision Making

5. **Consumer Behaviour Models** **23**
Economic or Marshallian Model, Disposable Personal Income, Learning or Pavlovian Model, Psychoanalytical Model, Sociological Model, Howard-Sheth Model, Nicosia Model, Summary

6. Cultural & Environmental Influences on Consumer Behaviour **33**

Introduction, Culture -Meaning, Characteristics of Culture, Types of Culture, Hofstede's Five Dimensions of Culture, Cultural Influences, Variation in Cultural Values, Subcultures and Consumer Behaviour, Cross Cultural Consumer Behaviour, Cross Cultural Marketing: Objectives and Policies, Problems in Cross Cultural Marketing, Cross-Cultural Consumer Analysis, Tangible Benefits of Global Brand Building, Strategic Implications, Cultural Variations & Non-Verbal Communication, Time, Space, Friendship, Agreements, Things, Symbols and Colours, Symbol of Numbers

7. Groups, Social Class & Reference Groups **51**

Introduction, Meaning of Group, Types of Groups, Consumer-Relevant Groups, The Family, Friendship Groups, Formal Social Groups, Shopping Groups, Consumer Action Groups, Work Groups, Social Class, Characteristics of the Social Classes, Reference Groups, Broadening Concept of the Reference Group, Types of Reference Groups, Factors Affecting Reference Group Influence, Information and Experience, Credibility, Attractiveness, and Power of the Reference Group, Conspicuousness of the Product, Reference Group Impact on Product and Brand Choice, Reference Groups and Consumer Conformity, Benefits of the Reference Group Appeal, Increased Brand Awareness, Reduced Perceived Risk

8. Family Influences & Decision Making **65**

Introduction, The Family, Meaning of a Family, Meaning of Household, Structural Variables Affecting Families and Households, Sociological Variables Affecting Families and Households, Functions of the Family, Family Life Cycles, Characteristics, Young Singles, Newly Married Couples, Full Nest I, Full Nest II, Full Nest III, Married, No Kids, Older Singles, Empty Nest I, Empty Nest II, Solitary Survivor, Retired Solitary Survivor, Decision-Making in a Family, Role Behaviour, Individual Roles in Family Purchases, Family Roles, Key Family Consumption Roles, Influencing Spouses and Resolving Consumer Conflicts, Children, Teenagers and Post Teens, Family marketing, Influences on the Decision Process, Influence by Decision Stage, Influence of employment, Influence of Gender

9. Opinion Leadership & Diffusion of Innovations **79**

Opinion Leadership, Meaning, Characteristics of Opinion Leaders, A Profile of Opinion Leaders, Frequency and Overlap of Opinion, Interpersonal Flow of Communication, Opinion Leadership and the Firm's Marketing Strategy, Diffusion of Innovations, Diffusion, The

Diffusion Process, Influence of Product Characteristics on diffusion, Classification of Adopters, Innovators, Early Adopters, Early Majority, Late Majority, Laggards, Non Adopter Categories, Role of Personal Influence, Market Strategy Related to Diffusion, Diffusion Enhancement Strategies

10. Consumer Behaviour Applications & Consumerism 95
Strategic Market Planning, Types of Marketing Strategies, Meaning, Marketing Segmentation, Developing a Target Market Strategy, Positioning, Product Positioning Strategy, Product Positioning Process, Perceptual Mapping, Marketing Communication, Review, Importance of Marketing Communication, Marketing Communication through Products, Price-Status, Store Choice & Shopping Behaviour, Consumer Outlet Selection, Consumer Shopping Behaviour, Stages of the Consumer Buying Process, Purchase Timing Behaviour, In-store Stimuli, Store Image and Loyalty, In-store Choice, Behaviour Basis, Tying them Together, Store Loyalty, Consumerism, History, Consumerism in India, Consumer Rights, Summary

11. The Borderless Consumer Market and Buying Behaviour 135
Introduction, The Borderless Consumer Market, Buyer - An Enigma, Internet User Profile, Internet Influencing the Consumer Behaviour

12. Consumer Buying Habits and Perceptions of Emerging Non-store Choices 145
Introduction, Importance of Consumer Perception, Formation of Perceptions, Marketer's Concern, Consumer Perceptions in the Service Sector

13. Research and Applications of Responses to Direct Marketing Approaches 151
Introduction, Direct Marketing, Research and Database Development, Characteristics of a Good Database, Direct Marketing Mix, Communication Programme, Customer Service, Timing and Sequencing, The Research Process, Scales Used to Measure the Attitude of the Customers in the Customer Intelligence System, Tools for Data Collection, Future of Direct Marketing in India and the Consumer Behaviour

14. Issues of Privacy and Ethics 167
Consumer Privacy, Ethics in Business and its Relevance to Consumer Behaviour, Ethics is not a Matter of Choice, Ethics from the Top, Ethics: A Journey, Ethical Purchasing, Understanding Buying Ethically, Shopping Tips for the Ethical Shopper, Deviant Consumer Behaviour,

Fraudulent Consumer Behaviour, Ethically Questionable Consumer Behaviour, Benefiting from Illegal Activity

15. The Psychology of Marketing **175**

Introduction, Methods in Consumer Research, Culture and Subculture, Demographics, Segmentation, Targeting, and Positioning, Information Search and Decision Making, Families and Family Decision Making, Group Influences, Perception, Learning and Memory, Diffusion of Innovation, Attitudes, E-Commerce, Economics of Electronic Commerce, Selling Online is Usually More Expensive, Issues in Web Site Design, Web Site Traffic Generation, Search Engine Optimization, Organizational Buyers

16. Consumer Buying Behaviour **235**

Consumer Decision-Making, Group/Social Variables impacting Buying Behaviour, Reference Groups, Ethnicity - Culture/Sub culture, Individual/Psychological Variables Impacting Buying Behaviour, Learning, Attitude, Perception, Risk, Organizational Buying Behaviour, Organizational Decision-Making, Group/Social Variables that Impact Organizational Buying Behaviour, Individual/Psychological Variables that Impact Organizational Buying Behaviour, Customer Relationship Management (CRM)

17. Consumer Psychology **245**

Consumer Research Methods, Primary and Secondary Research Methods, Culture and Subculture, Dealing with Culture , Warning about Stereotyping , Cultural Lessons, Cultural Characteristics as a Continuum , Hofstede's Dimensions , High vs. Low Context Cultures, Ethnocentrism and the Self-reference Criterion, Language Issues, Demographics, Segmentation, Targeting, and Positioning , Information Search and Decision Making, Families and Family Decision Making, Family Decision Making, Group Influences, Perception, Factors in Perception, Learning and Memory, Vicarious Learning, Diffusion of Innovation, Attitudes, Beliefs, Affect, Behavioral Intention, Attitude-Behavior Consistency, Attitude Change Strategies, One-sided vs. Two-sided Appeals , The Elaboration Likelihood Model (ELM) and Celebrity Endorsements, Appeal Approaches, Economics of Electronic Commerce, Issues in Web Site Design, Web Site Traffic Generation, Search Engine Optimization, Search Engine Rankings, Types of Search Engines, Text Optimization, Link Optimization, Organizational Buyers

Bibliography **301**

Index **309**

Preface

Consumer behaviour pertains to the buying behavior of the Consumer including the family, household or individual. The consumer market refers to the individual consumption of final consumers. There are mainly four features affecting the consumer in their buying decision. First factor is cultural, including insight of the consumers, subculture- set of people who share valued founded on common life, and social class- member who shares similar values.

Second is the social factor including groups-membership, aspirational and reference, family- family members, and social roles and status.

The third factor is personal factor. These are age and life cycle, occupation, economics situation, lifestyle, and personal and self concept.

The fourth factor is psychological factor. These are motivation- a need that is sufficient pressing to direct to seek satisfaction of the need, perception- the process by which people select, organize, and interpret the information to form of meaningful picture of the word.

This volume presents complete treatment of the subject with numerous examples. It emphasizes on consumer decision making and intelligibly explains all the five stages; problem recognition, information search, and evaluation of alternatives, purchase and post-purchase behaviour.

It also clearly enlightens outlet selection and purchase. The external environment and its influence on deciding factors are also highlighted. These external environmental factors are demographical, political, cultural and technological factors. Also along with these factors, the internal factors, i.e., attitudes, personality, beliefs, memory and values have also been discussed in detail. Different marketing strategies and marketing implications have been added. Changing consumer behaviour has also been discussed in detail.

Modern-day developments like net-consumer behaviour have also been discussed. Relevant examples, charts and tables are additional highlights of this book. With its lucid style and organized approach, this volume would be exceedingly useful for students of consumer behaviour. Consultants and professional persons would also find this text to be a priceless reference source.

A valuable source of knowledge for all students, teachers, consultants and lay person who are interested in gaining knowledge of consumer behaviour.

1

Consumer Behaviour and Marketing Action

Consumer behaviour is comparatively a new field of study which has evolved just after the Second World War. The sellers market has disappeared and buyers market has come up. This led to paradigm shift of the manufacturer's attention from product to consumer and specially focused on the consumer behaviour.

The evaluation of marketing concept from mere selling concept to consumer- oriented marketing has resulted into buyer behaviour becoming an independent discipline. The growth of consumerism and consumer legislation emphasizes the importance that is given to the consumer.

Consumer behaviour is a study of how individuals make decision to spend their available resources (time, money and effort) or consumption related aspects (What they buy? When they buy?, How they buy? etc.). The heterogeneity among people makes understanding consumer behaviour a challenging task to marketers.

Hence marketers felt the need to obtain an in-depth knowledge of consumers buying behaviour. Finally this knowledge acted as an imperative tool in the hands of marketers to forecast the future buying behaviour of customers and devise four marketing strategies in order to create long term customer relationship.

CONSUMER BEHAVIOUR

It is mainly the study of individuals, or organizations and the processes consumers use to search, select, use and dispose of products, services, experience, or ideas to satisfy needs and its impact on the consumer and the society.

CUSTOMERS VERSUS CONSUMERS

The term 'customer' is specific in terms of brand, company, or shop. It refers to person who customarily or regularly purchases particular brand, purchases a particular company's product, or purchases from a particular shop. Thus a person who shops at Bata Stores or who uses Raymonds clothing is a customer of these firms. Whereas the 'consumer' is a person who generally engages in the activities -search, select, use and dispose of products, services, experience, or ideas.

CONSUMER MOTIVES

Consumer has a motive for purchasing a particular product. Motive may be a strong feeling, urge, instinct, desire or emotion that makes the buyer to make a decision to buy. Buying motives thus are defined as 'those influences or considerations which provide the impulse to buy, induce action or determine choice in the purchase of goods or service. These motives are generally controlled by economic, social, psychological influences etc.

MOTIVES INFLUENCING PURCHASE DECISION

The buying motives may be classified into two categories:

i. Product Motives

ii. Patronage Motives

NATURE OF MOTIVE PURCHASE DECISION

- Desire for money: Purchasing when price falls down
- Vanity: Getting costly Items, to be admired by others
- Fear: Purchasing Insurance policy
- Pride: Purchasing premium products
- Fashion: Rural people imitate urban
- Possession: purchasing antiques
- Health: Purchasing health foods .membership in health clubs
- Comfort: Purchasing micro-oven, washing machine, mixy
- Love and affection: Purchasing gift items

i. Product Motives: Product motives may be defined as those impulses, desires and considerations which make the buyer purchase a product. These may still be classified on the basis of nature of satisfaction:

a. Emotional Product Motives: Emotional Product Motives are those impulses which persuade the consumer on the basis of his emotion. The buyer does not try to reason out or logically analyse the need for purchase. He makes a buying to satisfy pride, sense of ego, urge to initiate others, and his desire to be unique.

b. Rational Product Motives: Rational Product Motives are defined as those impulses which arise on the basis of logical analysis and proper evaluation. The buyer makes rational decision after chief evaluation of the purpose, alternatives available, cost benefit, and such valid reasons.

ii. Patronage Motives: Patronage motives may be defined as consideration or impulses which persuade the buyer to patronage specific shops. Just like product motives patronage can also be grouped as emotional and rational.

Emotional Patronage Motives those that persuade a customer to buy from specific shops, without any logical reason behind this action. He may be subjective for shopping in his favourite place. Rational Patronage Motives are those which arise when selecting a place depending on the buyer satisfaction that it offers a wide selection, it has latest models, offers good after-sales service etc. Knowledge of buyer motives of consumers is useful for marketers to anticipate market trends and formulate effective marketing strategies.

NEED FOR STUDY OF CONSUMER BEHAVIOUR

The study of consumer behaviour helps everybody as all are consumers. It is essential for marketers to understand consumers to survive and succeed in these competitive marketing environment. The following reasons highlight the importance of studying consumer behaviour as a discipline.

IMPORTANCE IN DAY TO DAY LIFE

The purpose of studying a discipline is to help oneself to better appreciate its contributions. The reason to study consumer behaviour is because of the role it plays in the lives of humans. Most of the free time is spent in the market place, shopping or engaging in other activities. The extra time is usually passed in knowing and thinking about products and services, discussing with friends about them, and watching advertisements related to them. The usage of them significantly reveals our life styles. All these reasons suggest the need for study. However, the purpose may be to attend immediate and tangible reasons.

PERTINENCE TO DECISION MAKING

Consumer behaviour is said to be an applied discipline as some decisions are significantly affected by their behaviour or expected actions. The two perspectives that seek application of its knowledge are micro and societal perspectives.

The micro perspectives involve understanding the consumer for the purpose of helping a firm or organization to achieve its objectives. The people involved in this field try to understand consumers in order to be more effective at their tasks. Whereas the societal or macro perspective applies knowledge of consumers to aggregate-level faced by mass or society as a whole. The behaviour of consumer has significant influence on the quality and level of the standard of living.

ORGANIZATIONAL BUYER VERSUS INDIVIDUAL BUYER

The obvious difference between industrial or institutional markets and consumer markets is that, instead of purchases being made for individual consumption industrial markets are made for business use. There are several factors that differentiate consumer markets and their buying behaviour from organizational market and their buying behaviour. The key factors of that differentiation are:

i. Market Structure and Demand: The distinguishing factors of market structure and demand are as follows: In organizations buyers are more geographically concentrated than consumer markets. Organizational buyers are few in number but they are bulk buyers compared to individual buyers. Organizational buyer markets are either vertical or horizontal. In vertical structures they cater only one or two industries, whereas in horizontal structure the buyer base is too broad. Organizational demand is derived from consumer demand. The nature of the demand is fluctuational and inelastic.

ii. Buyer Characteristics: The distinguishing factors of buyer characteristics are as follows: Many individuals or group involvement is seen in decision making process. Organizational buyers are quite knowledgeable and professional. The buying motive is mostly rational than individual buyer.

iii. Decision Process and Buying Patterns: The major differences are as follows: In organizational buying lot of formalities like proposals, quotations, procedures are to be followed unlike consumer buying. Decision process is much complex with high financial risk, technical aspects, multiple influencing factors etc. Organizational buying requires more extensive negotiation over larger time period than consumer buying.

Note: Colonial Group (Colonial) is a privately-held company. It acts as a holding company for various subsidiaries which provide storage and distribution services for liquid and dry bulk products, including bulk chemicals, motor fuels, industrial fuel oil, and retail gas. The company through its subsidiaries also provides ship bunkering, commercial shipping, and tug and barge services. It primarily operates in the US and Puerto Rico. Colonial is headquartered in Savannah, Georgia and employs about 1,100 people. For detailed information related to this chapter reader can visit www.colonialgroupinc.com

2

Consumer Involvement

Some consumers are characterized as being more involved in products and shopping than others. A consumer who is highly involved with a product would be interested in knowing a lot about it before purchasing. Hence he reads brochures thoroughly, compares brands and models available at different outlets, asks questions, and looks for recommendations. Thus consumer involvement can be defined as state of awareness that motivates consumers to seek out, attend to, and think about product information prior to purchase.

CAUSES OF CONSUMER INVOLVEMENT

The factors that influences consumer involvement include personal, product and situational.

PERSONAL FACTORS

Self-concept, needs, and values are the three personal factors that influence the extent of consumer involvement in a product or service. The more product image, the value symbolism inherent in it and the needs it serves are fitting together with the consumer self-image, values and needs, the more likely the consumer is to feel to be involved in it. Celebrities for example share a certain self-image, certain values, and certain needs. They tend to use products and services that reflect their life style. They get highly involved in purchasing prestigious products like designer wear, imported cars, health care products etc.

PRODUCT FACTORS

The consumer involvement grows as the level of perceived risk in the purchase of a good or service increases. It is likely that consumers will feel more involved in the purchase of their house than in the purchase of tooth paste, it is a more riskier purchase. Product differentiation affects involvement. The involvement increases as the number of alternatives that they have to choose from increases. This may be due to the fact that consumers feel variety which means greater risk. The pleasure one gets by using a product or service can also influence involvement. Some products are a greater source of pleasure to the consumer than others. Tea and coffee have a high level of hedonic (pleasure) value compared to, say household cleaners. Hence the involvement is high. Involvement increases when a product gains public attention. Any product that is socially visible or that is consumed in public, demands high involvement. For example, involvement in the purchase of car is more than the purchase of household items.

SITUATIONAL FACTORS

The situation in which the product is brought or used can generate emotional involvement. The reason for purchase or purchase occasion affects involvement. For example, buying a pair of socks for yourself is far less involved than buying a gift for a close friend. Social pressure can significantly increase involvement. One is likely to be more self conscious about the products and brands one looks at when shopping with friends than when shopping alone. The need to make a fast decision also influences involvement. A consumer who needs a new refrigerator and sees a 'one-day-only sale' at an appliances retailer does not have the time to shop around and compare different brands and prices. The eminence of the decision heightens involvement. The involvement is high when the decision is irrevocable, for example when the retailer does not accept return or exchange on the sale items. Thus involvement may be from outside the individual, as with situational involvement or from with in the individual as with enduring involvement. It can be induced by a host of personal-product-and situation related factors, many of which can be controlled by the marketer. It affects the ways in which consumers see, process, and send information to others.

TYPES OF INVOLVEMENT

The two types of involvement are:

a. Situation

b. Enduring

Involvement has various facets of consumer behaviour such as search for information, information processing, and information transmission.

SITUATIONAL INVOLVEMENT

Situational involvement is temporary and refers to emotional feelings of a consumer, experiences in a particular situation when one thinks of about a specific product.

ENDURING INVOLVEMENT

Enduring involvement is persistent over time and refers to feelings experienced toward a product category across different situations. For example, holiday-makers renting a resort for their trip are highly involved in their choice, but their involvement is temporary. Whereas involvement of a person whose hobby is bike racing endures overtime and affects his responses in any situation related to pre-purchase, purchase and post-purchase of sport bikes. It is observed that involvement is triggered by special situation in the case of holiday makers, but in the second case, in comes from, and is a part of the consumer. The contrast between situational and enduring involvement is important. When marketers measure involvement they examine the extent to which it can be induced by the product or selling situation. After noticing the type of involvement they are facing, marketers work to control products or selling situations.

EFFECTS OF CONSUMER INVOLVEMENT

Involvement with the product makes consumers process product-related information more readily. This information is processed thoroughly, hence, it is retained for a long-time. Because of this the consumers become emotionally high and tend to engage in extended problem solving and word-of-mouth communications. These result into three categories: search for information, processing information, and information transmission.

Customers who are highly involved tend to search for information and shop around more when compared with the customers having low involvement. For example, the customer who is highly involved with cars and thinks about buying it is likely to gather information. He sees for alternative models to figure the advantages and disadvantages of each.

The more they are involved, the more they learn about the alternatives within that category. To gather the information they use various sources. One such behaviour is to shop around, where they visit various outlets and talk to sales people. The customers of this kind should be encouraged buy retailers to visit the outlets to know, and compare various models to meet information needs.

STAGES IN PROCESSING OF INFORMATION

Processing of information means depth of comprehension, extent of cognitive elaboration, and the extent of emotional arousal of information as discussed below.

Depth of Comprehension

Highly involved customers tend to process product information at deeper levels of understanding than the ones with low involvement. For example educated parents in urban areas are highly involved in baby food purchase decisions than rural uneducated parents. They also retain this information for long time. In this case marketers need to provide information cues to help the consumers to retrieve information from memory. But when the target is low involvement consumers, marketers should make the necessary information as accessible as possible at the time of selection and buying of the product.

Extent of Cognitive Elaboration

Highly involved customers think more about product choices than consumers with low involvement. Their deep understanding involves support arguments and/or counter arguments. That is, highly involved consumers tend to generate cognitive responses either in support of the product information or against the information provided by the marketers. If we talk of the previous example, marketing baby food products, the product all though effective may have significant side effects like obesity. Educated parents are likely to give this the great deal of thought before giving it to their children. To ensure that the parents generate positive thoughts, the marketers have to mention a quality argument that the product benefits outweigh its negative effects. If the arguments are less informed and not persuasive, it is likely to produce negative thoughts resulting in an unfavourable attitude towards the product.

Level of Emotional Arousal

Highly involved consumers are more emotional than less involved consumers. The highly involved react more strongly to the product-related information which may act for or against marketers. This is because the negative interpretation is likely to be exaggerated more number of times causing the customers to reject the product.

Information Transmission

Transmission of information is the extent to which greatly involved customers send information about the product to others. This is done usually through word of-mouth communication. The researchers have shown that if consumers are highly involved they talk about the product frequently than others.

Satisfied consumers are likely to speak favourable about the product, while unsatisfied speak negatively. Therefore, marketers catering to highly involved consumers should attempt to enhance consumer satisfaction and decrease dissatisfaction. For example, customer happy with ONIDA television communicates the same to others through word-of-mouth.

MODELS REGARDING CONSUMER INVOLVEMENT

There are four prominent models of consumer behaviour based on involvement which help marketers in making strategic decision particularly in marketing communication related strategies. The four models are as follows.

LOW INVOLVEMENT LEARNING MODEL

Low Involvement products are those which are at low risk, by virtue of being inexpensive, and repeatedly used by consumers. Marketers try to sell the products without changing the attitudes of consumers.

New product beliefs replace old brand perceptions. Marketers achieve low-involvement learning through proper positioning. For example, writing pen with the 'uninterrupted flow', and tooth paste with 'mouth wash' positioning attracts new consumers.

LEARN-FEEL-DO HIERARCHY MODEL

Buying decisions vary according to the way they are taken. Some decisions are taken with lot of thinking, others are taken with great feelings. Some are made through force of habit and others are made consciously. The learn-feel-do hierarchy is simple matrix that attributes consumer choice to information (learn), attitude (feel), and behaviour (do) issues.

The matrix has four quadrants, each specifying a major marketing communication goal to be informative, to be effective, to be habit forming, or promote self-satisfaction. Thinking and feeling are shown as a continuum -some decisions involve one or the other and many involve elements of both. High and low importance is also represented as a continuum.

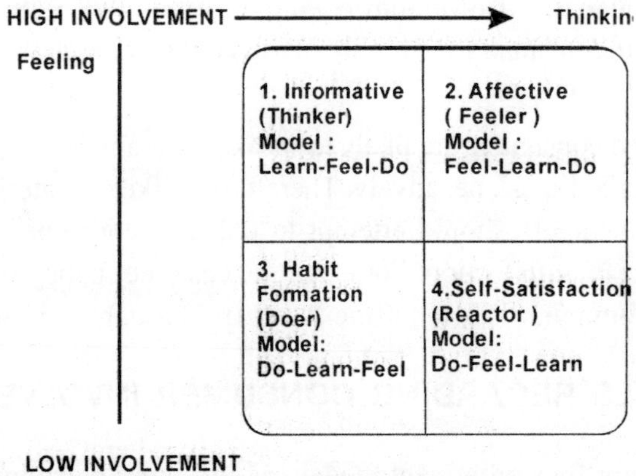

HIGH INVOLVEMENT/HIGH THINKING

Purchases in first quadrant require more information, both because of the importance of the product to the consumer and thinking issues related to the purchases. Major purchases such as cars, houses and other expensive and infrequently buying items come under this category. The strategy model is learn-feel-do. Marketers have to furnish full information to get consumer acceptance of the product.

HIGH INVOLVEMENT/HIGH FEELING

The purchase decisions in second quadrant involve low amount of information than feeling. Typical purchases tied to self-esteem-jewellery, apparel, cosmetics and accessories come under this category. The strategy model is feel-learn do. To encourage purchases marketers must approach customers with emotion and appeal.

LOW INVOLVEMENT/LOW FEELING

The purchases in this quadrant are motivated primarily by the need to satisfy personal tastes, many of which are influenced by self-image. Products like news paper, soft drinks, Liquor etc., fall under this category. Group influences often lead to the purchase of these items. The strategy model is do-feel-learn. It helps marketers to promote products through reference groups and other social factors.

LOW INVOLVEMENT/LOW THINKING

It involves less in thinking and more of habitual buying. Products like stationery, groceries, food etc., fall under this category. Over a period of time any product can fall in this segment. The role of information is to differentiate any 'point of difference' from competitors. Brand loyalty may result simply from the habit. The strategy model is do-learn-feel. It suggests that marketers induce trial through various sales promotion techniques.

LEVEL OF MESSAGE PROCESSING MODEL

Consumer attention to advertisements or any other marketing communication depends upon four levels of consumer involvement: Pre-attention, focal attention, comprehension and elaboration. Each calls for different level of message processing. Pre-attention demands only limited message processing -the consumer only identifies the product. Focal attention involves basic information as product name on use. In comprehension level the message is analysed, through elaboration the content of the message is integrated with other information that helps to build attitude towards the product. It is suggested that marketers make advertisements that can induce elaboration.

PRODUCT VERSUS BRAND INVOLVEMENT MODEL

Sometimes consumer is involved with the product category but may not be necessarily involved with the particular brand or vice versa. For example, house wives know more about kitchen ware but may not know the details of various brands. According to the consumer involvement in either product or particular brand, consumer types can be divided into four categories as described below.

- Brand Loyals: These consumers are highly involved with both the product category and with particular brand. For example, cigarette smokers and paper readers fall in this category.
- Information Seekers: These buyers are involved more with product category but may not have preferred brand. They are likely to see information to decide a particular brand. For examples, air-conditioners and washing machine buyers fall under this category.
- Routine Brand Buyers: These consumers are not highly involved with the product category but may be involved with the particular brand with in that category. They have low emotional attachment with the product category and tied mainly with their brand. For example users of particular brand of soap for years, regular visitors to particular restaurant fall in this category.
- Brand Switching: Consumers in this category have no emotional attachment either with product category or any brand with in

it. They typically respond to price. For example stationery items, fashion products come under this category.

Note: Toys "R" Us (TRU) is a privately held retailer of toys, baby products and children's apparels. The company operates in the US, Australia, Austria, Canada, France, Germany, Japan, Portugal, Spain, Switzerland and the UK. It is headquartered in Wayne, New Jersey and employs about 69,000 people. Reader can visit their site www.toysrus.com For a detailed study of connected to this chapter.

3

Consumer Decision Making Process

The most important environment in which firms operate is their customer environment because the basic belief of marketing oriented company - that the customer is the centrepoint around which the business revolves. Therefore, marketing people need to understand the processes that their customers go through while making decision.

The consumer decision making process involves series of related and sequential stages of activities. The process begins with the discovery and recognition of an unsatisfied need or want. It becomes a drive. Consumer begins search for information. This search gives rise to various alternatives and finally the purchase decision is made. Then buyer evaluates the post purchase behaviour to know the level of satisfaction. The process is explained below with the help of diagram.

STAGES IN DECISION MAKING PROCESS

1. Need Recognition: When a person has an unsatisfied need, the buying process begins to satisfy the needs. The need may be activated by internal or external factors. The intensity of the want will indicate the speed with which a person will move to fulfil the want. On the basis of need and its urgency, forms the order of priority. Marketers should provide required information of selling points.
2. Information Search: Identified needs can be satisfied only when desired product is known and also easily available. Different products are available in the market, but consumer must know which product or brand gives him maximum satisfaction. And the person has to search out for relevant information of the product, brand or location. Consumers can use many sources e.g., neighbours, friends and family. Marketers also provide

relevant information through advertisements, retailers, dealers, packaging and sales promotion, and window displaying. Mass media like news papers, radio, and television provide information. Now a days internet has become an important and reliable source of information. Marketers are expected to provide latest, reliable and adequate information.

3. Evaluation of Alternatives: This is a critical stage in the process of buying. Following are important elements in the process of alternatives evaluation:

   - A product is viewed as a bundle of attributes. These attributes or features are used for evaluating products or brands. For example, in washing machine consumer considers price, capacity, technology, quality, model and size.
   - Factors like company, brand image, country, distribution network and after-sales service also become critical in evaluation.
   - Marketers should understand the importance of these factors to consumers of these factor to consumers while manufacturing and marketing their products.

4. Purchase Decision: Outcome of the evaluation develops likes and dislikes about alternative products or brands in consumers. This attitude towards the brand influences a decision as to buy or not to buy. Thus the prospective buyer heads towards final selection. In addition to all the above factors, situational factors like finance options, dealer terms, falling prices etc., are also considered.

5. Post-Purchase Behaviour: This behaviour of consumer is more important as for as marketer is concerned. Consumer gets brand preference only when that brand lives up to his expectation. This brand preference naturally repeats sales of marketer. A satisfied buyer is a silent advertisement. But, if the used brand does not yield desired satisfaction, negative feeling will occur and that will lead to the formation of negative attitude towards brand. This phenomenon is called cognitive dissonance. Marketers try to use this phenomenon to attract user of other brands to their brands. Different promotional-mix elements can help marketers to retain his customers as well as to attract new customers.

RULES REGARDING CONSUMER DECISION

These are generally referred to as information processing strategies. These are procedures that help consumers to evaluate various options and reduce the risk of making complex decisions by providing the guidelines. Decision rules have been broadly classified into two categories:

1. Compensatory Decision Rules: Consumers evaluate brand or model in terms of each attribute and computes a weighted score for each brand. The computed score reflects the brand's relative merit as a potential purchase choice. The assumption is that consumer will select the brand that scores highest among alternative brands. The unique feature of this rule is that it balances the positive evaluation of a brand on one attribute to balance out a negative evaluation on some other attribute. For example, positive attribute like high fuel efficiency is balanced with the negative evaluation of high maintenance cost.
2. Noncompensarory Decision Rules: In contrast to the above rule noncompensatory rules do not allow consumers to balance positive evaluation of a brand on one attribute against negative evaluation on some other attribute.

There are three types of noncompensatory rules.

- Conjunctive Decision Rule: In conjunctive decision rule the consumer establishes a different, minimally acceptable level as a cut off point for each attribute. In this the option is eliminated for further consideration if a specific brand or model falls below the cut off point on any attribute.
- Disjunctive Rule: It is the 'mirror image' of conjunctive rule. Here the consumer establishes a separate minimally acceptable cut off level for each attribute. In this case if an option meets or exceeds the cut off establishes for any one attribute it is accepted.
- Lexicographic Decision Rule: In this rule the consumer initially ranks the attributes in terms of perceived relevance or importance. Later he compares different alternatives in terms of the single attribute that is considered most important. On this top ranked alternative, regardless of the score on any other attribute, if one option scores sufficiently high it is selected and the process ends.

LEVELS OF CONSUMER DECISION MAKING

The consumer decision making process is complex with varying degree. All purchase decisions do not require extensive effort. On continuum of effort ranging from very high to very low, it can be distinguished into three specific levels of consumer decision making:

1. Extensive Problem Solving (EPS): When consumers buy a new or unfamiliar product it usually involves the need to obtain substantial information and a long time to choose. They must form the concept of a new product category and determine the criteria to be used in choosing the product or brand.
2. Limited Problem Solving (LPS): Sometimes consumers are familiar with both product category and various brands in that category, but they have not fully established brand preferences. They search for additional information helped them to discriminate among various brands.
3. Routine Problem Solving (RPS): When consumers have already purchased a product or brand, they require little or no information to choose the product. Consumers are generally involved in habitual and automatic purchases.

Note: ConocoPhillips is the third-largest integrated energy company in the US and the second-largest refiner in the country. The company is engaged in the exploration and production of petroleum, natural gas, chemicals, and polymers businesses. It has operations in over 40 countries. ConocoPhillips is headquartered in Houston, Texas and employs about 33,800 people. For a very good study of "Consumer Decision Making Process" see www.conocophillips. com

4

Consumer Behaviour and Marketing Implications

The basic belief of marketing-oriented company is that the customer is the hub around which the business revolves. Therefore, understanding what makes people in general buy and what makes your customer in particular buy is a vital part of business success. Market itself means - customer, around whom all marketing strategies are formulated and implemented. In order to meet competition at the market place, the marketing managers are using various methods to add value to the final product which will reach the hands of the consumers. It means in ever changing marketing environment, there is a growing concern or awareness among marketers to go for a careful study of the consumer behaviour around which all marketing activities are made. Following are the key marketing implications of consumer behaviour.

CONSUMER BEHAVIOUR AND MARKETING STRATEGIES

Understanding the consumer behaviour is the basic for marketing strategy formulation. Consumers reaction to this strategy determines the organization success or failure. In this competitive environment Organizations can survive only by offering more customer value - difference between all the benefits derived from a total product and all the costs of acquiring those benefits -than competitors. Providing superior customer value requires the organization to do a better job of anticipating and reacting to the customer needs than the competitor. Marketing strategy is basically the answer to the question: How will company provide superior customer value to its target market? The answer to this question requires formulation of marketing -mix - product, price, place and promotion- strategies. The right combination of these elements meets customer expectation and provides customer value. For example, marketer of a bike must know the customers performance expectations, desired service, Price willing to pay, information he seeks and after-sales service to provide superior customer value.

CONSUMER BEHAVIOUR AND MARKETING SEGMENTATION

The most important marketing decision a firm makes is the selection of one or more segments to focus their marketing effort. Marketers do not create segments but they find it in the market place. Market segmentation is the study of market place in order to discover viable group of consumers who are homogeneous in their approach in selecting and using goods or services. Since market segment has unique needs, a firm that develops a product focusing solely on the needs of that segment will be able to meet the target group desire and provides more customer value than competitor. For example, right segment for 'Femina' magazine is educated urban women. The success of this magazine depends on their understanding of the urban woman.

CONSUMER BEHAVIOUR AND PRODUCT POSITIONING

Product positioning is placing the product, service, company, or shop in the mind of consumer or target group. Through positioning marketers seek the right fit between a product and desired customer benefits. The right positioning means understanding the consumer perception process in general and perception of company's product in particular. For example, Samsung brand is perceived as premium brand by few customers and value-driven brand by others in the market, but marketer must find out what makes their target market to perceive differently and position it accordingly.

CONSUMER BEHAVIOUR AND MARKETING RESEARCH

Studying consumer behaviour enables marketing researchers to predict how consumers will react to promotional messages and to understand why they make the purchase decision they do. Marketers realized that if they know more about the consumer decision making criteria, they can design marketing strategies and promotional messages that will influence consumers more effectively. The importance of consumer behaviour made marketers to think of a separate branch in marketing research -Consumer research, to deal exclusively for consumer related issues. The current focus of consumer research is on study of underlying needs and motives in taking purchase decisions, consumer learning process and attitude formation process.

CONSUMER BEHAVIOUR AND NON-PROFIT AND SOCIETAL MARKETING

A sound knowledge of consumer behaviour can help the organizations that sell ideas and concepts of social relevance. Institutions that promote family planning, AIDS free society, governmental agencies, religion orders and universities also appeal to the public for their support in order to satisfy some want or need in society. The knowledge about potential contributors, what motivate their generosity, how these motives can be effectively appealed is useful for the organizations involved in these activities.

CONSUMER BEHAVIOUR AND GOVERNMENTAL DECISION MAKING

To major areas where consumer behaviour study helps government is in policy making on various services, and in designing consumer protection legislation. The knowledge of people's attitudes, beliefs, perceptions and habits provides adequate understanding of consumers.

Note: Unisys Corporation (Unisys) is a global information technology (IT) company. The company offers systems integration and consulting services, outsourcing services, infrastructure services, maintenance services and high-end server technology. It primarily operates in the US and the UK. The company is headquartered in Blue Bell, Pennsylvania and employs 29,000 people. For further knowledge regarding this chapter reader can visit www.unisys.com

5

Consumer Behaviour Models

ECONOMIC OR MARSHALLIAN MODEL

This theory was first advanced by the economists. They gave formal explanation of buyer behaviour. According to this theory the consumers are assumed to be rational and conscious about economic calculations. They follow the law of marginal utility. An individual buyer seeks to spend his money on such goods which give maximum satisfaction (utility) according to his interests and at relative cost. The buying behaviour is determined by the income - its distribution and level -affects the purchasing power. The economic factors which affect the buyer's behaviour are:

DISPOSABLE PERSONAL INCOME

The economists attempted to establish relationship between income and spending. Disposable personal income represents potential purchasing power that a buyer has. The change in income has direct relation on buying habits. Personal consumption spending tends both to rise and fall at a slower rate than what disposable personal income does.

- Size of family income: Size of family and size of family income affect the spending and saving patterns. Usually large families spend more and small families spend less in comparison.
- Income Expectation: The income expected to get in future has direct relation with the buying behaviour. The expectation of higher or lower income has a direct effect on spending plans.
- Tendency to Spend and to Save: This goes to the habit of spending or saving with the disposable income of buyers. If the buyers give importance to the present needs, they dispose of their income. And buyers spend less if they give importance to future needs.

- Liquidity of Funds: The present buying plans are greatly influenced by liquidity of assets readily convertible into cash. For example, readily marketable shares and bonds, bank balances come into this category. However, this convertable assets influence and offer freedom to buyer, who actually buys with current income.
- Consumer Credit: Facility of consumer credit system -hire purchase, instalment purchase etc., play an important role in purchase decision. A buyer can command more purchasing power. 'Buy now and pay later' plays its role effectively in the rapid growth of market for car, scooter, washing machine, furniture, television and so on. The economic model of consumer behaviour is unidimensional. It is based on certain predictions of buying behaviour. They are:
- Lower the price of the product, higher the sales
- Lower the size of substitute product, lower the sale of this product
- Higher the real income, higher the sales of this product
- Higher the promotional expenses, higher will be the sales

However, 'lower the price of a product, higher the sales' may not hold good, as buyer may feel that the product is sub-standard one. The behavioural researchers believe that this model ignores all the other aspects such as perception, motivation, learning, attitude and personality, and sociocultural factors. Further, it is also observed that consumer also gets influenced by other marketing variables such as products, effective distribution network and marketing communication. Hence, it is felt that the economic model is inadequate. It assumes that market is homogeneous where markets are assumed to be heterogeneous.

LEARNING OR PAVLOVIAN MODEL

Psychology has contributed a lot to the marketers in understanding the buyers. It explains how consumers learn about a product and the way they can recall from the memory, and the development of buying habits. All theories of buyer's behaviour have been primarily based on a learning, viz., Stimulation-Response or S-R model, this theory of learning is explained as a process of repetition, motivation, conditioning and relationship. Repetition improves learning. For example, when advertisements are repeated, people may be able to understand further about the product. This is aimed at repeated advertisements for drawing the attention and interest of the people. According to stimulus-response theory learning involves the following steps.

- Drive: It is a strong internal stimulus which impels action and when it is directed towards a drive reducing object, it becomes a motive. A drive thus motivates a person for action to satisfy the need. Drives may be primary-thrust, hunger etc., and secondary -desire for money, pride etc.
- Cues: These are weak stimuli. They determine when the buyer will respond.
- Response: Response is the feedback reaction of the buyer. It is an answer given to drive or cue. The individual has to choose some specific response in order to fulfil the drive or the need which was acting as a stimulus. For example, a hunger drive can be satisfied by visiting a shop known through an advertisement and buying the readymade food product. If that experience is satisfactory, this response of satisfaction is strengthened.

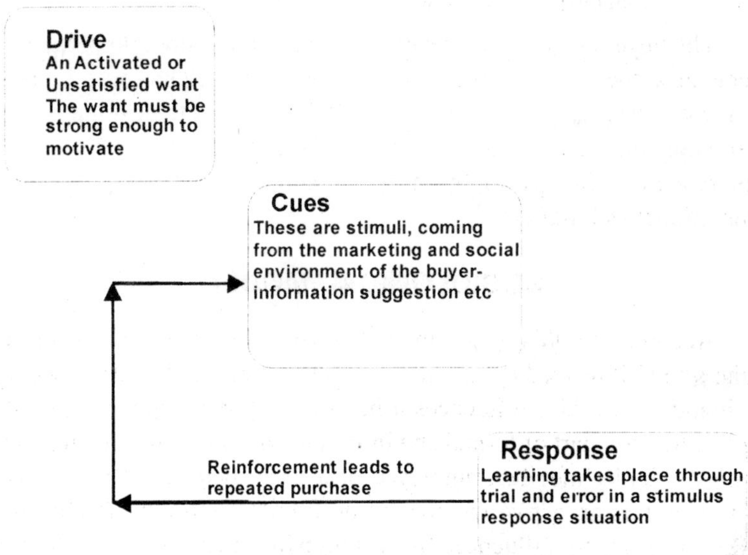

Thus this learning of links which mean stimulus, cue and response results in habits. Along with this attitudes and beliefs also learnt. As it becomes a habit, the decision process for the individual becomes routine affair. Thus, learning model has the following prediction:

- Learning refers to change in behaviour brought about by practice or experience. Everything one does or thinks is learnt.
- Product features such as price, quality, service, brand, package etc., acts as cues or hints influencing consumer behaviour
- Marketing communications such as advertising, sales promotion etc., also act as guides persuading buyer to purchase the product.
- Response is decision to purchase.

PSYCHOANALYTICAL MODEL

Sigmund Freud developed this theory. According to him human personality has three parts:

1. The Id, is the source of all mental energy that drives us to action
2. The super ego, the internal representation of what is social is approved conscience
3. The Ego, the conscious director of id impulses for finding him satisfaction in socially acceptable manner.

The buyer behaviour depends upon the relative strength of the three elements in the personal ability. Motivational research has been involved in investigating motives of consumer behaviour so as to develop suitable marketing implications accordingly. This approach has been used to generate idea for developing-design, features, advertising and other promotional techniques.

SOCIOLOGICAL MODEL

According to this theory the individual decision and behaviour are quite often influenced by the family and the society. He gets influenced by it and in turn also influences it in its path of development. He plays many roles as a part of formal and informal associations or organizations i.e., as a family member, employee of a firm, member of professional forum, and as an active member of an informal cultural organization. Hence he is largely influenced by the group in which he is a member. For example, the decision may be made by one, actual buying may be done by another, and the product is used by yet another member of the family. Here, a mother takes a decision to buy a tiny cycle for her child, the cycle is purchased by the father and the user is the child.

HOWARD-SHETH MODEL

The Howard -Sheth model shows the processes and variables influencing the buyer behaviour before and during the purchase. It emphasizes three key variables-perception, learning and attitude formation. It explains the way consumers compare available products in order to choose the best which fits their needs and desires. Consumers learn by finding out the relevant information about products through two sources of information:

- Social sources
- Commercial sources

The gathered information is used for comparison of alternative brands according to various choice criteria. The basic structure of the model is given below:

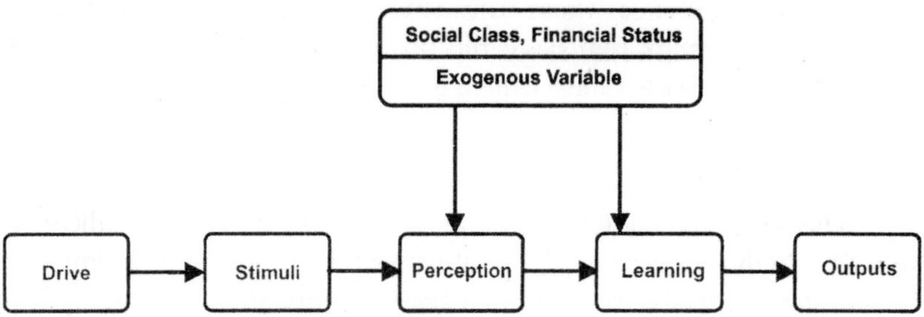

Social Class, Financial Status

Exogenous Variable

Drive Stimuli Perception Learning Outputs

Basic Structure of Buying Behaviour

The following predictions can be made about the model

- Stimuli or perceived learning occurs and results in output.
- Output occurs on the basis of the perception and learning-non observable variables.
- Exogenous or outside variables such as social class, financial status etc., are used to predict perception and learning.

This model describes the buying behaviour in various stages:

Stage 1: Motives are based on needs demanding satisfaction. They lead to goal directed behaviour satisfaction. Motives ignite a drive to search and secure information from alternatives. Stimulus-input variables are marketing programme and social environment.

Input or stimuli:

- Product themselves in the market
- Commercial information on them, say quality, price, availability and distinctiveness
- Product information obtained from friends acquaintances and reference groups.

Thus, a number of products or brands are perceived and considered by the consumers mind. In this manner the resulting perception is selected.

Stage 2: While evaluating, many brands are eliminated or left out for further consideration. Now, only few will receive further consideration. Each will have plus/minus points. These choice considerations act as connecting links between motives and selected brands choice consideration which provide a structure to motives and the process of learning and experience. These considerations develop as criteria/rule to decide on the goods that have the prospects of yielding maximum satisfaction. The market must offer a good marketing-mix that is used by the buyer to influence the choice criteria.

Stage 3: The choice criteria gives rise to predisposition-the relative preference in favour of particular brand. Sudden hindrances may sometimes stop the process. This may be in form of price, inadequate supply of brand, external variables such as financial status, time pressure etc. If they do not occur, the preference results in a response output such as attention, comprehension, attitude, buying intention and preferably actual purchase.

Stage 4: Feedback of purchase experience is sent to the buyer which shows if the actual satisfaction was equal to the expected satisfaction. Satisfaction leads to repurchase, and repeat orders indicate brand loyalty.

The marketer is interested in this outcome. Buying behaviour is influenced by motives (rational/emotional curiosity) attitudes, perception, social factors and personal factors. Thus models of buyer behaviour are generally based on certain factors internal to the consumer e.g., learning, personality, attitudes and perceptions. The external factors may be in the form of group, cultural and inter-personal influences and effects advertising and communications. The action of individuals is the result of both internal/external factors and interactions to the consumer decision making processes. The modern concepts of the buying behaviour state that the behaviour is the result of interaction between people centred factors and situation centred factors. The marketer is expected to be aware of the person centred factors such as buyer motivation, learning, perceptions, attitudes, values and beliefs.

Similarly, marketers must be aware of social environment and internal personal interactions influencing the buyer behaviour.

Outside Variables:

- Personality
- Social Class
- Financial Status and Trial
- Culture
- Importance of Purchase
- Time Pressure

Black Box of Buyer Behaviour

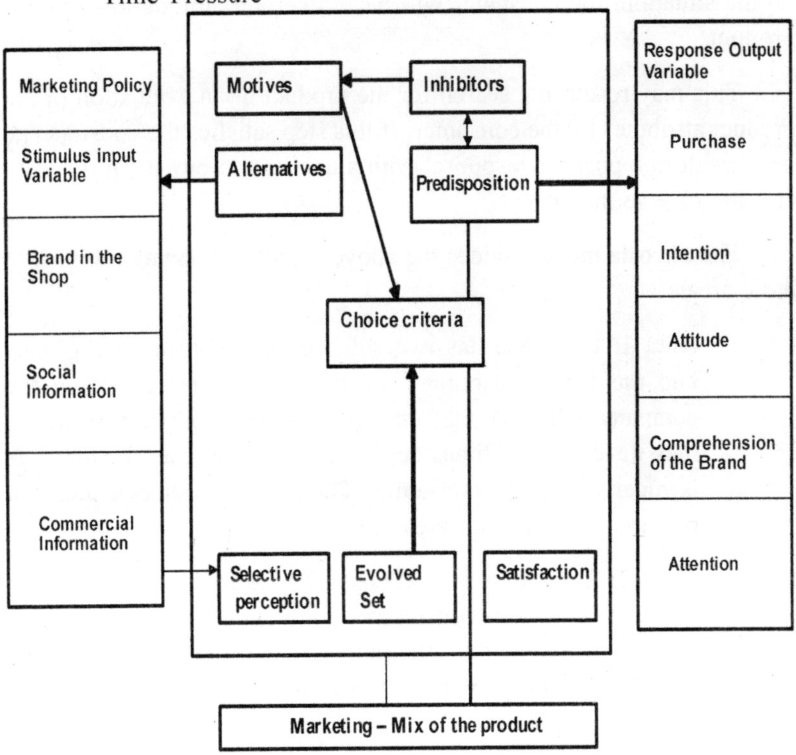

Howard - Sheth Brand Buyer Behaviour Model

NICOSIA MODEL

The buyer behaviour model is taken from the marketing mans point of view. It is also called systems model as the human is analysed as a system, with stimuli as the input to the system and the human behaviour as an output of the system.

Francesco Nicosia, an expert in consumer motivation and behaviour has developed this in 1966. He tried to explain buyer behaviour by establishing a link between the organization and its prospective consumer.

Here the messages from the company initially influence the predisposition of the consumer towards the product and service. Based on the situation, the consumer will have a certain attitude towards the product.

This may result in a search for the product or an evaluation of the product attributes by the consumer. If this step satisfies the consumer, it may result in a positive response, with a decision to buy the product or else the reverse may occur.

The Nicosia model divides the above activity explanation into four basic areas:

- Area 1: Field one has two sub areas-the consumer attributes and the firms attributes. The advertising message from the company will reach the consumers attributes. Certain attributes may develop sometimes depending upon the way the message is received by the consumer. The newly developed attribute becomes the input for area 2.
- Area 2: This area is related to the search and evaluation undertaken by the consumer of the advertised product and also to verify if other alternatives are variable. If the above step motivates to buy the product/service, it becomes the input for the third area.
- Area 3: This area explains as how the consumer actually buys the product.
- Area 4: This is related to the uses of the purchase items. This can also be used as an out put to receive feedback on sales results to the firm.

Nicosia Model

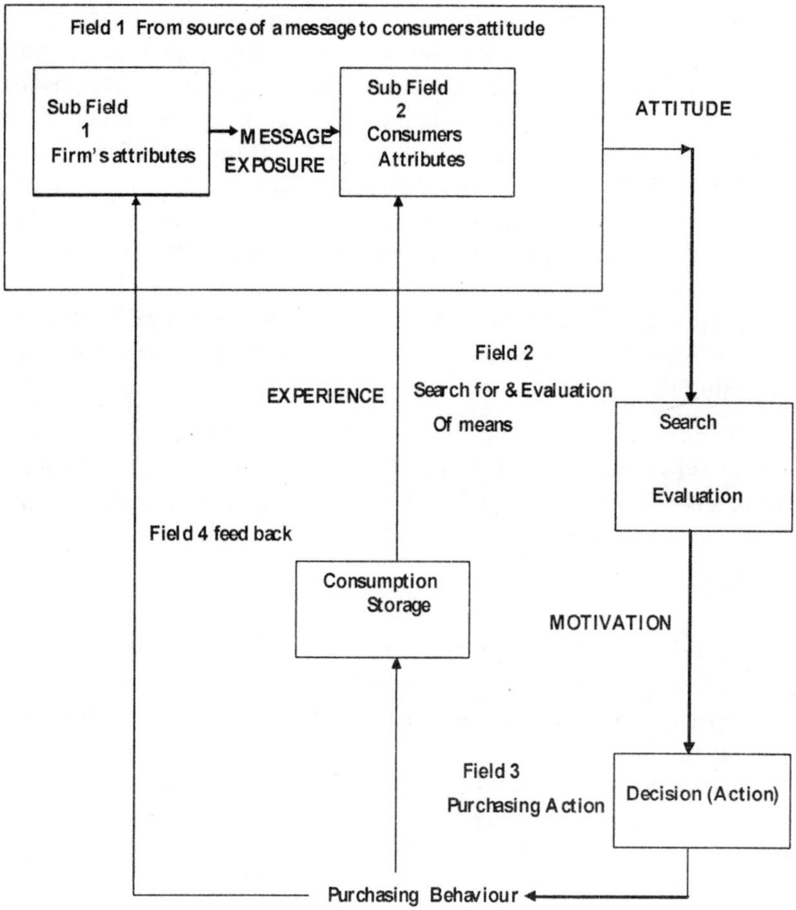

SUMMARY

The heterogeneity among people across the world makes understanding consumer buying behaviour an intricate and challenging task. Product motives and patronage motives play a crucial role in consumer purchases. Like individuals organizations also make many buying decisions. The major factors that distinguish it from consumer decision are Market structure and Demand, Buyer characteristics, and Decision process and buying patterns. The degree of involvement has a lot of impact on search of information, Information processing, and Transmission of information. The various models of consumer involvement help marketers to study purchase behaviour across product segments.

Consumers usually go through five stages in arriving at a purchase decision. In the first stage, the customer identifies an unsatisfied need. In the second stage consumer collect information about the product and brands. In a third stage, the consumer evaluates all the alternatives with the help of available information. Later in stage four, the customer makes a purchase decision. And finally in the fifth stage, consumer experiences post-purchase satisfaction or dissatisfaction. Organizational buyer has different decision making criteria. Decision making rules - Compensatory and Noncompensatory - simplify the complex nature of decision making to consumers. Understanding consumer behaviour is the basis of the formulation of marketing strategies. Consumer behaviour studies help in designing effective marketing strategies like, Marketing-mix Strategy, Market Segmentation Strategy, Product Positioning Strategy, and Marketing Research.

As consumer behaviour is very complex to understand, consumer models aid marketer to put their effort to understand in right direction. The models - Economic. Learning, Psychoanalytic, sociological, Howard-Sheth and Nicosia enables marketers to understand and predict consumer behaviour in the market place.

Note: VeriSign is a provider of infrastructure services for the internet and communications networks. The company's offerings include authentication, validation and payment services for websites, enterprises and service providers, to conduct e-commerce and communication over IP networks. The company primarily operates in the US. It is headquartered in Mountain View, California and employs 3,297 people. For a very good case study regarding this topic, reader can visit company's website www.verisign.com

6

Cultural & Environmental Influences on Consumer Behaviour

INTRODUCTION

Everybody in this world is a consumer. Everyday of our life we are buying and consuming an incredible variety of goods and services. However, we all have different tastes, likes and dislikes and adopt different behaviour patterns while making purchase decisions. Many factors affect how we, as individuals and as societies, live, buy, and consume. External influences such as culture, ethnicity, and social class influence how individual consumers buy and use products, and help explain how groups of consumers behave. The study of culture encompasses all aspects of a society such as its religion, knowledge, language, laws, customs, traditions, music, art, technology, work patterns, products, etc. Culture is an extremely critical and all pervasive influence in our life.

CULTURE -MEANING

For the purpose of studying consumer behaviour, culture can be defined as the sum total of learned beliefs, values and customs that serve to guide and direct the consumer behaviour of all members of that society. Howard and Sheth have defined culture as "A selective, manmade way of responding to experience, a set of behavioural pattern". Thus, culture consists of traditional ideas and in particular the values, which are attached to these ideas. It includes knowledge, belief, art, morale, law, customs and all other habits acquired by man as a member of society. An accepted concept about culture is that includes a set of learned beliefs, values, attitudes, habits and forms of behaviour that are shared by a society and are transmitted from generation to generation within that society.

Culture is learned through the following three ways:

1. Formal learning: parents and elders teach children the proper way to behave. For instance, you have been taught that you need to study to be successful and happy in life. This learning may influence your response both as a student and individual towards education.
2. Informal learning: we learn by imitating the behaviour of our parents, friends, or by watching TV and film actors in action
3. Technical learning: instructions are given about the specific method by which certain things to done such as painting, dancing, singing etc.

CHARACTERISTICS OF CULTURE

- Culture is learned.
- Culture regulates society -Norms, standards of behaviour, rewards and punishments.
- Culture makes life more efficient
- All members follow same norms.
- Culture is adaptive.
- Culture is environmental.
- Multiple cultures are nested hierarchically.

Culture also determines what is acceptable with product advertising. Culture determines what people wear, eat, reside and travel. Cultural values in India are good health, education, respect for age and seniority. But in our culture today, time scarcity is a growing problem, which implies a change in meals. Some changes in our culture:

1. Convenience: as more and more women are joining the work force there is an increasing demand for products that help lighten and relieve the daily household chores, and make life more convenient. This is reflected in the soaring sale of Washing machines, microwaves, Pressure cookers, Mixer-grinders, food processors, frozen food etc.
2. Education: People in our society today wish to acquire relevant education and skills that would help improve their career prospects. This is evident from the fact that so many professional, career oriented educational centres are coming up, and still they cannot seem to meet the demand. As a specific

instance count the number of institutions offering courses and training in computers that has opened in your city.

3. Physical appearance: Today, physical fitness, good health and smart appearance are on premium today. Slimming centres and beauty parlours are mushrooming in all major cities of the country. Cosmetics for both women and men are being sold in increasing numbers. Even exclusive shops are retailing designer clothes.
4. Materialism: There is a very definite shift in the people's cultural value from spiritualism towards materialism. We are spending more money than ever before on acquiring products such as air-conditioners, cars CD players etc, which adds to our physical comfort as well as status.

TYPES OF CULTURE

- National culture
- culture prevalent in a nation, common to everyone
- Popular culture
- of the masses with norms of mass appeal
- Subculture
- The culture of a group within the larger society
- Group identification based on nationality of origin, race, region, age, religion, gender, etc.
- Corporate culture
- The company's values, rituals, customs, myths and heroes

HOFSTEDE'S FIVE DIMENSIONS OF CULTURE

Culture has a profound impact on the way consumers perceive themselves, products they buy and use, purchasing processes, and the organizations from which they purchase. Marketers, however, are giving more attention, to understanding macro cultures and how they affect consumer behaviour. Hofstede found five dimensions of culture that are common among 66 countries. These dimensions serve as a foundation for characterizing, comparing and contrasting specific national cultures, and they are helpful in identifying environmentally sensitive segments of the market.

1. Individualism versus collectivism (Pursuit of self-or group interest): Individualism describes the relationship between an

individual and fellow individuals, or the collectivity that prevails in society. Table below depicts the attitudinal and behavioural differences associated with individualism and collectivism.

Table: Individualism versus Collectivism

	Individualism (E.g., United States, Australia, Canada Etc)	***Collectivism (E.g., Hong Kong, Japan, India)***
Self construal	Defined by internal attributes, personal traits	Defined by important others, family and friends
Role of others Values	Self-evaluation e.g., standards of social comparison, sources of appraisal regarding self. Emphasis on separateness, individuality	Self-definition e.g., relationships with others define self and affect personal preferences. Emphasis on connectedness, relationships
Motivational drives Behaviour	Focus differentiation, relatively greater need to unique Reflective of personal preferences and needs	Focus on similarity, relatively greater need to blend in Influenced by preferences, needs of close others

2. Power distance (Social inequality and submission to authority): Power distance reflects the degree to which a society accepts inequality in power at different levels in organizations and institutions. It can affect preferences for centralization of authority, acceptance of differential rewards, and the ways people of unequal status work together.
3. Uncertainty avoidance (Tolerance/avoidance of ambiguity): Uncertainty avoidance concerns the different ways in which societies react to the uncertainties and ambiguities inherent in life. Some societies need well-defined rules or rituals to guide behaviour, whereas others are tolerant of deviant ideas and behaviour.
4. Masculinity/femininity (Segregation of male and female roles in society): This factor determines the extent to which societies hold values traditionally regarded as predominantly masculine or feminine. For instance, assertiveness, respect for achievement, and the acquisition of money and material possessions are identified with masculinity; and nurturing, concern for the environment and championing the underdog are associated with a culture's feminity.
5. Abstract versus associative thinking: Creation of value in products based on cause/effect logic or association among events without a logical link

CULTURAL INFLUENCES

Culture is that complex whole which includes knowledge, belief, art, law, morals, customs and any other capabilities and habits acquired by humans as members of society. Culture influences the pattern of living, of consumption, of decision-making by individuals. Culture is acquired. It can be acquired from the family, from the region or from all that has been around us while we were growing up and learning the ways of the world. Culture forms a boundary within which an individual thinks and acts. When one thinks and acts beyond these boundaries, he is adopting a cross-cultural behaviour and there are cross-cultural influences as well.

The nature of cultural influences is such that we are seldom aware of them. One feels, behaves, and thinks like the other members of the same culture. It is all pervasive and is present everywhere. Material culture influences technology and how it brings cultural changes like use of telephones, mobile phones, clothing styles and fashions, gives the marketers a chance to improve the product, packing, etc. to meet the needs of the customers.

Norms are the boundaries that culture sets on the behaviour. Norms are derived from cultural values, which are widely told beliefs that specify what is desirable and what is not. Most individuals obey norms because it is natural to obey them. Culture outlines many business norms, family norms, behaviour norms, etc. How we greet people, how close one should stand to others while conducting business, the dress we wear and any other patterns of behaviour.

Culture keeps changing slowly over time; and is not static. Changes take place due to rapid technologies. In case of emergency, war, or natural calamities, marketers and managers must understand the existing culture as well as the changing culture and culture of the country where the goods are to be marketed. Major companies have adapted themselves to international culture and are accepted globally. Coca Cola is sold all over the world. Procter & Gamble and other companies give cross-cultural training to their employees.

By making cross-cultural mistakes, many companies have difficulty in pushing their products for example, (i) Coca Cola had to withdraw its 2 litres bottle from Spain, because it did not fit in the local refrigerator; (ii) Many countries are very traditional and do not like women displayed on the products. This acts as a detriment to business in those countries.

VARIATION IN CULTURAL VALUES

I. Other Oriented Values

This shows the relationship between individuals and the society. The relationship influences marketing practices. If the society values collective activity, decisions will be taken in a group. It gives rise to following questions which affect consumer behaviour.

- Individual/collective: Whether individual initiation has more value than collective activity?
- Romantic orientation: This depicts whether the communication is more effective which emphasises courtship or otherwise. In many countries a romantic theme is more successful.
- Adult/child theme: Is family life concentrated round children or adults? What role do children play in decision-making?
- Masculine/Feminine: Whether the society is male dominant or women dominant or balanced.
- Competitive/Cooperation: Whether competition leads to success. This is achieved by forming alliances with others.
- Youth/age: Are prestige roles assigned to younger or older members of the society. American society is youth oriented and Korean is age oriented. Decisions are taken by mature people in Korea.

II. Environment Oriented Values:

- Cleanliness: If a culture lays too much stress on cleanliness. There is scope for the sale of beauty creams, soaps, deodorants, insecticides, washing powder, vacuum cleaner, etc. In western countries, a lot of emphasis is placed on this aspect and perfumes and deodorants are widely used.
- Performance/status: A status oriented society cares for higher standards of living, and chooses quality goods and established brand names and high prices items. This is true for the United States, Japan, Singapore, Malaysia, Indonesia, Thailand and most Arabic countries. In performance oriented societies, where rewards and prestige is based on an individual's performance, less importance is given to brand names. Products which function equally well and may not be big brand names are used. Germans do not give the same amount of emphasis to brand names. The marketers adopt strategies accordingly.

- Tradition/change: Traditional oriented societies stick to the old product and resist innovation or new techniques. In traditional societies, there is less scope for new products, and old traditional products are in greater demand. In some societies which are upwardly mobile, consumers are looking for modern methods, new products, new models and new techniques.
- Risk taking/security: An individual who is in a secure position and takes a risk can be either considered venturesome or foolhardy. This depends on the culture of the society. For developing new entrepreneurs risk taking is a must. It leads to new product development, new advertising themes and new channels of distribution. Security oriented societies have little chances of development and innovation.
- Problem solving/fatalist: A society can be optimistic and have a problem solving attitude or, be inactive and depend on fate. This has marketing implications on the registering of complaints when consumers are dissatisfied with the purchase of the products. Advertising plays an important part and gives guidance to the consumer, and removes these doubts to a great extent.
- Nature: There are differences in attitude over nature and its preservation. Consumers stress on packing materials that are recyclable and environment friendly. Some countries give great importance to stop environmental pollution and to recycling of products. Companies like P&G, Colgate-Palmolive captured a great extent of the market by offering products which are less harmful to the environment. They also use ingredients in the products which are not harmful in any way.

III. Self-Oriented Values

- Active/passive: Whether a physically active approach to life is valued more highly than a less active orientation. An active approach leads to taking action all the time and not doing anything. In many countries, women are also taking an active part in all activities. This makes the society a highly active one, where everybody is involved in work.
- Material/non-material: In many societies money is given more importance, and a lot of emphasis is on being material minded. While in many societies things like comfort, leisure and relationships get precedence over being materialistic. Materialism can be of two types.

- Instrumental materialism, which is the acquisition of things to enable one to do something or achieve something. Cars are used for transportation. People like to possess things of material value which would help them to bring efficiency.
- Terminal materialism, is the requisition of materialism for the sake of owing it rather than for use-Art is acquired for owing it. Cultural differences play art important role in this type of materialism. Instrumental materialism is common in the United States of America, where as Japanese advertisements are mostly dominating terminal materialism.
- Hard work/leisure: This has marketing implications on labour saving products and instant foods. Some societies value hard work and consider it as a fuller life. Others adopt labour saving devices and instant foods to have more leisure time at their disposal.
- Postponed gratification/immediate gratification: Should one save for the rainy day or live for the day? Sacrifice the present for the future, or live only for the day? Some countries like The Netherlands and Germany consider buying against credit cards as living beyond one's means, whereas credit cards are very popular in America and other countries having a different cultural orientation, some prefer cash to debt. Some societies save for tomorrow; others enjoy the present and spend lavishly.
- Sexual gratification/Abstinence: Some traditional societies curb their desires, food, drinks or sex, beyond a certain requirement. Muslim cultures are very conservative, and do not want their women to be seen in public or be exposed, so the Polaroid camera which gives instant photographs can be purchased and pictures can be taken by the family members without their women being exposed to the developers in a photo lab.
- Humour/serious: Should we take life lightly and laugh it off on certain issues or, take everything seriously? This is an-other aspect of culture. Advertising personnel selling techniques and promotion may revolve around these themes and the way the appeal for a product is to be made in various cultures.

SUBCULTURES AND CONSUMER BEHAVIOUR

Culture can be divided into subcultures. A subculture is an identifiable distinct, cultural group, which, while following the dominant cultural values of the overall society also has its own belief, values and customs that set them apart from other members of the same society.

Sub-culture categories are:

- Nationality: Indian, Srilanka, Pakistan
- Religion: Hinduism, Islam
- Race: Asian, black, white
- Age: young, middle aged, elderly
- Sex: Male, Female
- Occupation: Farmer, teacher, business
- Social class: upper, middle, lower
- Geographic regions: South India, North-eastern India

1. Regional, Ethnic, and Religious Influences on Consumer Behaviour: The three major aspects of culture that have important effects on consumer behaviour are regional, ethnic, and religious differences. Firstly, consumption patterns may differ in various regions of India and the world, and marketing strategy can sometimes be tailored specifically to these regions. Secondly, our country has a number of different ethnic groups, and population trends will dramatically alter the demographic profile of the country in the next 50 years. The very diverse Asian American subculture is described as young and having higher socioeconomic status, placing strong value on the family and the group, and being strongly brand loyal. In spite of its diversity, marketing strategies can be developed for this group. Finally, religious beliefs and values can influence consumer. Many marketers are now becoming multicultural in their marketing activities by trying to appeal to a variety of cultures at the same time. Although the diversity of the Indian melting pot may be unique, there are many important ethnic groups in other areas of the world.

2. Age, Gender, and Household Influences on Consumer Behaviour: Among the four major age groups, Teens, who need to establish an identity, are the consumers of tomorrow and have an increasing influence on family decisions. The somewhat disillusioned Generation X consists of smart and cynical consumers who can easily see through obvious marketing attempts. Baby boomers grew up in a very dynamic

and fast-changing world, and this has affected their values for individualism and freedom. The 50 and older segment can be divided into two groups-the young again and the grey market. Neither group likes to be thought of as old. The affect of gender differences on consumer behaviour is examined next. Sex roles are changing. Women are becoming more professional and independent, and men are becoming more sensitive and caring. Also, men and women can differ in terms of traits, information processing, decision styles, and consumption patterns. Gender is consistent throughout lifetime, influencing customer values and preferences. Gender shows different consumption patterns and perceptions of consumption situations -E.g. the wedding ceremony. Households play a key role in consumer behaviour. The proportion of nontraditional households has increased due to factors such as

- Later marriages,
- Cohabitation,
- Dual-career families,
- Increased divorce, and
- Fewer children.

Households also exert an important influence on acquisition and consumption patterns. First, household members can play different roles in the decision process (gatekeeper, influencer, decider, buyer, and user). Second, husbands and wives vary in their influence in the decision process, depending on the situation husband-dominant, wife-dominant, autonomic, or syncratic.

3. Psychographics: Values, Personality, and Lifestyles: The roles of psychographics in affecting consumer behaviour are detailed below.

Values are enduring beliefs about things that are important. They are learned through the processes of socialization and acculturation. Our values exist in an organized value system, with some values being viewed as more important than others. Some are regarded as terminal values and reflect desired end states that guide behaviour across many different situations. Instrumental values are those needed to achieve these desired end states. Domain-specific values are those that are relevant within a given sphere of activity. Western cultures tend to place a relatively high value on mater[illegible] goods, youth, the home, family and children, work and play, health, hedonism, and technology. Marketers use tools like value segmentation to identify consumer groups with common values. Personality consists of the distinctive patterns of behaviours, tendencies, qualities, and personal dispositions that make people different from one another. Approaches to the study of personality include:

- The psychoanalytic approach, which sees personality arising from unconscious internal struggles within the mind at key stages of development;
- Trait theories, which attempt to identify a set of personality characteristics that describe and differentiate individuals, such as introversion, extroversion, and stability;
- Phenomenological approaches, which propose that personality is shaped by an individual's interpretation of life events
- Social-psychological theories, which focus on how individuals act in social situations (e.g., compliant, detached, or aggressive); and
- Behavioural approaches, which view an individual's personality in terms of past rewards and punishments.

Marketers also measure lifestyles, which are patterns of behaviour (or activities, interests, and opinions). These lifestyles can provide some additional insight into consumers' consumption patterns. Finally, some marketing researchers use Psychographic techniques that involve all of these factors to predict consumer behaviour. One of the most well known Psychographic tools is the Values and Lifestyle Survey (VALS). The newer VALS2 identifies eight segments of consumers who are similar in their resources and self-orientations.

CROSS CULTURAL CONSUMER BEHAVIOUR

CROSS CULTURAL MARKETING: OBJECTIVES AND POLICIES

Cross-cultural marketing is defined as "the effort to determine to what extent the consumers of two or more nations are similar or different. This will facilitate marketers to understand the psychological, social and cultural aspects of foreign consumers they wish to target, so as to design effective marketing strategies for each of the specific national markets involved."

A company can enter a foreign market as a:

- Domestic exporter
- Foreign importer
- Foreign government-solicit the firm to sell abroad

The firm's objectives could be:

- To determine how consumers in two or more societies are similar/different and devise suitable, appropriate strategies.
- Devise individualized marketing strategy if cultural beliefs, values and customs of a specific country are different.

Characteristic features of a firm going global:

- High market share in the domestic market.
- Advantageous economies of scale.
- Access to marketing/manufacturing bases across global borders.
- Availability of resources and capability to absorb huge losses.
- Product/technology clout.
- Cost and differentiation advantages.

PROBLEMS IN CROSS CULTURAL MARKETING

- Problems related to product selection: The marketer going for cross cultural marketing has to select the customers/market not on the basis of the superficial similarities of age or income, but by using the real motivating factors that prompt them to accept or reject products.
- Problems related to promotion/marketing communication: e.g. Ariel in the middle east and also Pepsi
- Problems related to pricing: the marketer has to adjust his pricing policies according to the local economic conditions and customs.
- Problems related to selection of distribution channels: in Japan, P & G used this to sell soap

CROSS-CULTURAL CONSUMER ANALYSIS

To determine whether and how to enter a foreign market, we need to conduct some form of cross-cultural consumer analysis. Cross-cultural consumer analysis can be defined as the effort to determine to what extent the consumers of two or more nations are similar or different.

Such analysis can provide marketers with an understanding of the psychological, social, and cultural characteristics of the foreign consumers they wish to target, so that they can design effective marketing strategies for the specific national markets involved.

Similarities and differences among people

A major objective of cross-cultural consumer analysis is to determine how consumers in two or more societies are similar and how they are different.

Alternative Multinational Strategies

Some of us may argue as markets are becoming more and more similar, standardized marketing strategies are becoming more and more feasible. But, some more would argue back that differences between consumers of various nations are far too great to permit a standardized marketing strategy. Whether to use shared needs and values as a segmentation strategy or to use national borders as a segmentation strategy? Shared needs and values would mean to appeal to consumers in different countries in terms of their common needs, values, and goals. Using national borders as a segmentation strategy would mean to use relatively different local or specific marketing strategies for members of distinctive cultures or countries.

Table: Alternative Global Marketing Strategies.

Product Strategy	*Standardized Communications*	*Localized Communications*
Standardized Product	*Global strategy*: Uniform product/ Uniform Message	*Mixed strategy*: Uniform Product/ Customized message
Localized Product	*Mixed Strategy*: Customized Product/ Uniform Message	*Local strategy*: Customized Product/ Customized Message

1. Favouring a World Brand: A lot of companies have created world brand products that are manufactured, packaged, and positioned in exactly the same way regardless of the country in which they are sold. For instance, Sony sells its Walkman in this fashion.
2. Adaptive Global Marketing: In contrast to the above, some other organizations imbibe a strategy that adapts their advertising messages to the specific values of particular cultures. A very good example here would be that of McDonald's, which tries to localize its advertising to consumers in each of the cross-cultural markets in which it operates.

TANGIBLE BENEFITS OF GLOBAL BRAND BUILDING

Global brand building drastically reduces marketing investments. A strong brand needs lower and lower levels of incremental investment to sustain itself over time. A new and unknown player will have to spend two to four times more than the market leader to achieve the same share of mind. Given the huge difference in business volumes, the pressure of the bottom-line is much higher for an unestablished player.

Strong global brands always account for more stable businesses. Global brand building commands a premium. As long as there is a distinct value attached to your offering, the consumer will always be willing to pay more for it. That is the only reason why an unknown brand called Titan could command a substantial premium over HMT. That is the same reason why a brand such as BPL at a higher cost beat the stuffing out of companies such as Akai, Sony and Philips in the CTV wars.

Global brand building builds entry barriers. Human beings as a species love status quo. Therefore, a brand which is entrenched in the consumer's mind is very difficult to dislodge.

Global brand building increases cash flow efficiency: Global brand building also increases value of the business due to the international presence. Phillip Morris bought Kraft from General Foods in 1991 for $13 billion, more than three times its book value. Coca-Cola paid $60 million to acquire Thumbs-Up from Parle. Neither buyer had any lacunae in manufacturing, finance or human resources. They merely bought business with very powerful brand equities and therefore paid more than the net worth of the businesses.

STRATEGIC IMPLICATIONS

There is an assumption that the world is becoming homogenised; yet national and sub-regional cultures do exist. This makes global branding a tough challenge and one that is handled differently from organization to organization. Some companies pursue strategies based upon the identification of common elements among countries, whilst others find it more profitable to adapt and adjust according to specific conditions in various markets. There are five basic propositions that a global brand manager has to take note of while developing strategy at the global level.

Many marketers operate in global markets with a strategy still rooted in the domestic market. The strategy needs to embrace the opportunities and the costs of working in multiple countries. The marketer has to look for his competitive advantage outside the country of origin. What will allow one to compete and win in a strange country? Are the product and the brand in particular needed in another culture? Only careful consideration of these questions will create the right platform for a global branding strategy.

CULTURAL VARIATIONS & NON-VERBAL COMMUNICATION

In a culture we have many variations in non-verbal communications. Each culture assigns a meaning to non-verbal signs utilised by it. There are some variables in non-verbal communication. These are:

TIME

Time is a resource which is distributed equally amongst everybody. Every person has the same amount of time at his disposal. What view individuals and societies take of time makes them different. Some can be classified under monochromic culture and others in polychromic culture. Some of the important differences between monochromic a polychromic culture are give in the table below.

Table: Differences between Monochronic and Polychronic Culture

Monochronic Culture	*Polychronic Culture*
Do one thing at a time.	Do many things at once.
Concentrate on the job.	Highly distractible and subject to interruption.
Take deadlines and schedules seriously.	Consider deadlines and schedules secondary.
Committed to job.	Committed to people and relationships.
Adhere religiously to plans.	Change plan often and easily.
Emphasise promptness.	Base promptness on relationship.
Accustomed to short term relationships.	Prefer long term relationships

The meaning of time may be different in different cultures. Some people take time in making decisions according to the importance of decisions. Some insist on coming to the point directly in business transactions and are well prepared. Some keep appointments by the minute, others make people wait for a long time.

SPACE

Space may be related to prestige rather than the need. The higher the office, the bigger the office space and so on. Americans have the offices of executives on the top floor and tend to separate the office of subordinates. Japanese have their discount stores on the upper floor. Some cultures and individuals maintain a fair distance while transacting, others co-mingle easily. Americans maintain a fair distance while interacting with associates. Arabs stand very close to each other.

FRIENDSHIP

Friendship plays an important role in business transactions. Good personal relationship and feelings matter most in a long term agreement. Social contacts developed by parties gain priority over technical specifications. Americans make friends easily, and drop them easily as well, because of both social and geographical mobility.

Some cultures like Indian or Latin Americans have lasting relationships that endure for a long time and so does the business. Personal ties, personal trust leads to cooperation and a lot of transaction can take place between parties. Some want to transact business only with those whom they get along and, making money is secondary.

AGREEMENTS

All business when transacted is done under some agreements. These agreements may be written or just on an understanding between the two parties. Most people enter into an agreement, but friendship and kinship are also given a lot of importance. Verbal commitments are also binding in some cultures, where signing a contract is just a mere formality.

THINGS

Different cultures attach different meaning to things. Things include products as well as gifts given in certain business and social situations. An appropriate product in the form of a gift is to be carefully chosen. The gifts can be big or small. They can be given openly or presented privately. This depends on the practices followed in that particular country. Some want to make a show of the gift, by giving it in front of others. Others are secretive about it.

SYMBOLS AND COLOURS

Different countries attach different meanings to symbols, numbers and colours. Symbols can be flowers, triangles, pictures and animals, etc. Some numbers are considered lucky, and others not so lucky, or even unlucky, like 13, 4, etc. Colours have different interpretations. Pink is associated with a female, and blue with the male in the US, whereas it is just the opposite in Holland.

A list of colours and their interpretations is given below:

White: Symbol of mourning or death in the Far East, happiness, purity and peace in the United States.

Purple: Associated with death in many Latin American countries. Blue: Symbolises feminity in Holland and masculinity in the United States, Sweden, India, etc.

Red: Colour for brides and children in India. Sign of masculinity in the UK and France, negative in Nigeria, Germany and positive in Denmark, Rumania and Argentina.

Yellow: Sign of death in Mexico, infidelity in France, celebrations in many countries including India.

White lilies: Suggestion of death in England.

SYMBOL OF NUMBERS

7: Lucky in India, USA, Morocco, Nicaragua and Czechoslovakia.

13: Unlucky in many countries including India.

4: Symbol of death in Japan. Packing in 4s is avoided.

Triangle: Negative in Hong Kong and Taiwan, positive in Columbia.

Owl: Wisdom in the United States, bad luck in India.

Deer: Speed, grace in the United States; Homosexuality in Brazil.

These are accepted norms of behaviour. Some behaviour may be rude or abusive in one culture and quite acceptable in other cultures, e.g. sitting with legs crossed or sitting in a manner that shows the sole of a shoe. In Japan it is considered impolite to say no directly to a business offer. They put it differently, by saying it is very difficult, which means no. The exchange of business cards in Japan is essential, and indicates the level of your status in your business. Similarly, there are many different habits and ways of doing things socially that affect the making of advertisement. Eating with the fork in the right hand and the left hand kept under the table is quite common in America, whereas, in European culture, the fork should be in the left hand and the right hand holding the knife or spoon. These non-verbal communications in different countries or different languages have a direct bearing on the marketing activity and must be taken care of. As people recognise verbal languages, they act accordingly. In a similar manner, non-verbal communication must also be recognised and understood so that there is less misinterpretation. The advertisement of the communication we want to give should be appropriate and match with the culture of the country.

Note: Coca-Cola Enterprises (CCE) is the world's largest marketer, producer, and distributor of Coca-Cola products. The company is the sole licensed bottler for products of The Coca-Cola Company in Belgium, continental France, Great Britain, Luxembourg, Monaco, and the Netherlands. The company primarily operates in North America. It is headquartered in Atlanta, Georgia and employs 72,000 people. For detailed information & understanding more on "Cultural & Environmental"Influences on Consumer Behaviour" reader may visit this site www.cokecce.com

7

Groups, Social Class & Reference Groups

INTRODUCTION

With the exception of those very few people who can be classified as hermits, people tend to be involved with others on a rather constant basis. Like almost all behaviour, an individual's social relationships are of-ten motivated by the expectation that they will help in the satisfaction of specific needs. For example, a person might become a volunteer ambulance driver to satisfy a need for community recognition. Another person might join a computer club in an effort to find compatible friends to satisfy social needs. A third person might join a health food cooperative to obtain the benefits of group buying power. These are just a few of the almost infinite number of reasons why people involve themselves with others.

MEANING OF GROUP

A group may be defined as two or more people who interact to accomplish some goals. Within the broad scope of this definition are both an intimate "group" of two neighbours who informally attend a fashion show together and a larger, more formal group, such as a neighbourhood.

TYPES OF GROUPS

To simplify our discussion, we will consider four different types of group classification: primary versus secondary groups, formal versus informal groups, large versus small groups, and membership versus symbolic groups.

1. Primary versus Secondary Groups: If a person interacts on a regular basis with other individuals (with members of his or her family, with neighbours, or with co-workers whose opinions are valued), then these individuals can be considered as a primary group for that person. On the other hand, if a person interacts only occasionally with such others, or does not consider their opinions to be important, then these others constitute a secondary group for that person. From this definition, it can be seen that the critical distinctions between primary and secondary groups are the frequency with which the individual interacts with them and. the importance of the groups to the individual.

2. Formal versus Informal Groups: Another useful way to classify groups is by the extent of their formality; that is, the extent to which the group structure, the members' roles, and the group's purpose are clearly defined. If a group has a highly defined structure (e.g., a formal membership list), specific roles and authority levels (a president, treasurer, and secretary), and specific goals (to support a political candidate, improve their children's education, increase the knowledge or skills of members), then it would be classified as a formal group. The local chapter of the American Red Cross, with elected officers and members who meet regularly to discuss topics of civic interest, would be classified as a formal group. On the other hand, if a group is more loosely defined, if it consists, say, of four women who were in the same college sorority and who meet for dinner once a month, or three co-workers who, with their spouses, see each other frequently then it is considered an informal group.

3. Large versus Small Groups: It is often desirable to distinguish between groups in terms of their size or complexity. A large group might be thought of as one in which a single member is not likely to know more than a few of the group's members personally, or be fully aware of the specific roles or activities of more than a limited number of other group members. Examples of large groups include such complex organizations as General Motors, with its numerous subordinate divisions, and the American Bar Association, with its many state, county, and city chapters. In contrast, members of a small group are likely to know every member personally and to be aware of

every member's specific role or activities in the group. For example, each staff member of a college newspaper is likely to know all the other members and be aware of their duties and interests within the group. In the realm of consumer behaviour, we are principally concerned with the study of small groups, since such groups are more likely to influence the consumption behaviour of group members.

4. Membership versus Symbolic Groups: Another useful way to classify groups is by membership versus symbolic groups. A membership group is a group to which a person either belongs or would qualify for membership. For example, the group of women with whom a young homemaker plays golf weekly or with whom she hopes to play golf when an opening occurs would be considered, for her, a membership group. In contrast, a group in which an individual is not likely to receive membership, despite acting like a member by adopting the group's values, attitudes, and behaviour, is considered a symbolic group. Clearly, actual membership groups offer a more direct, and thus a more compelling, influence on consumer behaviour. In summary, we can say that small, informal, primary membership groups are of the great interest to marketers because they exert the greatest potential influence on consumer purchase decisions.

CONSUMER-RELEVANT GROUPS

To more fully comprehend the kind of impact that specific groups have on individuals, we will examine six basic consumer-relevant groups: the Family, Friendship groups, Formal social groups, Shopping groups, Consumer action groups and Work groups.

THE FAMILY

An individual's family is the most important group to influence his or her consumer decisions. The family's importance in this regard is due to the frequency of contact that the individual has with other family members and that the family has a greater extent of influence on the establishment of a wide range of values, attitudes, and behaviour.

FRIENDSHIP GROUPS

Friendship groups are informal groups because they are, usually unstructured and lack specific authority levels. In terms of relative influence, after an individual's family, it is friends who are most likely to influence the individual's purchase decisions. Seeking and maintaining friendships is a basic drive of most people. Friends fulfil a wide range of needs: they provide companionship, security, and opportunities to discuss problems that an individual may be reluctant to discuss with members of his or her own family. Friendships are also a sign of maturity and independence, for they represent a breaking away from the family and the forming of social ties with the outside world. Consumers are more likely to seek information from those friends they feel have values or outlooks similar to their own.

FORMAL SOCIAL GROUPS

In contrast to the relative intimacy of friendship groups, formal social groups are more remote and serve a different function for the individual. A person joins a formal social group to fulfil such specific goals as making new friends, meeting "important" people (e.g., for career advancement), or promoting a specific cause. Because members of a formal social group often consume certain products together, such groups are of interest to marketers. For example, the membership list of a men's club would be of interest to local men, Insurance agents, automobile agents, tax accountants.

Membership in a formal social group may influence a consumer's behaviour in several ways. For example, members of such groups have frequent opportunity to informally discuss products, services, or stores. Some members may copy the, consumption behaviour of other members whom they admire.

SHOPPING GROUPS

Two or more people who shop together-whether for food, for clothing, or simply to pass the time, can be called a shopping group. Such groups are often offshoots of family or friendship groups. People like to shop with others who they feel have more experience with or knowledge about a desired product or service. Shopping with others also provides an element of social fun to an often boring but necessary task. In addition, it reduces the risk that a purchase decision will be socially unacceptable.

Relatively few marketing or consumer behaviour studies have examined the nature of shopping groups. However, one study of the in-store behaviour of shoppers revealed some differences between group and individual shopping. The research found that shopping parties of at least three persons deviated more from their original purchase plans (they bought either more or less than originally planned) than did either single shoppers or two-party groups. The study also found that shopping groups tended to cover more territory in the store than individuals shopping alone, and thus had more opportunity to see and examine merchandise and to make unplanned purchases.

A special type of shopping group is the in-home shopping group, which typically consists of a group of women who gather together in the home of a friend, to attend a "party" devoted to the marketing of a specific line of products. The in-home party approach provides marketers with an opportunity to demonstrate the features of their products simultaneously to a group of potential customers. The undecided guests often overcome a reluctance to buy when they see their friends make positive purchase decisions. Furthermore, some of the guests may feel obliged to buy because they are guests in the home of the sponsoring hostess.

CONSUMER ACTION GROUPS

A particular kind of consumer group-a consumer action group-has emerged in response to the consumerist movement. This type of consumer group has become increasingly visible since the 1960s and has been able to influence product design and marketing practices of both manufacturers and retailers. Consumer action groups can be divided into two broad categories: those that organize to correct a specific consumer abuse and then disband, and those that organize to address broader, more pervasive, problem areas and operate over an extended or indefinite period of time. A group of tenants who band together to dramatize their dissatisfaction with the quality of service provided by their landlord, or a group of irate community members who unite to block the entrance of a fast-food outlet into their middle-class neighbourhood, are examples of temporary, cause-specific consumer action groups.

WORK GROUPS

The sheer amount of time that people spend at their jobs, frequently more than thirty-five hours per week, provides ample opportunity for work groups to serve as a major influence on the consumption behaviour of members. Both the formal work group and the informal friendship/ work group have the potential for influencing consumer behaviour. The formal work group consists of those individuals who work together as a team. Their direct and sustained work relationship offers substantial opportunity for one or more members to influence the consumer-related attitudes and activities of other team members. Members of informal work groups may influence the consumption behaviour of other members during coffee or lunch breaks or after-hours meetings.

SOCIAL CLASS

Social class is more of a continuum, i.e., a range of social positions, on which each member of society can be place. But, social researchers have divided this continuum into a small number of specific classes. Thus, we go by this framework, social class is used to assign individuals or families to a social-class category. Social class can be defined as 'The division of members of a society into a hierarchy of distinct status classes, so that members of each class have relatively the same status and the members of all other classes have either more or less status.'

CHARACTERISTICS OF THE SOCIAL CLASSES

The main characteristics of Social class:

1. Persons within a given social class tend to behave more alike
2. Social class is hierarchical
3. Social class is not measured by a single variable but is measured as a weighted function of one's occupation, income, wealth, education, status, prestige, etc.
4. Social class is continuous rather than concrete, with individuals able to move into a higher social class or drop into a lower class.

Factors responsible for Social Stratification

S. No	*Status, Value & Prestige Enjoyed*	*Social Class*	*Factors Affecting Social Class*
1	*Low*	*Lower Class*	Lower level occupation with no authority, less income, and no education or minimum education, For example, labour class or clerks etc.
2	*Medium*	*Middle Class*	Graduates, or postgraduates, executives' managers of companies with authority, drawing handsome salary of which certain amount can be saved and invested. For example, executives or middle level managers of companies.
3	*High*	*Higher Class*	Authoritative person, drawing handsome salary, very often professionally qualified, working in a very senior position or a person born into a rich family, with a good background of education.

Impact of social class:

- Provides a sense of identity
- Imposes a set of 'normative' behaviours
- Classes share values, possessions, customs and activities
- Marketing response to customers of different economic means
- Marketing to the low-income consumer
- Some marketers ambivalent as not perceived as long-term customers constitutes a substantial group
- Target with value-oriented strategies

REFERENCE GROUPS

Reference groups are groups that serve as a frame of reference for individuals in their purchase decisions. This basic concept provides a valuable perspective for understanding the impact of other people on an individual's consumption beliefs, attitudes, and behaviour. It also provides some insight into methods that Groups can be used to effect desired changes in consumer behaviour.

A reference group is any person or group that serves as a point of companion (or reference) for an individual in the formation of either general or specific values, attitudes, or behaviour. The usefulness of this concept is enhanced by the fact that it places no restrictions on group size or membership, nor does it require that consumers identify with a tangible group (i.e., the group can be symbolic: prosperous business people, rock stars, and sports heroes).

Reference groups that influence general values or behaviour are called normative reference groups. An example of a child's normative reference group is the immediate family, which is likely to play an important role in moulding the child's general consumer values and behaviour (e.g., which foods to select for good nutrition, appropriate ways to dress for specific occasions, how and where to shop, what constitutes "good" value).

Reference groups that serve as benchmarks for specific or narrowly defined attitudes or behaviour are called comparative reference groups. A comparative reference group might be a neighbouring family whose lifestyle appears to be admirable and worthy of imitation (the way they maintain their home, their choice of home furnishings and cars, the number and types of vacations they take).

Both normative and comparative reference groups are important. Normative reference groups influence the development of a basic code of behaviour; comparative reference groups influence the expression of specific consumer attitudes and behaviour. It is likely that the specific influences of comparative reference groups are to some measure dependent upon the basic values and behaviour patterns established early in a person's development by normative reference groups.

BROADENING CONCEPT OF THE REFERENCE GROUP

Like many other concepts borrowed from the behavioural sciences, the meaning of reference group has changed over the years. As originally employed, reference groups were narrowly defined to include only those groups with which a person interacted on a direct basis (e.g., family and close friends). However, the concept has gradually broadened to include both direct and indirect individual or group influences. Indirect reference groups consist of those individuals or groups with whom a person does not have direct face-to-face contact, such as movie stars, sports heroes, political leaders, or TV personalities. Referents that a person might use in evaluating his or her own general or specific attitudes or behaviour vary from an individual to several family members to a broader kinship, from a voluntary association to a social class, a profession, an ethnic group, a community, or even a nation.

TYPES OF REFERENCE GROUPS

Reference groups can be classified in terms of a person's membership or degree of involvement with the group and in terms of the positive or negative influences they have on his or her values, attitudes, and behaviour. Four types of reference groups that emerge from a cross-classification of these factors: contactual groups, aspirational groups, disclaimant groups, and avoidance groups.

1. A contactual group is a group in which a person holds membership or has regular face-to-face contact and of whose values, attitudes, and standards he or she approves. Thus a contactual group has a positive influence on an individual's attitudes or behaviour.
2. An aspirational group is a group in which a person does not hold membership and does not have face-to-face contact, but wants to be a member. Thus it serves as a positive influence on that person's attitudes or behaviour.

3. A disclaimant group is a group in which a person holds membership or has face-to-face contact but disapproves of the group's values, attitudes, and behaviour. Thus the person tends to adopt attitudes and behaviour that are in opposition to the norms of the group.
4. An avoidance group is a group in which a person does not hold membership and does not have face-to-face contact and disapproves of the group's values, attitudes, and behaviour. Thus 'the person tends to adopt attitudes and behaviour that are in opposition to those of the group.

Consider Ram, a senior majoring in advertising at the state university in the southwestern United States. The school's Advertising Club, of which he is vice-president, serves as one of Ram's contractual groups. Ram believes that continuing his education to obtain an MBA will enhance his career opportunities. It is clear that individuals who hold the MBA degree serve as an aspirational group for him. Still further, although he enjoys his position as a reporter on the university's newspaper, the recent editorials (endorsed by most of the staff) urging students to adopt a more conservative political philosophy run counter to his own views. Thus the newspaper staff is currently a disclaimant group. Finally, Ram personally knows a number of students who have quit college during their final year; these former students serve as an avoidance group.

FACTORS AFFECTING REFERENCE GROUP INFLUENCE

The degree of influence that a reference group exerts on an individual's behaviour usually depends on the nature of the individual and the product and on specific social factors. This section discusses how and why some of these factors operate to influence consumer behaviour.

INFORMATION AND EXPERIENCE

An individual who has firsthand experience with a product or service, or can easily obtain full information about it, is less likely to be influenced by the advice or example of others. On the other hand, a person who has little or no firsthand experience with a product or service, and does not expect to have access to objective information about it (e.g., a person who believes that relevant, advertising may be misleading or deceptive), is more likely to seek out the advice or example of others. Research on imitative behaviour provides some interesting insights on how insufficient experience or information concerning a product makes consumers more susceptible to the influence either positive or negative, of others. For example, if a medical school student wants to impress his new girl-friend, he may take her to a restaurant that he knows from experience to be good or to one that has been highly recommended by the local newspaper's Dining-Out Guide. If he has neither personal experience nor information he regards as valid, he may seek the advice of friends or imitate the behaviour of others by taking her to a restaurant he knows is frequented by physicians whom he admires.

CREDIBILITY, ATTRACTIVENESS, AND POWER OF THE REFERENCE GROUP

A reference group that is perceived as credible, attractive, or powerful can induce consumer attitude and behaviour change. For example, when consumers are concerned with obtaining accurate information about the performance or quality of a product or service, they are likely to be persuaded by those they consider to be trustworthy and knowledgeable. That is, they are more likely to be persuaded by sources with high credibility. When consumers are primarily concerned with the acceptance or approval of others they like, with whom they identify, or who offer them status or other benefits, they are likely to adopt their product, brand, or other behavioural characteristics.

When consumers are primarily concerned with the power that a person or group can exert over them, they might choose products or services that con-form to the norms of that person or group in order to avoid ridicule or punishment. However, unlike other reference groups that consumers follow either because they are credible or because they are attractive, power groups are not likely to cause attitude change. Individuals may conform to the behaviour of a powerful person or group but are not likely to experience a change in their own attitudes. Different reference groups may influence the beliefs, attitudes, and behaviour of an individual at different points in time or under different circum-stances. For example, the dress habits of a young female attorney may vary, depending on her place and role. She may conform to the dress code of her office by wearing conservative business suits by day and drastically alter her mode of dress after work by wearing more conspicuous, flamboyant styles.

CONSPICUOUSNESS OF THE PRODUCT

The potential influence of a reference group varies according to how visually or verbally conspicuous a product is to others. A visually conspicuous product is one that can be seen and identified by others, and that will stand out and be noticed (e.g., a luxury item or novelty product). Even if a product is not visually conspicuous, it may be verbally conspicuous it may be highly interesting or it may be easily described to others. Products that are especially conspicuous and status-revealing (a new automobile, fashion clothing, home furniture) are most likely to be purchased with an eye to the reactions of relevant others. Products that are less conspicuous (canned fruits, laundry soaps) are less likely to be purchased with a reference group in mind. The success of a brand of status running shoes like Reebok is aided by the fact that it is relatively easy to spot a person wearing them-given the distinctive flag symbol on the side of each shoe.

REFERENCE GROUP IMPACT ON PRODUCT AND BRAND CHOICE

In some cases, and for some products, reference groups may influence both a person's product category and brand (or type) choices. Such products are called pro-duct-plus, brand-plus items. In other cases, reference groups influence only the product category decision. Such products are called product-plus, brand-minus items. In still other cases, reference groups influence the brand (or type) decision. These products are called product-minus, brand-Plus items. Finally, in some cases, reference groups influence neither the product category nor the brand decision; these products are called product-minus, brand-minus items. The idea of classifying products and brands into four groups in terms of the suitability of a reference group appeal was first suggested in the mid-1950s, along with an initial classification of a small number of product categories.

REFERENCE GROUPS AND CONSUMER CONFORMITY

Marketers are particularly interested in the ability of reference groups to change consumer attitudes and behaviour (i.e., to encourage conformity). To be capable of such influence, a reference group must

1. Inform or make the individual aware of a specific product or brand;
2. Provide the individual with the opportunity to compare his or her own thinking with the attitudes and behaviour of the group;
3. Influence the individual to adopt attitudes and behaviour that are consistent with the norms of the group;
4. Legitimize an individual's decision to use the same products as the group.

The ability of reference groups to influence consumer conformity is demonstrated by the results of a classic experiment designed to compare the effects.

BENEFITS OF THE REFERENCE GROUP APPEAL

Reference group appeals have two principal benefits for the advertiser: they increase brand awareness and they serve to reduce perceived risk.

INCREASED BRAND AWARENESS

Reference group appeals provide the advertiser with the opportunity to gain and retain the attention of prospective consumers with greater ease and effectiveness than is possible with many other types of promotional campaigns. This is particularly true of the celebrity form of reference group appeal, where the personality employed is generally well known to the relevant target segment. Celebrities tend to draw attention to the product through their own popularity. This gives the advertiser a competitive advantage in gaining audience attention, particularly on television where there are so many brief and similar commercial announcements.

REDUCED PERCEIVED RISK

The use of one or more reference group appeals may also serve to lower the consumer's perceived risk in purchasing a specific product. The example set by the endorser or testimonial-giver may demonstrate to the consumer that uncertainty about the product purchase is unwarranted:

Following are examples of how reference group appeals serve to lower the consumer's perceived risk.

- Celebrity. Consumers who admire a particular celebrity often have the following reactions to the celebrity's endorsement or testimonial. For e.g. "She wouldn't do a commercial for that product if she didn't believe it was really good."
- Expert. When consumers are concerned about the technical aspects of a product, they welcome the comments of an acknowledged or apparent expert. For e.g. "If he says it works, then it really must work."
- Common Man. When consumers are worried about how a product will affect them personally, they are likely to be influenced by a common man endorsement or testimonial. For e.g. "People just like me are using that product,"

Note: Foster Farms is a US based privately held company, which primarily provides poultry products such as turkey and chicken to grocery and foodservice companies. The company's product range encompasses over 750 different items, including fresh chicken and turkey, deli meats, prepared entrees and corn dogs. It is headquartered in Livingston, California and employs about 10,000 people. For a case study visit company's site www.fosterfarms.com

8

Family Influences & Decision Making

INTRODUCTION

The family is a major influence on the consumer behaviour of its members. There are many examples of how the family influences the consumption behaviour of its members. A child learns how to enjoy candy by observing an older brother or sister; learns the use and value of money by listening to and watching his or her parents.

Decisions about a new car, a vacation trip, or whether to go to a local or an out-of-town college are consumption decisions usually made within the context of a family setting. As a major consumption unit, the family is also a prime target for the marketing of many products and services.

THE FAMILY

The importance of the family or household unit in consumer behaviour arises for two reasons:

1. Many products are purchased by a family unit.
2. Individuals' buying decisions may be heavily influenced by other family members.

How families or households make purchase decisions depends on the roles of the various family members in the purchase, consumption, and influence of products. Household products like food and soaps may be purchased by a person but consumed by many, whereas personal care items, such as cosmetics or shaving cream, might be purchased by an individual family member for his or her own consumption. Homes and cars, on the other hand, are often purchased by both spouses, perhaps with involvement from children or other member of the extended family.

Visits to shopping malls often involve multiple family members buying clothing and accessories, something with a heavy dose of influence by family members-children may buy clothing paid for and approved of by parents, whereas teenagers may influence the clothing purchase of a parent.

Regardless of how many family members are present when items are being purchased, the other family members play an important role in the purchase. Just because of being mother for two young children, it is her responsibility for buying food for the family and act as an individual in the market. It does not mean that her decisions are not influenced by the preferences and power of other family members. Although marketing communications are usually directed to individuals, marketers should consider the consumption circumstances and the family structure before deciding on specific communication or advertising methods to attract their segment.

MEANING OF A FAMILY

A family is a group of two or more persons related by blood, marriage, or adoption who reside together. The nuclear family is the immediate group of father, mother, and child(ren) living together. The extended family is the nuclear family, plus other relatives, such as grandparents, uncles and aunts, cousins, and parents-in-law. The family into which one is born is called the family of orientation, whereas the one established by marriage is the family of procreation. In a more dynamic sense, the individuals who constitute a family might be described as members of the most basic social group who live together and interact to satisfy their personal and mutual needs.

MEANING OF HOUSEHOLD

The term household is used to describe all person, both related and unrelated, who occupy a housing unit. There are significant differences between the terms household and family even though they are sometimes used interchangeably. It is important to distinguish between these terms when examining data. The term household is becoming a more important unit of analysis for marketers because of the rapid growth in nontraditional families and non-family households. Among non-family households, the great majority consist of people living alone. The remaining non-family households include those consisting of elderly people living with non-family members. For example, persons of Opposite Sex Sharing Living Quarters, friends living together, and same sex couples.

STRUCTURAL VARIABLES AFFECTING FAMILIES AND HOUSEHOLDS

Structural variables include the age of the head of household or family, marital status, presence of children, and employment status. For example, consumer analysts have enormous interest in whether families have children and how many they have. Children increase family demand for clothing, food, furniture, homes, medical care, and education, while they decrease demand for many discretionary items, including travel, higher-priced restaurants, and adult clothing.

Other structural changes affect the types of products that are manufactured. For example, in Japan, high-tech companies have formed a consortium to standardize technology that has been developed to monitor and manage households.

SOCIOLOGICAL VARIABLES AFFECTING FAMILIES AND HOUSEHOLDS

Marketers can understand family and household decisions better by examining the sociological dimensions of how families make consumer decisions. Three sociological variables that help explain how family's function includes cohesion, adaptability, and communication.

- Cohesion is the emotional bonding between family members. It measures how close to each other family members feel on an emotional level. Cohesion reflects a sense of connectedness to or separateness from other family members.
- Adaptability measures the ability of a family to change its power structure, role relationships, and relationship rules in response to situational and developmental stress. The degree of adaptability shows how well a family can meet the challenges presented by changing situations.
- Communication is a facilitating dimension, critical to movement on the other two dimensions. Positive communication skills (such as empathy, reflective listening, supportive comments) enable family members to share their changing needs as they relate to cohesion and adaptability. Negative communication skills (such as double messages, double binds, criticism) minimize the ability to share feelings, thereby restricting movement in the dimensions of cohesion and adaptability. Understanding whether family members are satisfied with family purchase requires communication within the family.

To determine how the family makes its purchase decisions and how the family affects the future purchase behaviour of its members, it is useful to understand the functions provided and the roles played by family members to fulfil their consumption needs.

FUNCTIONS OF THE FAMILY

Four basic functions provided by the family are particularly relevant to a discussion of consumer behaviour. These include:

1. Economic Well-Being: Providing financial means to its dependents is unquestionably a basic family function. How the family divides its responsibilities for providing economic well-being has changed considerably during the past 25 years. The traditional roles of husband as economic provider and wife as homemaker and child rearer are still valid. The economic role of children has changed.

   Today, even if some teenage children work, they rarely assist the family financially. Their parents are still expected to provide for their needs. But some of them get enough pocket-money to decide their consumption of discretionary items.

2. Emotional Support: The provision of emotional nourishment (including love, affection, and intimacy) to its members is an important basic function of the contemporary family. In fulfilling this function, the family provides support and encouragement and assists its members in coping with personal or social problems.

   To make it easier for working parents to show their love affection and support for their children, greeting-card companies have been marketing cards especially for parent to give to their children. For instance, in most communities, many educational and psychological centres are available that are designed to assist parents who want to help their children improve their learning and communication skills, or generally, better adjust to their environments.

3. Suitable Family Lifestyles: Another important family function in terms of consumer behaviour is the establishment of a suitable lifestyle for the family. Family lifestyle commitments, including the allocation of time, greatly influence consumption patterns. For example, the increase in the number of married

women working outside the home has reduced the time they have available for household chores, and has created a market for convenience products and fast-food restaurants.

Also, with both parents working, an increased emphasis is placed on the notion of "quality time", rather than the "quantity of time" spent with children and other family members. Realizing the scarcity of quality family time, Hotels feature a variety of weekend packages targeted to couples and their children.

4. Socialization of Children and Other Family Members: The socialization of family members, especially young children, is a central family function. In large part, this process consists of imparting to children the basic value and modes of behaviour consistent with the culture.

   These generally include moral and religious principles, interpersonal skills, dress and grooming standard, appropriate manners and speech, and the selection of suitable educational and occupational or career goals.

   Socialization skills (manners, goals, values, and other qualities) are imparted to a child directly through instruction and indirectly through observation of the behaviour of parents and older siblings. Marketers often target parents looking for assistance in the task of socializing preadolescent children.

FAMILY LIFE CYCLES

Families pass through a series of stages that change them over time. This process historically has been called the family life cycle (FLC). The concept may need to be changed to household life cycle (HLC) or consumer life cycle (CLC) in the future to reflect changes in society. However, we will use the term FLC to show how the life cycle affects consumer behaviour.

CHARACTERISTICS

The traditional FLC describes family patterns as consumers marry, have children, leave home, lose a spouse, and retire. These stages are described in Table below, along with consumer behaviours associated with each stage. But consumers don't necessarily have to pass through all these stages-thy can skip multiple stages

Table: Consumer Activities Occurring in Various Life Cycles

Stages in Family Life Cycle	*Economic Circumstances*	*Likely Buying Behaviour*
Bachelorhood (Young, single staying alone)	Earning reasonable good salary, no financial burdens	Buy, basic kitchen equipment basic furniture, two wheeler, vacation with friends
Parenthood (young married just attained parenthood)	Better off financially, though home purchases at peak, less liquid assets, not able to save more.	Buys baby food, toys, diapers, chest & cough medicines
Post parenthood (growing children or grown up children)	Financial position improved with wife working, probability of home ownership on the higher side).	Concentrates on home improvements. Buy more tasteful furniture, car, home appliances, and magazines. Interested in vacation packages.
Dissolution (retired & lone surviving spouse)	Income though good, not interested in spending. At times drastic cut in income is likely.	Buy more medicinal products and other products like the retired people. Seeks more of attention, affection and security conscious.

YOUNG SINGLES

Young singles may live alone, with their nuclear families, or with friends, or they may co-habitate with partners in this stage. Although earnings tend to be relatively low, these consumers usually don't have many financial obligations and don't feel the need to save for their futures or retirement. Many of them find themselves spending as much as they make on cars, furnishings for first residences away from home, fashions, recreation, alcoholic beverages, food away from home, vacations, and other products.

NEWLY MARRIED COUPLES

Newly married couples without children are usually better off financially than they were when they were single, since they often have two incomes available to spend on one household. These families tend to spend a substantial amount of their incomes on cars, clothing, vacations, and other leisure activities. They also have the highest purchase rate and highest average purchases of durable good (particularly furniture and appliances) and appear to be more susceptible to advertising.

FULL NEST I

With the arrival of the first child, parents begin to change their roles in the family, and decide if one parent will stay to care for the child or if they will both work and buy daycare services. In this stage, families are likely to move into their first home; purchases furniture and furnishings for the child; and purchase new items such as baby food, toys, sleds, and skates. These requirements reduce families' ability to save, and the husband and wife are often dissatisfied with their financial position.

FULL NEST II

In this stage, the youngest child has reached school age, the employed spouse's income has improved. Consequently, the family's financial position usually improves, but the family finds itself consuming more and in larger quantities. Consumption patterns continue to be heavily influenced by the children, since the family tends to buy large-sized packages of food and cleaning suppliers, bicycles, music lessons, clothing, sports equipment, and a computer.

FULL NEST III

As the family grows older and parents enter their min-40s, their financial position usually continues to improve because the primary wage earner's income rises, the second wage earner is receiving a higher salary, and the children earn from occasional and part-time employment. The family typically replaces some worn pieces of furniture, buys some luxury appliances, and spends money on education. Families also spend more on computers in this stage, buying additional PCs for their older children. Depending on where children go to college and how many are seeking higher education, the financial position of the family may be tighter than other instances.

MARRIED, NO KIDS

Couples who marry and do not have children are likely to have more disposable income to spend on charities, travel, and entertainment than others in their age range. Not only do they have fewer expenses, these couples are more likely to be dual-wage earners, making it easier for them to retire earlier if they save appropriately.

OLDER SINGLES

Single, age 40 or older, may be single again (ending married status because of divorce or death of a spouse), or never married (because they prefer to live independently or because they co-habitate with partners), either group of which may or may not have children living in the household. This group now has more available income to spend on travel and leisure but feels the pressure to save for the future, since there is no second income on which to rely as they get older.

EMPTY NEST I

At this stage, the family is most satisfied with its financial position. The children have left home and are financially independent allowing the family to save more. In this stage discretionary income is spent on what the couple wants rather than on what the children need. Therefore, they spend on home improvements, luxury items, vacations, sports utility vehicles, food away from home, travel, and product for their grand children.

EMPTY NEST II

But this time, the income earners have retired, usually resulting in a reduction in income and disposable income. Expenditures become health oriented, centering on such items as medical appliances and health, and medicines. But many of these families continue to be active and in good health, allowing them to spend time traveling, exercising, and volunteering. Many continue working part time to supplement their retirement and keep them socially involved.

SOLITARY SURVIVOR

Solitary survivors be either employed or not employed. If the surviving spouse has worked outside the home in the past, he or she usually continues employment or goes back to work to live on earned income (rather than saving) and remain socially active. Expenditures for clothing and food usually decline in this stage, with income spent on health care, sickness care, travel entertainment, and services.. Those who are not employed are often on fixed incomes and may move in with friends to share housing expenses and companionship, and some may choose to remarry.

RETIRED SOLITARY SURVIVOR

Retired solitary survivors follow the same general consumption patterns as solitary survivors; however, their income may not be as high. Depending on how much they have been able to save throughout their lifetimes, they can afford to buy a wide range of products. These individuals have special needs for attention, affection, and security based on their lifestyle choices. Marketers use the descriptions of these FLC stages when analyzing marketing and communication strategies for products and services, but they often add additional information about consumer markets to analyze their needs, identify niches, and develop consumer-specific marketing strategies.

DECISION-MAKING IN A FAMILY

Families use products even though individuals usually buy them. Determining what products should be bought, which retail outlet to use, how and when products are used, and who should buy them is a complicated process involving a variety or roles and actors.

ROLE BEHAVIOUR

Families and other groups exhibit what sociologist Talcott Parsons called instrumental and expressive role behaviours.

- Instrumental roles, also known as functional or economic roles, involve financial, performance, and other functions performed by group members.
- Expressive roles involve supporting other family members in the decision-making process and expressing the family's aesthetic or emotional needs, including upholding family norms.

INDIVIDUAL ROLES IN FAMILY PURCHASES

Family consumption decisions involve at least five definable roles, which may be assumed by spouses, children, or other members of a household. Both multiple roles and multiple actors are normal. Marketers need to communicate with consumers assuming each of these roles, remembering that different family members will assume different roles depending on the situation and product. Children, for example, are users of cereals, toys, clothing, and many other products but may not be the buyers. One or both of the parents may be the decider and the buyer, although the children may be important as influencers and users.

FAMILY ROLES

For a family to function as a cohesive unit, roles or tasks-such as doing the laundry, preparing meals, setting the dinner table, taking out the garbage, walking the dog must be carried out by one or more family members. In our dynamic society, etc. family-related roles are constantly changing.

KEY FAMILY CONSUMPTION ROLES

The roles played by the different family members will vary from product to product. While shopping in the market, a housewife comes across a new variety of juice that she buys for the family. Her decision to purchase does not directly involve the influence of other family members. She is the decider, buyer; but she may or may not be the preparer and is not the only user. In case of products such as television, car, music systems, furniture or any other product which is likely to be used by some or all the family members, the purchase decision is likely to be joint or group decision.

There are eight distinct roles in the family decision-making process. A look at these roles provides further insight into how family members act in their various consumption-related roles:

- Influencers: Those family members who provide information and advice and thus influence the purchase. The housewife tells her family about the new eatery that has opened in the neighbourhood and her favourable description about it influences her husband and teenaged children.
- Gatekeepers: Those family members who control the flow of information about a product/service thus influencing the decisions of other family members. The teenaged son who wants a racing bicycle, may withhold from his father much of the relevant information on all brands except the one that he fancies, thereby influencing his father's decision in favour of his preferred brand.
- Deciders: Family members who have the power to unilaterally or jointly decide whether or not to buy a product or service. The husband and wife may jointly decide about the purchase of a new refrigerator.
- Buyers: Those family members who actually buy a particular product or service. A housewife may be the person who actually buys all the foodstuffs, rations and toiletries, which are consumed by all the family members.
- Preparers: Those family members who transform or prepare the product into the form in which it is actually consumed. The housewife may prepare the family meal using raw vegetables, lentils, spices, oil and other ingredients.
- Users: Those family members who use or consume a particular product or service. All family members may use the car, watch the television, and listen to the stereo music system
- Maintainers: Family member(s) who service or repair the product so that it will provide continued satisfaction.
- Disposers: Family member(s) who initiate or carry out the disposal or discontinuation of a particular product or service.

INFLUENCING SPOUSES AND RESOLVING CONSUMER CONFLICTS

When making consumer decisions, husbands and wives commonly attempt to influence each other to arrive at what they feel to be the best outcome. Six influence strategies for resolving husband/wife consumption-related conflicts have been identified:

- Expert: At attempt by a spouse to use his or her superior information about decision alternatives to influence the other spouse.
- Legitimacy: An attempt by a spouse to influence the other spouse on the basis of position in the household.
- Bargaining: An attempt by a spouse to secure influence now that will be exchanged with the other spouse at some future date.
- Reward: An attempt by a spouse to influence the behaviour of the other spouse by offering a reward.
- Emotional: An attempt by spouse to use an emotion-laden reaction to influence the other spouse's behaviour.
- Impression: Any persuasive attempts by one spouse to influence the behaviour of the other.

These influence strategies tend to be used by either husbands or wives when they find themselves in disagreement or in conflict with the other spouse regarding specific consumer decision. For instance, we all have experienced occasions on which different restaurants to visit, see different movies, or go on a different type of family vacation. These are only a few examples of the almost endless possibilities of potential family consumption conflicts that might need to be resolved.

CHILDREN

As any parent knows, young children attempt to influence family decisions as soon as they possess the basic communication skills needed to interact with other family members ("Buy me a cookie", "I want a Barbie doll", "Let's eat at McDonald's".). Older children are likely to participate more directly in family consumption activities. In a study of children aged 6 to 14, more than half indicated that they influenced family purchase decisions, such as choice of vacations, stereo equipment, and home computers. Other research indicates that children play relatively important roles when it comes to initiating interest in a new computer and in the actual purchase decision.

The parent-child relationship, as it relates to consumer behaviour, can be viewed as an influence versus yield situation. Specifically, children attempt to influence their parents to make a purchase (to yield). In observing shoppers in a supermarket, it is quite evident that children attempt to influence their parents to make purchases of special interest (e.g., laundry detergents) for which they see ads on TV.

TEENAGERS AND POST TEENS

A significant number of teenagers have discretionary spending in terms of spending patterns. High school students (those in grades 7 through 12) are most interested in sports and fitness. Boys between the ages of 16 and 19 spend most of their money on movies, dating, entertainment, vehicle expenses, and clothing, while girls of that age spend most of their money on clothing, cosmetics, and fragrances.

The teen market can be segmented in terms of lifestyle groups. Table below presents a four-category segmentation schema of the teenage market. Such segmentation framework has value for marketers who wish to focus their marketing efforts on a particular subgroup of teens.

Table: Lifestyle Segmentation of the Teen Market

Segment Name	*Key Characteristics*
Socially driven	Primarily female; active and extroverted. They are optimistic and plan to attend College.
Versatile Participant	Slightly more females than males: responsible teens, but less optimistic and less likely to plan to attend college than the Social Driven. They are comfortable in social and solitary situations.
Passive Introverts	Slightly more males than females: withdrawn, self-conscious, and the least comfortable in social situations. They are less optimistic about, the future, and spend the least.
Sports Oriented	Primarily males: outgoing, active, and greatly interested in participating in and watching sports. Sports influence their self-image and what they buy.

FAMILY MARKETING

Family marketing focuses on the relationships between family members based on the roles they assume, including the relationship between purchaser and family consumer and between purchaser and purchase decision maker. Family marketing identifies scenarios where some purchase might have more than one decision maker, whereas some have more than one consumer.

Although these answers may not identify all essential relationships marketers should consider, they do identify a family marketing plan, which creates a relationship between individuals and products based on the role each individual has in the influence or purchase of products. In the restaurant industry, the trend has been to focus on marketing to the family as a single unit. Admittedly, the appeal to families arose from the restaurant industry's desire to grow sales and profits.

INFLUENCES ON THE DECISION PROCESS

How do husbands and wives perceive their relative influence on decision making across the decision stages? And what does this mean for marketers? Joint decisions tend to be made about vacations, televisions, refrigerators, and living room furniture.

Autonomic decision-making tends to be present in decisions about categories that include women's jewelry, men's leisure clothing, indoor paint and wallpaper, and luggage. By understanding where on this "map" the decisions to buy particular products fall, marketers can being to determine which aspects of specific product to advertise to different household members and which media will reach the influential family member.

INFLUENCE BY DECISION STAGE

Spouses exert different degrees if influence when passing through the different stages of the decision-making process. This movement from information search to final decision may be minimal in the case of many low-involvement goods but more pronounced for goods that are risky or have high involvement for the family.

Movement is most pronounced for refrigerators, family autos, upholstered living room furniture, and carpets or rugs. Vacations are perhaps the most democratic of a family's purchase decisions. Separate campaigns may be timed to coincide with specialized interests, especially for products with a long planning cycle.

INFLUENCE OF EMPLOYMENT

In the past, marketers were able to refer to the traditional role structure categories to determine which family member was most likely to purchase a specific product. Although traditional buying roles still apply, husbands in dual-income marriages may be willing to stop at the grocery store to pick up a few items, and working wives may drop the family car at the service station for an oil change. However, contemporary couples are not inclined to shift traditional joint buying responsibilities to only one spouse, but they are willing to shop jointly for major items.

INFLUENCE OF GENDER

As the gender gap narrows, husband and wife decisions are increasingly made jointly. Qualls studied family decisions concerning vacations, automobiles, children's education, housing, insurance, and savings. Prior studies showed that decisions regarding these products were usually reported as wife or husband dominant. Qualls found overwhelmingly that joint decisions are now the norm for these products, with 80 percent of children's education and housing decisions made jointly. Increasing resources of women and shift toward egalitarianism are producing more joint decision-making in product and service categories of perceived high risk.

Note: Perdue Incorporated (Perdue) is a privately held producer and distributor of poultry products. The company also provides other agricultural products. The company primarily operates in the US. It is headquartered in Salisbury, Maryland and employs about 20,000 people. The company generates $4,100 million revenue annually. For a detailed example in "Family Influences & Decision Making" visit www.perdue.com.

9

Opinion Leadership & Diffusion of Innovations

OPINION LEADERSHIP

An issue of considerable importance to consumers and marketers alike-the informal influence that others have on consumers' behaviour and the dynamic processes that impact consumers' behaviour is the nature and dynamics of the influence that friends, neighbours, and the acquaintances have on our-consumer related decisions. This influence is often called word-of-mouth communications or the opinion leadership process. We also consider the personality and motivations of those who influence, i.e., opinion leaders and those who are influenced, i.e., opinion receivers.

MEANING

Opinion Leadership is the process by which one person (opinion leader) informally influences the actions or attitudes of others, who may be opinion seekers or merely opinion recipients. The definition of opinion leadership emphasizes on informal influence. This informal flow of opinion related influence between two or more people is referred to as word-of-mouth communication.

The person is the opinion leader and may become an opinion receiver. Individuals who actively seek information and advice about products are often called opinion seekers.

These opinion leaders are very often a part of the social groups and also have social communication network. The biggest advantage of the informal word-of-mouth communication is that it is informal and interpersonal in nature and this takes place between people who are not directly associated with the commercial selling source or the firm. Very often, we can see that the formal word-of-mouth communication is more influential than mass advertising in determining which product or brand is bought.

Opinion Leaders

Self-Improvement Motivations

- Reduce post purchase uncertainty or dissonance
- Gain attention or status
- Assert superiority and expertise
- Feel like an adventurer
- Experience the power of "Converting" others

Product-Involvement Motivations

- Express satisfaction or dissatisfaction with a product or service

Social Involvement Motivations

- Express neighbourliness and friendship by discussing products or services that may be useful to others

Message Involvement Motivations

- Express one's reaction to a stimulating advertisement by telling others about it

Opinion Receivers

- Reduce the risk of making a purchase commitment
- Reduce research time
- Learn how to use or consume a product
- Learn what products are new in the marketplace
- Buy products that have the approval of others, thereby ensuring acceptance

CHARACTERISTICS OF OPINION LEADERS

Let us now take a look at the main characteristics of opinion leaders. Some of the main features that all opinion leaders have are: Characteristics of Opinion Leaders

Opinion leaders are more knowledgeable, and have a keen level of interest.

- More involved in the product category
- Have local friendship and social interaction

- Can disseminate information
- Have high credibility
- Have more self-confidence, are more sociable and cosmopolitan, can take risks.

Opinion leaders are activated greatly to reduce distance process for the products they have bought; may want to influence neighbours and friends. They involve themselves, to confirm their own judgement. They are younger, have more education, have a higher income, and higher occupational status.

They are exposed to media. See more movies and television. Also read information magazines and technical publication devoted to the product category. Having greater knowledge about the product, they can disseminate more and true information about the products and their usage. Opinion leaders are therefore a case of study to marketers and their strategies are evaluated and formed, keeping the opinion leaders and their roles in mind.

1. Opinion leaders are perceived to be highly credible sources of product related information. Opinion leaders are persons who are considered to be knowledgeable. They often voice their opinion based on first hand information.
2. Opinion leaders are gregarious people and also have a lot of experience: Their experience as a shopper and user sets them apart from other people. Since most of their advice is based on first hand experience, opinion receivers have a lot of confidence in their advice. Besides, because of their gregarious nature, people enjoy interacting with them.
3. Opinion leaders usually provide unbiased information, i.e., they provide both favourable and unfavourable information to the opinion seekers: This adds credibility to them and opinion seekers have faith that they are receiving correct information.
4. Opinion leaders are both sources of information and advice.
5. Opinion leaders have got greater exposure to the media, especially in their area of leadership
6. Opinion leaders tend to be consumer innovators.
7. Opinion leaders have got some personal product specific characteristics like personality traits, social status and demographic characteristics

A PROFILE OF OPINION LEADERS

Now we need to study a profile of opinion leader so that we can identify them. It would be a very difficult job to exactly identify the profile of opinion leader, but we have a generalized profile as shown in table below:

Profile of Opinion Leaders

General attributes across product categories	Category specific attributes
Innovativeness	Interest
Willingness to talk	Knowledge
Self-Confidence	Special-interest
Gregariousness	Media exposure
Cognitive differentiation	Same age
	Same social status
	Social exposure outside group

FREQUENCY AND OVERLAP OF OPINION

Often we can see that more than half of the people studied in any consumer research project are classified as opinion leaders with respect to some self-selected product category. The frequency of consumer opinion leadership suggests that people are sufficiently interested in at least one product or product category to talk about it and give advice concerning it to others.

Market research suggests the existence of a special category of opinion leaders, the market maven. These are the consumers who possess a wide range of information about many different types of products, retail outlets, and other dimensions of markets.

Some important characteristics associated with market maven are:

- They both initiate discussions with other consumers and respond to requests for market information.
- Although they appear to fit the profile of opinion leaders in that they have high levels of brand awareness and tend to try more brands, unlike opinion leaders their influence extends beyond the realm of high-involvement products.
- Market mavens are also distinguishable from other opinion leaders because their influence stems not so much from product experience but from a more general knowledge or market expertise that leads them to an early awareness of a wide array of new products and services.

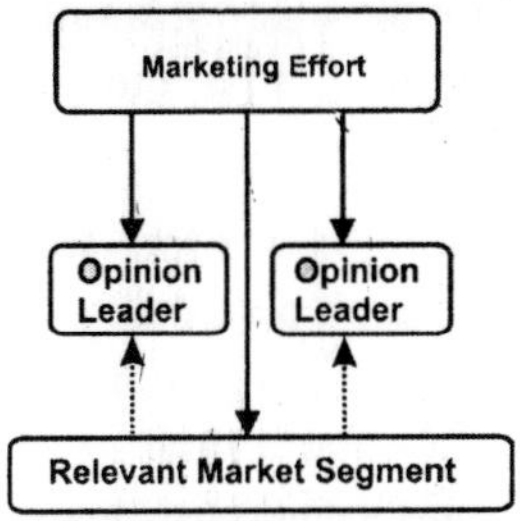

Fig. Information Flow

The figure shows that the opinion leaders seek relevant information from the mass media and other sources, and transmit the same to members of the group. The dashed line shows the feedback from the group to the opinion leaders.

INTERPERSONAL FLOW OF COMMUNICATION

You might have observed that ideas often flow from radio and print media to opinion leaders and from them to the general public. This is the concept behind the two-step flow of communication. This so-called two-step flow of communication theory portrays opinion leaders as direct receivers of information from impersonal mass-media sources, which in turn transmit (and interpret) this information to the masses. This theory views the opinion leader as a middleman between the impersonal mass media and the majority of society. A more comprehensive model of the interpersonal flow of communication depicts the transmission of information from the media as a Multistep flow. The revised model takes into account the fact that information and influence often are two-way processes in which opinion leaders both influence and are influenced by opinion receivers.

OPINION LEADERSHIP AND THE FIRM'S MARKETING STRATEGY

Marketers have long been aware of the power that opinion leadership exerts on consumers' preferences and actual purchase behaviour. Many marketers look for an opportunity to encourage word-of-mouth communications and other favourable informal conversations. New product designers take advantage of the effectiveness of word-of-mouth communication by deliberately designing products to have word-of-mouth potential. A new product should give customers something to talk about.

Proof of the power of word-of-mouth is the cases in which critics hate a movie and the viewing public like it and tell their friends. In instances where informal word of mouth does not spontaneously emerge from the uniqueness of the product or its marketing strategy, some marketers have deliberately attempted to stimulate or to simulate opinion leadership.

There are different opinion leaders for different products. The marketer must determine through research, experience or logic, the role an opinion leader plays in the existing situation for a product or service. Consumers talk to each other about their experiences and performance of the product. If their experiences do not meet expectations then there is cause for concern, and the marketer must take relevant steps to redress their complaints.

This can be reduced by utilising the knowledge of opinion leaders, which are rather difficult to identify. Opinion leaders are gregarious and tend to belong to clubs and associations. Some product categories have professional opinion leaders who are also very influential.

Hairstylists serve as, opinion leaders for hair-care products. For healthcare products-pharmacists are important opinion leaders. Computer professionals can give an opinion about the purchase of personal computers. The idea is to identify the opinion leaders, and then undertake a marketing research on them and formulate a marketing strategy.

The marketing research conducted on opinion leaders gives ideas of the likes and dislikes of the product users and their categories. Various tests should include the product use test, the pre-testing of the advertising copy, the media preferred for customers to respond favourably to the firm's marketing mix. The sampling should be done from amongst the opinion leaders. In retailing and personnel selling various techniques can be adopted to attract customers like, one meal extra for every three meals or, pay for two and take three or, a "fashion advisory board" can be constituted in clothing stores.

In advertising, people of prominence and, owners can be used and their experiences and satisfaction received can be projected through conversation and, by giving their impression to the general public and non-owners of the product. Opinion leaders can be used effectively in commercials to promote the product to the masses.

DIFFUSION OF INNOVATIONS

We as consumers always find a new innovation-idea or product or even new service attractive. However, for the firm which is trying its hand at the new innovation, there is always a question hanging around

'How fast will the diffusion of the innovation take place?" This is to say that any innovation has got an element of risk involved. The firm will introduce a new concept or a new product after an intensive research is carried out by it. Thus we see that the process of diffusion of innovation is very critical to a firm.

DIFFUSION

Diffusion is a macro process concerned with the spread of a new product an innovation from its source to the consuming public. Adoption is a micro process that focuses on the stages through which an individual consumer passes when deciding to accept or reject a new product. Diffusion of innovations is the process by which acceptance of an innovation (new products or new service or new idea) is spread by communication (mass media, sales people, informal conversation) to members of the target market over a period of time. Some new product innovation, which were easily accepted by customers

Examples of New Products/Services Easily Accepted by Consumers

New Product	*Benefit Communicated*
1. Vacuum cleaner (Eureka Forbes)	Compact, easy to use vacuum cleaner to keep home clan and tidy, home delivery after demonstration.
2. Fire extinguisher (Real Value)	Portal piece of safety equipment-fire extinguisher.
3. Plastic water tank (Sintex)	A convenient low cost alternative to the traditional metal or concrete water tank
4. Utensil cleaner cake (Rin cake)	Premixed scouring solution in the form of bar instead of waste prone powder.
5. Mosquito repellent matt (Good Knight)	A mosquito repellent-which has no smoke, no fumes, no ash, no cream, no mosquitoes
6. Diaper (Huggys)	Drier, more comfortable than cloth, disposable diaper for babies.

THE DIFFUSION PROCESS

The diffusion process follows a similar pattern, overtime, irrespective of the social group or innovation. The typical diffusion process shows a slow growth or adoption. It later rises rapidly, and then a period of slow growth is noticed. In fast diffusion process, the product clicks immediately. The spread of innovation is very quick. People patronise the product immediately, and later on there is again slow diffusion. In slow diffusion process, the product takes a lot of time to diffuse or spread, and the consumer follows a pattern of adoption slowly by getting acquainted with the product.

Diffusion is the process by which the acceptance of an innovation (a new product, a new service, new idea or new practice) is spread by communication (mass media, salespeople, or informal conversations) to members of a social system (a target market) over a period of time. These studies show that the products take a certain amount of time, from when it gets introduced to its saturation. The marketer therefore has to understand what determines the spread of innovation in a given market segment, and how do the early buying consumers differ from those of late purchasers. The four basic elements of this process are:

1. The Innovation: Various approaches which have been taken to define a new product or a new service include
   - Firm-oriented definitions: A firm oriented approach treats the newness of a product from the perspective of the company producing or marketing it. When the product is "new" to the firm it is considered to be new.
   - Product oriented definitions: Product-oriented approach focuses on the features inherent in the product itself and on the effects these features are likely to have on consumers' established usage patterns. Three types of product innovations could be: Continuous innovation having the least disruptive influence on established patterns involving the introduction of a modified product, rather than a totally new product. E.g., latest version of Microsoft Office; dynamically continuous innovation which may involve the creation of a new product or the modification of an existing product e.g., disposable diapers, CD players; discontinuous innovations requiring consumers to adopt new behaviour patterns e.g., TV, fax machines, Internet
   - Market oriented definitions: Judges the newness of a product in terms of how much exposure consumers have to the new product. The definitions could be:
   - A product id considered new if it has been purchased by a relatively small (fixed) percentage of the potential market.
   - A product is considered new if it has been on the market for a relatively short (specified) period of time.
   - Consumer oriented definitions: A new product is any product that a potential consumer judges to be new.
2. The channels of Communication: How quickly an innovation spreads through a market depends to a great extent on communications between the marketer and consumers, as well

as communication among consumers i.e., word-of-mouth communication. Thus this communication will include two types of communication:

- Communication between marketers and consumers
- Communication among consumers i.e., word of mouth.

Consumer information sources fall into four categories:

- Personal sources: Family, friends, neighbours, and acquaintances.
- Commercial sources: sales people, advertising, sales promotion techniques.

3. The Social System: The diffusion of a new product usually takes place in a social setting frequently referred to as a social system. In our case, the terms market segment and target segment may be more relevant than the term social system used in diffusion research. A social system is a physical, social, or cultural environment to which people belong and within which they function. For example, for new hybrid seed rice, the social system might consist of all farmers in a number of local villages. The key point to remember is that a social system's orientation is the climate in which marketers must operate to gain acceptance for their new products. For example, in recent years, the World has experienced a decline in the demand for red meat. The growing interest in health and fitness thought the nation has created a climate in which red meat is considered too high in fat and calorie content. At the same time, the consumption of chicken and fish has increased, because these foods satisfy the prevailing nutritional values of a great number of consumers.

4. Time: Time pervades the study of diffusion in three distinct but interrelated ways:

   - The amount of purchase time: Purchase time refers to the amount of time that elapses between consumers' initial awareness of a new product or service and the point at which they purchase or reject it. For instance, when the concept of "Home Land" super market was introduced by Asha Chavan in Pune, apart from offering a variety of quality products, also give an unconditional guarantee of replacement or refund, home delivery of all, even single item telephonic orders at no extra cost. And beyond business, Homeland also offers free services like phone, electricity, credit card and cell phone bill payments.

- The identification of adopter categories: The concept of adopter categories involves a classification scheme that indicates where a consumer stands in relation to other consumers in terms of time. Five adopter categories are frequently used viz., innovators, early adopters, early majority, late majority, and laggards.
- The rate of adoption: The rate of adoption is concerned with how long it takes a new product or service to be adopted by members of a social system i.e., how quickly it takes a new product to be accepted by those who will ultimately adopt it.

Table: Importance of Time in the Diffusion Process

Type of Time	*Meaning*	*Examples*
Purchase time	Time between awareness and purchase	If you look at your car's fuel meter and it reads "Empty" you stop at the next petrol pump you come to.
Adopter categories	A classification scheme that indicates where a consumer stands, in relation to others, when adopting a new product	If you are shopping for your second car, you may take a while to make a purchase, as long as your present car is working fine. Innovators are the first to adopt a new product, and laggards are the last
Rate of adoption	How long it takes a new product or service to be adopted by members of a social system	Black-and-white TVs were adopted by consumers much more quickly than their manufacturers had envisioned; in contrast, trash compactors have never been widely adopted

The marketing objective for launching new products is to gain wide acceptance from the market as quickly as possible. So as to obtain huge market share with the new product, marketers either adopt a Penetrating strategy, i.e., low introductory price to discourage competitors from entering the market or go for a Skimming strategy.

INFLUENCE OF PRODUCT CHARACTERISTICS ON DIFFUSION

The rate of spread of innovation depends on a number of factors listed below:

- Type of group: Some groups, who are young, affluent and highly educated, accept changes faster than the old, traditional and poor groups. This shows that the target market is an important determinant of the rate of diffusion.

- Perceived risk: The more the risk associated with changing to new innovation, the slower is the rate of diffusion. The risk consists of the product not performing as expected, the risk of the consequences of change-over, and the risk of reverting back to the old product, if not satisfied with the innovative product.
- Type of decision: An individual vs. a collective decision. Individual decisions lead to faster diffusion than collective ones.
- Marketing effort: This also affects the diffusion process. More aggressive marketing effort, consisting of high and continuous advertising expenditure, diffuses faster than otherwise.
- Trial: The trial can be taken at low cost and low risk, the diffusion is faster. Some products can be borrowed, rented or, their trial can be taken at retail outlets. These products like medicines and other low priced items have faster diffusion. These days even car outlets are giving free trials and rides to prospective customers, to make their new models of cars diffuse faster.
- Fulfilment of felt need: The faster a need is satisfied or fulfilled by a product, the greater is the rate of its diffusion.
- Compatibility: The more the product is compatible with the beliefs, attitudes and values of the individual or group the faster the diffusion vegetables soup for vegetarians, ordinary microwave no roasting.
- Relevant advantage: The advantage could be of price, quality, ease of handling, product quality. To have quick diffusion, the product must offer either a price advantage or a performance advantage. Washing machine is expensive, but a labour saving device.
- Complexity: If the product is complex (difficult to understand and use) the diffusion is slower. The product may be complex but its use must be easy. Complexity may be because of many attributes (at-tributes complexity which are difficult to understand). The other complexity may be trade off complexity. The trade off takes place between cost of purchase and economy. Convenience vs. space or speed of cooking, vs. quality of cooking, as in microwave ovens.
- Observability: The more easily the positive effects of the products can be observed, the more discussion takes place and faster the diffusion process, e.g. cell phones.

CLASSIFICATION OF ADOPTERS

Adopters can be classified into five groups based on the time when they adopt.

Innovators	The first 2.5 per cent to adopt innovation.
Early adopters	The next 13.5 per cent to adopt.
Early majority	The next 34 per cent to adopt.
Late majority	The next 34 per cent to adopt.
Laggards	The final 16 per cent to adopt.

INNOVATORS

Innovators are venturesome risk takers. They are younger, more educated and socially mobile. They have the capacity to absorb risk associated with the new product. They are cosmopolitan in outlook, are aware and make use of commercial media, and are eager to learn about new products, are progressive, ready to use new products.

EARLY ADOPTERS

They take a calculated risk before investing and using new innovations. They are opinion leaders and provide information to groups, but they are also concerned about failure. Therefore, they weigh advantages and disadvantages of the product before plunging in for a purchase.

EARLY MAJORITY

They tend to be more continuous and use the product after the innovators and early adopters seem to be satisfied with it. They are elders, well educated and less socially mobile. They rely heavily on inter-personal source of information. They constitute 34 per cent of the consumers.

LATE MAJORITY

They are doubtful and skeptical about the innovation of new products. They tend to use the product not so much because of innovation, but because of other pressures, non-availability of the product and social pressures. They have less social status, and are less socially mobile than the previous group.

LAGGARDS

They are more traditional. They possess limited social interaction and are oriented to the past. They adopt the innovations with great reluctance. They constitute a small portion of 16 per cent of the consumers.

Table: Adopter Categories

Adopter Category	Description	Relative percentage within which the population that eventually adopts
Innovators	Venturesome-very eager to try new ideas; acceptable if risk is daring; more cosmopolite social relationships; communicates with other innovators	2.5%
Early Adopters	Respect-more integrated into the local social system; the persons to check with before adopting a new idea; category contains greatest number of opinion leaders; are role models	13.5%
Early Majority	Deliberate-adopt new ideas just prior to the average time; seldom hold leadership positions; deliberate for some time before adopting	34.0%
Late majority	Skeptical-adopt new ideas just after the average time; adopting may be both an economic necessity and a reaction to peer pressures; innovations approached cautiously	34.0%
Laggards	Traditional-the last people to adopt an innovation; most "localite" in outlook; oriented to the past; suspicious of the new	16.0%

NON ADOPTER CATEGORIES

A classification of the non-adopter categories would include:

- The unaware group: Those consumers who are not aware of the new product
- Symbolic rejectors: Who, though aware of the product, have decided against buying it.
- Symbolic adopters: Who know the product will be useful or them but have not tried it.
- Trial adopters: Who have tried the product and also rejected the same.
- Trial rejectors

ROLE OF PERSONAL INFLUENCE

Personal influence is another important factor, which plays a role in the adoption process of new products. This refers to what effect the statements made abut 'a new product' by one person will have on another person's change in attitude or probability. This means that based on the comments or views expressed by ones personal friend or acquaintance one may change the decision to adopt a new product or innovation. It is usually observed that consumers and especially women prefer to consult one another's friends and value the opinions expressed by them about new products, the quality differences among the different brands, store at which to purchase to experience shopping and so on.

MARKET STRATEGY RELATED TO DIFFUSION

There are differences in the early purchasers or innovators and late purchasers (Laggards). The strategy for the target market adopted is a "moving target market" approach. First the general target market is selected, and then the focus shifts to innovators, early adopters, early majority, late majority and laggards. This takes place as the product keeps getting acceptance from the consumers. There is then a change in the media and advertising themes for different target groups.

DIFFUSION ENHANCEMENT STRATEGIES

The idea is to find out the diffusion inhibitors and to eliminate them for the enhancement of diffusion. For this the diffusion determinants are analysed, and diffusion strategies framed, as given in table below.

Table: Diffusion Enhancement Strategies

S.No.	*Diffusion Determinant*	**Diffusion Inhibitor**	*Diffusion Enhancement Strategies*
1.	Type of group	Conservative	Try other markets modern traditional and consumer
2.	Perceived risk	High	Give guarantees, reduce risk by endorsing with credible sources
3.	Type of decision	Group	Choose media to reach all decisions deciders and provide conflict reduction themes
4.	Marketing effort	Limited	Extensive and aggressive marketing effort
5.	Trial	Difficult	Distribute free samples to early adopters. Use high service outlets
6.	Fulfilment of felt need	Weak	Show importance of benefits use extensive advertising
7.	Compatibility	Conflict	Stress attributes consistent with values and norms
8.	Relevant advantage	Low	Lower the price-redesign the product
9.	Complexity	High	Use extensive marketing effort. Use skilled sales force. Use demonstration of product
10.	Observability	Low	Expose the product more through promotion and advertising

These diffusion inhibitors have to be analysed, and strategies formulated accordingly.

Note: Rich Products Corporation (Rich's) is a US-based privately held manufacturer of frozen foods. The company manufactures and markets products, including toppings and icings, breads and rolls, finished desserts and cakes, pizza dough and sweet goods, beverages, Italian specialties, barbeque, seafood and appetizers. The company primarily operates in the US. It is headquartered in Buffalo, New York and employs 7,200 people. For detailed information related to this chapter reader can visit www.rich.com

10

Consumer Behaviour Applications & Consumerism

Consumers have so many choices to make compared to ten or even twenty years ago. Today as always, business growth depends heavily on loyal customers who return because they are satisfied with the product and/or service they have received. But first companies have to bring consumers into the stores. The companies bring consumers into the store by marketing their product. Through out in this book you would realize that Consumer is the end all and by all. He reigns the market. It is necessary to discuss strategic market planning and marketing early in the course. A strategic market plan gives direction to a firm's efforts and better enables it to understand the dimensions of marketing research, consumer analysis, and product, distribution, promotion, and price planning.

The study of consumers helps firms and organizations improve their marketing strategies by understanding issues such as how

- The psychology of how consumers think, feel, reason, and select between different alternatives (e.g., brands, products);
- The psychology of how the consumer is influenced by his or her environment (e.g., culture, family, signs, media);
- The behaviour of consumers while shopping or making other marketing decisions;
- Limitations in consumer knowledge or information processing abilities influence decisions and marketing outcome;
- How consumer motivation and decision strategies differ between products that differ in their level of importance or interest that they entail for the consumer; and

- How marketers can adapt and improve their marketing campaigns and marketing strategies to more effectively reach the consumer.

Understanding these issues helps us adapt our strategies by taking the consumer into consideration. For example, by understanding that a number of different messages compete for our potential customers' attention, we learn that to be effective, advertisements must usually be repeated extensively.

We also learn that consumers will sometimes be persuaded more by logical arguments, but at other times will be persuaded more by emotional or symbolic appeals. By understanding the consumer, we will be able to make a more informed decision as to which strategy to employ.

There are four main applications of consumer behaviour:

- The most obvious is for marketing strategy-i.e., for making better marketing campaigns. For example, by understanding that consumers are more receptive to food advertising when they are hungry, we learn to schedule snack advertisements late in the afternoon.

  By understanding that new products are usually initially adopted by a few consumers and only spread later, and then only gradually, to the rest of the population, we learn that (1) companies that introduce new products must be well financed so that they can stay afloat until their products become a commercial success and (2) it is important to please initial customers, since they will in turn influence many subsequent customers' brand choices.
- A second application is public policy. In the 1980s, Acutance, a near miracle cure for acne, was introduced. Unfortunately, Acutance resulted in severe birth defects if taken by pregnant women. To get consumers' attention, the Federal Drug Administration (FDA) took the step of requiring that very graphic pictures of deformed babies be shown on the medicine containers.
- Social marketing involves getting ideas across to consumers rather than selling something.
- As a final benefit, studying consumer behaviour should make us better consumers.

STRATEGIC MARKET PLANNING

A Strategic marketing plan is an outline of the methods and resources required to achieve organizational goals within a specific target market(s).

"Describes the direction [an organization] will pursue within its chosen environment and guides the allocation of resources and effort" - Peter Bennett, Dictionary of Marketing Terms, AMA 1988

Strategic planning requires a general marketing orientation rather than a narrow functional orientation. According to Prof. Mohan Kuruvilla, visiting professor IIM (B) -All functional areas must include marketing and must be coordinated to reach organizational goals. It is a hierarchal process, from company wide to marketing specific. (Marketing concept, implemented from top down.)

A firm can be broken down into several strategic business units. Each Strategic Business Units (SBU) is a division, product line, or other profit centre within the parent company.

An SBU has its own strategic plan and can be considered a separate business entity competing with other SBU's for corporate resources.

For example Pepsico Companies SBUs include:

- KFC
- Pizza Hut
- Mountain Dew
- Lipton Tea Brands
- Lays

E.g. The College of Business and Economics is an SBU of the University of Delaware.

A strategic plan gives:

- Direction and better enables the company to understand market. function dimensions
- Makes sure that each division has clear integrated goals
- Different functional areas are encouraged to coordinate
- Assesses SW & OT (Strengths Weakness and opportunity & Threat)
- Assesses alternative actions
- It is a basis for allocating company resources
- A procedure to assess company performance

The strategic planning process may include the following, although this differs from one organization to another:

- Develop a SWOT analysis
- Develop Mission Statement that evolves from the SWOT analysis
- Develop Corporate Objectives that are consistent with the organization's mission statement.
- Develop corporate strategy to achieve the organization's objectives. [If the organization is made up of more than one SBU, then follow loop again for each SBU, then proceed]
- Marketing (and other functional objectives) must be designed to achieve the corporate objectives
- Marketing Strategy, designed to achieve the marketing objectives.

The strategic market planning process is based on the establishment of organizational goals and it must stay within the broader limits of the organizations mission that is developed taking into consideration the environmental opportunities and threats and the companies' resources and distinct competencies.

A firm can then assess its opportunities and develop a corporate strategy. Marketing objectives must be designed so that they can be accomplished through efficient use of the firm's resources.

Corporate strategy is concerned with issues such as diversification, competition, differentiation, interrelationships between business units and environmental issues. It attempts to match the resources of the organization with the opportunities and risks of the environment (SWOT). Corporate strategy is also concerned with defining the scope and roles of the SBU's of the firm so that they are coordinated to reach the ends desired.

TYPES OF MARKETING STRATEGIES

Every marketing strategy is unique, but if we abstract from the individualizing details, each can be reduced into a generic marketing strategy. There are a number of ways of categorizing these generic strategies. A brief description of the most common categorizing schemes is presented below:

Strategies based on market dominance -Market dominance is a measure of the strength of a brand, product, service, or firm, relative to competitive offerings. There is often a geographic element to the competitive landscape. In defining market dominance, you must see to what extent a product, brand, or firm controls a product category in a given geographic area.

There are several ways of calculating market dominance. The most direct is market share. This is the percentage of the total market serviced by a firm or brand.

In this scheme, firms are classified based on their market share or dominance of an industry. Typically there are four types of market dominance strategies:

- Leader -The market leader is dominant in its industry. It has substantial market share and often extensive distribution arrangements with retailers. It typically is the industry leader in developing innovative new business models and new products (although not always). It tends to be on the cutting edge of new technologies and new production processes. It sometimes has some market power in determining either price or output. Of the four dominance strategies, it has the most flexibility in crafting strategy. - E.g. Colgate dental care products
- Challenger -A market challenger is a firm in a strong, but not dominant position that is following an aggressive strategy of trying to gain market share. It typically targets the industry leader (for example, Pepsi targets Coke), but it could also target smaller, more vulnerable competitors. The fundamental principles involved are:
- Assess the strength of the target competitor. Consider the amount of support that the target might muster from allies.
- Choose only one target at a time.
- Find a weakness in the target's position. Attack at this point. Consider how long it will take for the target to realign their resources so as to reinforce this weak spot.
- Launch the attack on as narrow a front as possible. Whereas a defender must defend all their borders, an attacker has the advantage of being able to concentrate their forces at one place.
- Launch the attack quickly, then consolidate. E.g. When Coca Cola was the official sponsor for the Cricket world cup, they advertised as the "Official drink". Pepsi retaliated by advertising "Nothing official about it".

- Follower - A market follower is a firm in a strong, but not dominant position that is content to stay at that position. The rationale is that by developing strategies that are parallel to those of the market leader, they will gain much of the market from the leader while being exposed to very little risk. This "play it safe" strategy is how Burger King retains its position behind McDonalds. The advantages of this strategy are:
- No expensive R&D failures
- No risk of bad business model
- "Best practices" are already established
- Able to capitalize on the promotional activities of the market leader
- No risk of government anti-combines actions
- Minimal risk of competitive attacks
- Don't waste money in a head-on battle with the market leader
- Nicher -In this niche strategy the firm concentrates on a select few target markets. It is also called a focus strategy. It is hoped that by focusing ones marketing efforts on one or two narrow market segments and tailoring your marketing mix to these specialized markets, you can better meet the needs of that target market. The niche should be large enough to be profitable, but small enough to be ignored by the major industry players. Profit margins are emphasized rather than revenue or market share. The firm typically looks to gain a competitive advantage through effectiveness rather than efficiency. It is most suitable for relatively small firms and has much in common with guerrilla marketing warfare strategies. The most successful nichers tend to have the following characteristics:
- They tend to be in high value added industries and are able to obtain high margins.
- They tend to be highly focussed on a specific market segment.
- They tend to market high end products or services, and are able to use a premium pricing strategy.
- They tend to keep their operating expenses down by spending less on R&D, advertising, and personal selling. E.g. Mercedes Benz.
- Porter generic strategies -Michael Porter assessed strategy on the dimensions of strategic scope and strategic strength.

Strategic scope refers to the breadth of market penetration while strategic strength refers to the firm's sustainable competitive advantage. He felt three types were important:

- Cost leadership
- Product differentiation
- Market segmentation

In this strategy the firm concentrates on a select few target markets. It is also called a focus strategy or niche strategy. It is hoped that by focusing your marketing efforts on one or two narrow market segments and tailoring your marketing mix to these specialized markets, you can better meet the needs of that target market. The firm typically looks to gain a competitive advantage through effectiveness rather than efficiency. It is most suitable for relatively small firms but can be used by any company. As a focus strategy it may be used to select targets that are less vulnerable to substitutes or where a competition is weakest to earn above-average return on investments

- Innovation strategies -This deals with the firm's rate of new product development and business model innovation. It asks whether the company is on the cutting edge of technology and business innovation. There are three types:
- Pioneers
- Close followers
- Late followers
- Growth strategies -In this scheme we ask the question, "How should the firm grow?". There are a number of different ways of answering that question, but the most common gives four answers:
- Horizontal integration -In microeconomics and strategic management, the term horizontal integration describes a type of ownership and control. It is a strategy used by a business or corporation that seeks to sell a type of product in numerous markets. To get this market coverage, several small subsidiary companies are created. Each markets the product to a different market segment or to a different geographical area. This is sometimes referred to as the horizontal integration of marketing. The horizontal integration of production exists when a firm has plants in several locations producing similar products. Horizontal integration in marketing is much more common than

horizontal integration in production. It is contrasted with vertical integration

- Vertical integration -In microeconomics and strategic management, the term vertical integration describes a style of ownership and control. Vertically integrated companies are united through a hierarchy and share a common owner. Usually each member of the hierarchy produces a different product or service, and the products combine to satisfy a common need. It is contrasted with horizontal integration. Vertical integration is one method of avoiding the hold-up problem. One of the earliest, largest and most famous examples of vertical integration was the Carnegie Steel company. The company controlled not only the mills where the steel was manufactured, but the mines where the iron ore was extracted, the coal mines that supplied the coal, the ships that transported the iron ore and the railroads that transported the coal to the factory, the coke ovens where the coal was coked, etc.
- Diversification (or conglomeration) -Diversification is a means whereby a business builds up its revenue by recognising chances to create or obtain businesses that are not precisely linked to the company's existing businesses. There are three main types of diversification: concentric, horizontal and conglomerate.

Concentric diversification results in new product lines or services that have technological and/or marketing synergies with already accessible product lines, even though the products may attract a new customer base. Horizontal diversification happens when the company develops new products that could attract its present customer groups even though those new products may be technologically unconnected to the existing product lines. Conglomerate diversification happens where there is neither technological nor marketing synergy and required reaching new customer groups and individuals.

- Intensification
- Aggressiveness strategies - Business strategies can be categorized in many ways. One popular method is to assess strategies based on their degree of aggressiveness. Aggressiveness strategies are rated according to their marketing assertiveness, their risk propensity, financial leverage, product innovation, speed of decision making, and other measures of business aggressiveness. Typically the range of aggressiveness

strategies is classified into four categories: prospector, defender, analyzer, and reactor.

- Prospector -This is the most aggressive of the four strategies. It typically involves active programs to expand into new markets and stimulate new opportunities. New product development is vigorously pursued and attacks on competitors are a common way of obtaining additional market share. They respond quickly to any signs of market opportunity, and do so with little research or analysis. A large proportion of their revenue comes from new products or new markets
- Defender -This strategy entails a decision not to aggressively pursue markets. As a result, they tend to do none of the things prospectors do. A defender strategy entails finding, and maintaining a secure and relatively stable market. Rather than being on the cutting edge of technological innovation, product development, and market dynamics, a defender tries to insulate themselves from changes wherever possible. In their attempt to secure this stable market they either keep prices low, keep advertising and other promotional costs low, engage in vertical integration, offer a limited range of products or offer better quality or service. They tend to be slower in making decisions and will only commit to a change after extensive research and analysis.
- Analyser -The analyzer is in between the defender and prospector. They take less risk and make less mistakes than a prospector, but are less committed to stability than defenders. Most firms are analyzers. They are seldom a first mover in an industry but are often second or third place entrants. They tend to expand into areas close to their existing core competency. Rather than develop wholly new products, they make incremental improvements in existing products. Rather than expand into wholly new markets, they gradually expand existing markets. They try to maintain a balanced portfolio of products with some stable income generators and some potential winners. They watch closely the developments in their industry but don't act until they are sure that the time is right.
- Reactor -A reactor has no proactive strategy. They react to events as they occur. They respond only when they are forced to by macroenvironmental pressures. This is the least effective of the four strategies. It is without direction or focus.

- Warfare based strategies -are a type of strategies, used in business and marketing, that try to draw parallels between business and warfare, and then apply the principles of military strategy to business situations. In business we do not have enemies, but we do have competitors; and we do not fight for land, but we do compete for market share. It is argued that, in mature, low-growth markets, and when real GDP growth is negative or low, business operates as a zero-sum game. One person's gain is possible only at another person's expense. Success depends on battling competitors for market share. This scheme draws parallels between marketing strategies and military strategies. There are many types of marketing warfare strategies, but they can be grouped into:
- Offensive marketing warfare strategies -Attack the target competitor with an objective such as "liberating" some of its market share.
- Defensive marketing warfare strategies -Strategies intended to maintain your market share, profitability, sales revenue, or some other objective.
- Flanking marketing warfare strategies -Operate in areas of little importance to the competitor.
- Guerrilla marketing warfare strategies -Attack, retreat, hide, then do it again, and again, until the competitor moves on to other markets.

A basic tenet underlying marketing strategy is that there are distinct market segments each of which has its own needs, wants, desires, and interests.

MEANING

A market is: "An aggregate of people who, as individuals or organizations, have needs for products in a product class and who have the ability, willingness and authority to purchase such products (conditions needed for an exchange)."

Types of markets:

- Consumer Intend to consume or benefit, but not to make a profit.
- Organizational/Business For:
- Resale

- Direct use in production
- General daily operations.

MARKETING SEGMENTATION

To get a product or service to the right customer, a marketer would firstly segment the market, then target a single segment or series of segments, and finally position within the segment's. Segmentation is essentially the identification of subsets of buyers within a market who share similar needs and who demonstrate similar buyer behaviour. The world is made up from billions of buyers with their own sets of needs and behaviour. Segmentation aims to match groups of purchasers with the same set of needs and buyer behaviour. Such a group is known as a 'segment'.

The requirements for successful segmentation are:

- Homogeneity within the segment
- Heterogeneity between segments
- Segments are measurable and identifiable
- Segments are accessible and actionable
- Segment is large enough to be profitable.

E.g. The market for Laptops can be segmented into - Students, Business Executives, IT professionals - both backend and front end.

Criteria needed for segmentation are:

- Segments must have enough profit potential to justify developing and maintaining a Marketing Mix
- Consumer must have heterogeneous (different) needs for the product.
- Segmented consumer needs must be homogeneous (similar)
- Company must be able to reach a segment with a Marketing Mix.

Have you seen children making choice for themselves or for the family? How do you think they know what they want? How do marketers reach children? Yes, today they are an important part of our market. They not only make decisions regarding their cloths, they actually help parents make decision regarding high priced products and services such as televisions, clubs and hotels, car, shoes etc.

The marketers use various tools to reach them-some of the media channels they focus on:

- Cartoons Network
- Toon Disney
- POGO
- Nickelodeon
- Cereal boxes
- Sports illustrated for kids

Look at how media has changed recently due to changing demographics etc. and therefore the need of marketers to reach these groups. Media must respond because they are essentially financed by the marketers or at least heavily subsidized

Bases for Marketing Segmentation:

- Geographic variables -dividing the market into zones or geographical regions
- region of the world or country
- country size
- climate
- E.g. MTR chilly or any of their items price their products region-wise. Within Karnataka Rs.15/100grams AND Outside Karnataka Rs. 18/100 grams
- Demographic variables -is a shorthand term for 'population characteristics'. Demographics include race, age, income, mobility (in terms of travel time to work or number of vehicles available), educational attainment, home ownership, employment status, and even location. Distributions of values within a demographic variable, and across households, are both of interest, as well as trends over time.

Demographics are primarily used in economic and marketing research.

- Age
- Gender
- Sexual orientation
- Family size
- Family life cycle

- Income
- Occupation
- Education
- Socioeconomic status is the social science of the social and economic impacts of any product or service offering, market intervention or other event on an economy as a whole and on the companies, organizations and factors that influence how an intervention is likely to change a society will be unique to each situation, but generally may include, for example:
- Prevailing economic conditions
- Race or ethnicity
- The level of economic development and the extent of disparities within a society
- Political stability and the relationship between government and judiciary
- Levels of education, literacy and familiarity with technology
- Maturity and openness of markets
- Propensity for entrepreneurial activity
- Strength of tradition in terms of beliefs and behaviours
- religion
- nationality/race
- E.g. Spice Telecom has a special plan for the "Youth segment" called Spice youth, they have special benefits like 100 sms free, zero balance recharge.
- Psychographic variables are any attributes relating to personality, values, attitudes, interests, or lifestyles. They are also called IAO variables (Interests, Attitudes, and Opinions). They can be contrasted with demographic variables (such as age and gender), and behavioural variables (such as usage rate or loyalty). When a relatively complete assessment of a person or group's psychographic make-up is constructed, this is called a psychographic profile. Psychographic profiles are used in market segmentation and advertising. It only relates to one form not two as geodemographic which would relate to the geographical spread of different age groups across the India for example. The variables are:

- Personality
- Life style
- Value
- Attitude
- Behavioural variables - are any attributes relating to the behaviour or pattern of use of a product by the consumers.
- Benefit sought
- Product usage rate
- Brand loyalty
- Product end use
- Readiness-to-buy stage
- Decision making unit

When numerous variables are combined to give an in-depth understanding of a segment, this is referred to as depth segmentation. When enough information is combined to create a clear picture of a typical member of a segment, this is referred to as a buyer profile. When the profile is limited to demographic variables it is called a demographic profile (typically shortened to "a demographic"). A statistical technique commonly used in determining a profile is cluster analysis.

- Segmentation variables should be related to consumer needs for, and uses of, or behaviour toward the product. E.g. Stereo; age not religion.
- Segmentation variable must be measurable. No best way to segment the markets. Selecting inappropriate variable limits the chances of success.

DEVELOPING A TARGET MARKET STRATEGY

A Product will not sell by itself; It needs the best of strategies. After drawing a strong strategy plan, we need to develop a target market. Developing a target market strategy has three phases:

1. Analyzing consumer demand
2. Targeting the market(s)
    - Undifferentiated
    - Concentrated
    - Multi-segmented
3. Developing the marketing strategy

Selecting Target Markets by Analyzing Demand: Demand is the quantity of a good that consumers are not only willing to purchase but also have the capacity to buy at the given price. For example, a consumer may be willing to purchase 2 Kgs of potatoes if the price is Rs.3 per kg. However, the same consumer may be willing to purchase only 1 Kg if the price is Rs.5.00 per Kg. A demand schedule can be constructed that shows the quantity demanded at each given price. It can be represented on a graph as a line or curve by plotting the quantity demanded at each price. It can also be described mathematically by a demand equation. The main determinants of the quantity one is willing to purchase will typically be the price of the good, one's level of income, personal tastes, the price of substitute goods, and the price of complementary goods.

The capacity to buy is sometimes used to characterise demand as being merely an alternate form of supply. As marketers we need to aggregate consumers with similar needs. We need to identify demand patterns. Identification of demand could be done by asking the following questions and analyzing the same.

Do all potential customers have similar needs/desires or are there clusters? What are the demand patterns?

A marketer can normally identify 3 demand patterns, they are:

- Homogeneous Demand-uniform, everyone demands the product for the same reason(s). e.g. A prescribed textbook for a course
- Clustered Demand-consumer demand classified in 2 or more identifiable clusters. E.g. Automobiles:
- Luxury
- Cheap
- Sporty
- Spacious
- Diffused Demand-Product differentiation more costly and more difficult to communicate E.g. Cosmetic market; need to offer hundreds of shades of lipstick. Firms try to modify consumer demand to develop clusters of at least a moderate size.

Targeting The Market: After analyzing the demand pattern we as marketers, can identify how the consumers can be targeted. This would include 3 approaches in which a marketer can target its consumers.

- Undifferentiated Approach (Total Market Approach) - This approach does not differentiate the market according to any variable. In this case a Single Marketing Mix for the entire market identified is laid out. All consumers have similar needs for a specific kind of product. Homogeneous market, or demand is so diffused it is not worthwhile to differentiate, try to make demand more homogeneous. E.g. Nirma Detergent soap - for any kind of stain, for any kind of person or cloth one soap.

Single Marketing Mix consists of:

- Pricing strategy
- Promotional program aimed at everybody
- Type of product with little/no variation
- Distribution system aimed at entire market

The elements of the marketing mix do not change for different consumers; all elements are developed for all consumers. Examples include Staple foods-sugar and salt and farm produce. This approach is popular when large-scale production began. In today's competitive market this approach is out-dated and could cause a product to fail, as the competition is very high and the availability of alternatives are very extensive.

If this approach is incorporated into an organization it must be able to develop and maintain a single marketing mix. In this case the major objective is to maximize sales.

- Market Segmentation Approach - Indians are very price conscious people. They would like the best of products at a very economical price. Well there is another set of people who believe the higher the price better he quality of product. It can be understood that Individuals with diverse product needs have heterogeneous needs. Market segmentation is the process of dividing a total heterogeneous market into market groups consisting of people who have relatively similar product needs, there are clusters of needs. The purpose is to design a Marketing Mix (s) that more precisely matches the needs of individuals in a selected market segment(s). A market segment consists of individuals, groups or organizations with one or more characteristics that cause them to have relatively similar product needs. There are two Market Segmentation Strategies (remember these are strategies and not the basis of segmentation).
- Concentration Strategy - A firm that does targeting of only one segment with a unique marketing mix is referred as

concentrated marketing strategy. It the company is small or new to the field, it may decide to go for concentrated strategy. Here the complete market is not considered as one, but instead one homogeneous segment is selected. E.g. RECOVA - a facial cream for women who are in the age of 30 and above.

PROS include:

- It allows a firm to specialize in one product/one market group
- can focus all energies on satisfying one group's needs
- A firm with limited resources can compete with larger organizations.

CONS include:

- Puts all eggs in one basket.
- Small shift in the population or consumer tastes can greatly affect the firm.
- May have trouble expanding into new markets (especially up-market).

In this strategy the objective is not to maximize sales, it is efficiency, attracting a large portion of one section while controlling costs.

- Multi-segment strategy (or also called as differentiated marketing strategy) Here targeting is inclusive of many segments using individual marketing mixes is called differentiated marketing strategy. Here two or more segments are sought with a Marketing Mix for each segment, different marketing plan for each segment. This approach combines the best attributes of undifferentiated marketing and concentrated marketing. In this strategy, the firm will try to offer a product suitable for every purse, purpose and personality by adoption this strategy, it hopes to strengthen the overall identification of the company with the product category.

Example: Titan-watches ranging from Rs. 250 to more than a lakh, executive watches to sports watches, plastic to the hardest of metal, water proof.... etc.

Marriott International:

- Marriott Suites...Permanent vacationers
- Fairfield Inn...Economy Lodging
- Residence Inn...Extended Stay
- Courtyard By Marriott...Business Travellers

PROS include:

- Shift excess production capacity.
- Can achieve same market coverage as with mass marketing.
- Price differentials among different brands can be maintained Contact Lens!!
- Consumers in each segment may be willing to pay a premium for the tailor-made product.
- Less risk, as the marketer is not relying on one market.

CONS include:

- Demands a greater number of production processes.
- Costs and resources and increased marketing costs through selling through different channels and promoting more brands, using different packaging etc.
- Must be careful to maintain the product distinctiveness in each consumer group and guard its overall image

POSITIONING

In marketing, positioning is the technique by which marketers try to create an image or identity in the minds of their target market for its product, brand, or organization. It is the 'relative competitive comparison' their product occupies in a given market as perceived by the target market.

Positioning is something (perception) that is done in the minds of the target market. A product's position is how potential buyers see the product. Positioning is expressed relative to the position of competitors. The term was coined in 1969 by Al Ries and Jack Trout in the paper "Positioning" is a game people play in today's me-too market place" in the publication Industrial Marketing.

Simply, positioning is how your target market defines you in relation to your competitors.

A good position is:

- What makes you unique
- This is considered a benefit by your target market

Both of these conditions are necessary for a good positioning. So what if you are the only red-haired singer who only knows how to play a G minor chord? Does your target market consider this a good thing?

Positioning is important because you are competing with all the noise out there competing for your potential fans attention. If you can stand out with a unique benefit, you have a chance at getting their attention. It is important to understand your product from the customer's point of view relative to the competition.

PRODUCT POSITIONING STRATEGY

The ability to spot a positioning opportunity is a sure test of a person's marketing ability. Successful positioning strategies are usually rooted in a product's sustainable competitive advantage. A company that is more profitable than its rivals is exploiting some form of competitive advantage. The benchmark for profitability is the company's cost of capital. To consistently make profits in excess of its cost of capital economic rent - the company must possess some form of sustainable competitive advantage (SCA) to derive firm specific distinctive strategic positioning.

The most common basis for constructing a product positioning strategy are:

- Positioning on specific product features
- Positioning on specific benefits, needs, or solutions
- Positioning on specific use categories
- Positioning on specific usage occasions
- Positioning on a reason to choose an offering over the competition
- Positioning against another product
- Positioning through product class dissociation
- Positioning by cultural symbols

PRODUCT POSITIONING PROCESS

Generally, the product positioning process involves:

- Defining the market in which the product or brand will compete (who the relevant buyers are)
- Identifying the attributes (also called dimensions) that define the product 'space'
- Collecting information from a sample of customers about their perceptions of each product on the relevant attributes
- Determine each products' share of mind
- Determine each products' current location in the product space

- Determine the target market's preferred combination of attributes (referred to as an ideal vector)
- Examine the fit between:
- The position of your product
- The position of the ideal vector
- Finally, Position.

One of the main objectives of advertising and promotion is to establish what is called mind share (or share of mind). When people think of examples of a type or category of product, they think of a limited list (referred to as an evoked set). Any product included in an evoked set has mind share. For example, if you are considering purchasing a college education, you have several thousand colleges to choose from.

However your evoked set, those that you will consider, will probably be limited to about ten. Of these ten, the colleges that you are most familiar with will have the greatest proportion of your mind share. Marketers try to maximize their product's share. Mind share can be established to a greater or lesser degree depending on market segment.

A similar concept is top of mind. The more easily you remember a brand, the closer it is to your top of mind. This implies that you have not forgotten or buried the information.

The process is similar for positioning your company's services. Services, however, don't have the physical attributes of products -that is, we can't feel them or touch them or show nice product pictures. So you need to ask first your customers and then yourself, what value do clients get from my services? How are they better off from doing business with me? Also ask: is there a characteristic that makes my services different? Write out the value customers derive and the attributes your services offer to create the first draft of your positioning. Test it on people who don't really know what you do or what you sell, watch their facial expressions and listen for their response. When they want to know more because you've piqued their interest and started a conversation, you'll know you're on the right track.

Six-step template for successful positioning:

- What position do you currently own?
- What position do you want to own?
- Whom you have to defeat to own the position you want.
- Do you have the resources to do it?

- Can you persist until you get there?
- Are your tactics supporting the positioning objective you set?

Re-positioning involves changing the identity of a product, relative to the identity of competing products, in the collective minds of the target market.

De-positioning involves attempting to change the identity of competing products, relative to the identity of your own product, in the collective minds of the target market.

PERCEPTUAL MAPPING

Perceptual mapping is a graphics technique used by marketers that attempts to visually display the perceptions of customers or potential customers. Typically the position of a product, product line, brand, or company is displayed relative to their competition.

Perceptual maps can have any number of dimensions but the most common is two dimensions. Any more is a challenge to draw and confusing to interpret. The first perceptual map below shows consumer perceptions of various automobiles on the two dimensions of sportiness/conservative and classy/affordable. This sample of consumers felt Porsche was the sportiest and classiest of the cars in the study (top right corner). They felt Plymouth was most practical and conservative (bottom left corner).

Cars that are positioned close to each other are seen as similar on the relevant dimensions by the consumer. For example consumers see Buick, Chrysler, and Oldsmobile as similar. They are close competitors and form a competitive grouping. A company considering the introduction of a new model will look for an area on the map free from competitors. Some perceptual maps use different size circles to indicate the sales volume or market share of the various competing products.

Displaying consumers' perceptions of related products is only half the story. Many perceptual maps also display consumers' ideal points. These points reflect ideal combinations of the two dimensions as seen by a consumer. The next diagram shows a study of consumers' ideal points in the alcohol/spirits product space. Each dot represents one respondents ideal combination of the two dimensions. Areas where there is a cluster of ideal points (such as A) indicates a market segment. Areas without ideal points are sometimes referred to as demand voids.

A company considering introducing a new product will look for areas with a high density of ideal points. They will also look for areas without competitive rivals. This is best done by placing both the ideal points and the competing products on the same map.

Some maps plot ideal vectors instead of ideal points.

Perceptual maps need not come from a detailed study. There are also intuitive maps (also called judgmental maps or consensus maps) that are created by marketers based on their understanding of their industry. Management uses its best judgement. It is questionable how valuable this type of map is. Often they just give the appearance of credibility to management's preconceptions.

When detailed marketing research studies are done methodological problems can arise, but at least the information is coming directly from the consumer. There is an assortment of statistical procedures that can be used to convert the raw data collected in a survey into a perceptual map. Preference regression, Multi dimensional scaling will produce either ideal points or competitor positions. Factor analysis, discriminant analysis, cluster analysis, and log analysis can also be used. Some techniques are constructed from perceived differences between products, others are constructed from perceived similarities. Still others are constructed from cross price elasticity of demand data from electronic scanners.

MARKETING COMMUNICATION

To be a manager is to be a communicator - the two are inextricably linked. A great manager needs to communicate upwards, sideways and with his/her team all the time. Employees have a stake in the business, so it is essential that they are kept fully informed regularly and that their views and opinions are sought.

Communication is any process in which people share information, ideas, and feelings. It involves not only the spoken and written word, but also body language, personal mannerisms and style, and the physical environment anything that adds meaning to a message.

- Noise -is the interference that keeps a message from being understood or accurately interpreted.
- External noise: Comes from environment. i.e. loud music, hot sun, babies...
- Internal noise: Occurs in the minds of the sender receiver when their thoughts and feelings are focused on something other than the communication at hand.

- Semantic: Caused by people's emotional reaction to words.

Simply stated, the communication process involves a sender who transmits a message through a selected channel to the receiver. A simple communication process model is given here.

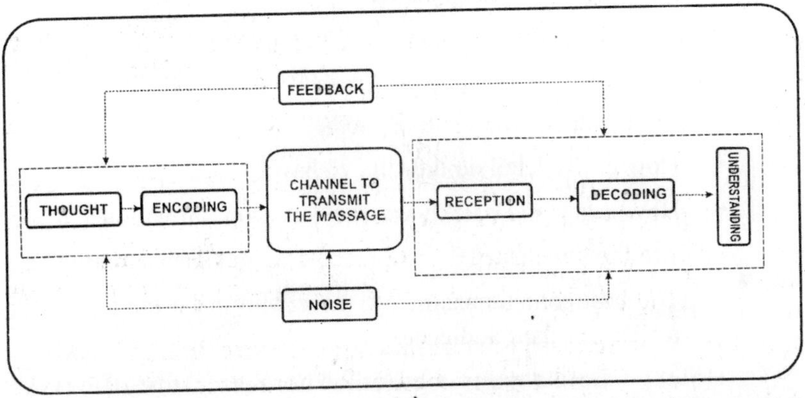

Most problems in business are caused by poor communication. What is more, one of the two most common reasons why employees feel demotivated is that they don't know what's going on and no-one's interested in their views. Good communication can improve the performance of your business, so take time to do it well. We will take you through the following essential pointers to effective communication:

Two-way communication

Ensure it is two-way. Many managers focus only on communications downwards - giving information to their people. However, for communication to be really effective it must be two-way. You need therefore, to give information to others and to gain information from them by asking questions.

What?: Decide what to communicate. Many managers are far too secretive. If you are keeping something from your team, ask yourself why. There may be a good reason, but most issues relating to the business, its performance and its future plans should be shared. This will create a greater sense of ownership and involvement amongst your team.

When?: Decide when to communicate. Communication should be timely. Share information as things happen. Avoid the temptation to store up your communication until the next monthly meeting! By then, it may seem like history and you may have lost the opportunity to gain the input of others.

Why?: Decide why you are communicating. This will influence how best to do it. Is it to share information? Is it to persuade? Influence? Is it to gain feedback? Is it to prompt action?

Tailoring the communication

Make it relevant to your audience. The art of good communication is to tailor the message to the recipient. Consider, for example:

- What is their reaction likely to be?
- How much detail do they like to have?
- How easily and quickly can they absorb information?
- Are they interested in hard facts, data and substantiation?
- The best communicators are those who make the effort to get it right for their audience.

How?: Choose your method. There are lots of ways to communicate. Select the right combination for the right circumstances. Here are a few:

Method	*Pros*	*Cons*
Telephone	• Two-way • Quick and easy	• Usually limited to one-to-one • No body language
Meeting	• Good way of sharing the same information with many people • Opportunity to explore and discuss • Good for gaining consensus • Good for building teams	• Takes time to arrange • Reliant on the skills of the person chairing the meeting • Takes the time of each participant
Letter	• Provides the writer with the opportunity to draft, re-write and re-write again until it's right • Allows copies to be taken and kept for the record	• Slower than telephone or email • One-way
E-mail	• Quick and easy • Information can be kept technology and stored • Lends itself to communicating the same information to a wide audience	• Relies on the technology being available • Can lead to over-communicating to e.g., copying everything to everyone
Presentation	• Formal • Can have great impact • Communicates a consistent message to a wide audience	• Cost • Time • Relies on the skills of the presenter

Presentation	• Formal • Can have great impact • Communicates a consistent message to a wide audience	• Cost • Time • Relies on the skills of the presenter
Informal chats	• Quick and easy • Timely – you can speak as and when things happen • Requires little preparation	• Can be disruptive • Can exclude employees based elsewhere
Newsletters / bulletins	• Good for business-wide communications • Can mix business and people information • Can engender a feeling of belonging and establish an organization culture	• Cost and time of production
Notice board	• Immediate • Can have impact • Reaches lots of people, including visitors	• Relies on employees taking the time to look at it • Needs regular updating

REVIEW

Review the effectiveness of each method from time to time, to ensure that you are using the most effective combination. For example, at the end of a team meeting, take five minutes to conduct a review - what went well? What could we do differently next time?

- Good communicators make the message interesting by giving a human twist, telling a story, using analogies, giving examples.... etc.
- The recall rate of the spoken word improves when supported by good visual aids, but is still only around 30%!

IMPORTANCE OF MARKETING COMMUNICATION

It is very important o have a communication flow between the firm and the consumer. In the absence of a direct face-to-face contact with the consumer, the marketer has to make provisions for developing a communication flow between them and their customers.

The Traditional view, the marketer's held, was that they can enter into a communication with their consumer through the development of a 'promotion mix', which includes personal selling, advertising, sales promotion and publicity.

However, in the existing competitive scenario, firms have realized that in order to woo and win over consumers, they have to develop a multi dimensional flow of communication network between them on one hand and with the consumers on the other side.

While the organization performs its role as an effective communicator, the firm is also a sender of market message and also a receiver of the market response.

MARKETING COMMUNICATION THROUGH PRODUCTS

According to Philip Kotler "A product is anything that can be offered to a market for attentions, acquisition, use or consumption that might satisfy a want or need. It includes physical objects, services, persons, places, organizations and ideas.

So a product is said to be the carrier of messages through its package, colour, size shape physical attributes, label and above all its brand name. The consumer does not consider the product as a non-living thing but instead he would assign meaning and significance to a product because of its brand personality or brand equity or image. E.g. Margo soap - conveys the message of a complete neem diet for the consumer skin and Lux soap - feel like a star.

PRICE-STATUS

Pricing as viewed today is the analysis of the consumer's perception of "value and sacrifice". In certain cases the consumer's view price as a status sign. This is very true in premium or higher priced products. E.g. Onida's Plasma TV.

Promotion - A vital Component in Marketing Communication

By using persuasive communication, the marketer seeks to transfer a set of meanings, feelings and tones about a product to some target audience. Such communication will affect the consumer's attitudes and motivation levels and can help in formulating conceptions of the advertised brand. Through advertising a marketer reaches the consumers by advocating the use or the usefulness of the product. It attracts consumers, increases their curiosity towards the product or increases the usage level of the product. Effective communication would convert competitor's consumers and help retain their own consumers.

Firms use consumer oriented franchise building promotions because they re-in force the consumer's brand understanding. Sales promotion tools like coupons, premium, catalogue, trade fairs, exhibitions, road shows and hoardings etc., convey a selling message along with the deal.

Both publicity and public relation can stimulate and provide support methods to communicate about the company and its products. They also enjoy more credibility with the public than advertising.

STORE CHOICE & SHOPPING BEHAVIOUR

CONSUMER OUTLET SELECTION

- Retail evolution and consumer choice. For many products, consumers frequently have numerous choices as to where they are going to actually obtain the product. Although we are used to thinking of buying automobiles only from dealerships, for example, it is today possible to buy them through brokers or fleet sales organizations that may both (1) offer a lower price and/or (2) provide the help of a neutral third party which does not have a vested interest in the sales of one make over the other. In general, the evolution of diversity in the retail scene has provided consumers with more choice. In the old days, most consumers had access only to "general" stores for most products. Gradually, in urban environments, specialty and discount stores evolved. Today, a consumer may generally choose to buy most products either at a relatively high price, frequently with a significant amount of service, in a specialty store, or with lower service in a discount store. A special case of the discount store is the category killer--a store that tends to specialize in some limited area (e.g., electronics), lacking the breadth of a traditional discount store often undercutting the traditional discount store on price (which they are able to do because of the bargaining power that results from high buying volumes of a narrow assortment of merchandise from the same manufacturer).
- "At home" shopping and electronic commerce. During the last several decades, the incidence of "at home" shopping has increased. The growth of catalogue sales can be traced to advances in computer technology and subsequent list availability (as we discussed in the section of direct marketing segmentation methods). A more recent development is Internet based marketing. Although sales are modest in this domain at the moment, it is too early to judge the total potential of this medium. Although many of the concerns that consumers hold about computer crime tend to be exaggerated and/or largely unwarranted, public fears are a major holdback. Another problem is the demographics of computer and Internet use--the majority of U.S. consumers, and certainly the great majority of residents of even highly industrialized countries, are not

regular Internet users. Certain products specifically aimed at heavy Internet users (e.g., records, software) and products/ services that require a high level of customization (e.g., airline tickets) may find good opportunities. An interesting problem with Internet commerce, which may well have spillover effects outside the realm of the Net, is the relative ease with which consumers may compare prices of different retailers, resulting in intense price competition. Note that recent legislation has limited taxation of Internet sales in the U.S., in a sense attempting to "jump start" this innovation.

- Store positioning. Positioning of retail stores is essential. In general, stores which excel on a significant dimension seem to perform better--for example, RPG's food world excels through its intense customer service, while Big Bazaar excels through its efficiency and low prices. Stores which fall somewhere in between--e.g., Nilgiris -tend to do less well since they get "stuck in the middle" and have to compete against both. Obviously, there is a limit to how strongly you can move toward one extreme. For example, if Food world were to double its prices and even double its service, that position would be untenable, and certain extreme discount stores that offer lower prices than Big Bazaar tend not to be successful because they are ultimately not satisfactory to consumers.

A grocery retail chain faces the following consumer behaviour issues:

- Should there be a reduction in number of stock keeping units (SKU) for a particular category?
- How should the sale of non-promoted categories be looked at in judging promotional effectiveness?
- Is there a need to classify variety seeking behaviour?
- How should one monitor consumption rates for packaged goods?
- What are the long term effects of promotion on consumer behaviour?

CONSUMER SHOPPING BEHAVIOUR

Definition of Buying Behaviour: Buying Behaviour is the decision processes and acts of people involved in buying and using products. As Marketers we need to understand our Consumer for the following reasons:

- Why consumers make the purchases that they make?
- What factors influence consumer purchases?
- The changing factors in our society.

Consumer Buying Behaviour refers to the buying behaviour of the ultimate consumer. A firm needs to analyze buying behaviour for:

- Buyers reactions to a firms marketing strategy has a great impact on the firms success.
- The marketing concept stresses that a firm should create a Marketing Mix (MM) that satisfies (gives utility to) customers, therefore need to analyze the what, where, when and how consumers buy.
- Marketers can better predict how consumers will respond to marketing strategies.

STAGES OF THE CONSUMER BUYING PROCESS

There are Six Stages to Consumer Buying Decision Process (For complex decisions). Actual purchasing is only one stage of the process. Not all decision processes lead to a purchase. All consumer decisions do not always include all 6 stages, determined by the degree of complexity.

The 6 stages are:

- Problem Recognition (awareness of need) - It is actual difference between the desired state and the actual condition. The stage where marketers help identify the deficit in assortment of products. Simple example Hunger stimulates your need to eat. This can be stimulated by the marketer through product information, in case the consumer did not know he was deficient? E.g. When we see a commercial for a new pair of shoes, It can stimulates your recognition that you need a new pair of shoes.
- Information search--can be both internal and external.
  a. Internal search, search your memory. This basically your experience or things that affect you which is stored in your memory.
  b. External search if you need more information. Friends and relatives (word of mouth), Marketer dominated sources like magazines, catalogue; comparison shopping; public sources etc. A successful information search leaves a buyer with possible alternatives.

Hungry, want to go out and eat, evoked set is

- Chinese food
- Indian food
- McDonalds
- Pizza Hut etc
- Evaluation of Alternatives-This is stage when you know that you have quite a lot of alternatives and you need to establish criteria for evaluation, features the buyer wants or does not want. We could Rank/weight alternatives or resume search. May decide that you want to eat something spicy, Indian gets highest rank etc.
- If not satisfied with your choice then return to the search phase. Can you think of another restaurant, next time? Look in the yellow pages etc.
- Information from different sources may be treated differently. Marketers try to influence by "framing" alternatives.
- Purchase decision--Choose buying alternative, includes product, package, store, method of purchase etc.
- Purchase--May differ from decision, time lapse between point 4 & 5, product availability. Most of the time the consumers make their purchase decision irrational or emotional. There need not be a rational process all the time. E.g. Ann purchased Levi Jeans just because her neighbour purchased it and she looks good in it. Ann never wears western clothes. In this example you can understand that Ann has been emotional when purchasing the jeans, as she might have assumed that she will also look good or just out of sheer jealously she has done it.
- Post-Purchase Evaluation-In this stage it is the outcome that is looked into. There are two major outcomes, they are Satisfaction or Dissatisfaction. Have you heard people asking for suggestions after the purchase, True a lot of them need the security of others who would make comments. It is like all human beings to have doubts on the purchase. E.g. A woman buys a pink colour saree and comes home, though she likes it she will ask her husband, her friends and every one close to her, their opinion about the saree. This is called Cognitive Dissonance, a inner feeling if she has made the right decision. This can be reduced by warranties, after sales communication

etc. Another example is after eating an Indian meal, may think that really you wanted a Chinese meal instead.

PURCHASE TIMING BEHAVIOUR

The economic assumption underlying the analysis of brand switching and purchase timing for a single product category is the reparability of consumers' utilities across the different product categories that constitute the basket of goods purchased by consumers. Most grocers generally store related categories together with the assumption that a household's choice in one category is not independent of its choice in the other. The decision of when to purchase one product category might depend on the decision for a related category.

Such an understanding is useful for the retailer because it helps in getting an idea about what kind of promotions will click with the consumers. A critical issue when studying household purchases of multiple categories is being able to identify the related product categories. This requires a complete characterization of the purchase behaviour of households in several different categories. Inter-purchase time also needs to be monitored. There are several sources of the observed correlation in the inter-purchase times across households. One source is related to the nature of the product categories themselves that induce the dependence. Consumers typically consume these products together and therefore purchase them together, for example, dhoop sticks and camphor. Other sources of the estimated correlation across categories are from (1) consumers visiting the store only on few occasions and consequently making purchases in all categories at the same time, like monthly purchase, (2) the retailer promoting 'unrelated' categories together, which results in the joint purchases of products in different categories, for example, a free toothbrush with a deodorant, or (3) the household exhausts its supply of both products at the same time, which prompts joint purchase. Interestingly, purchase timing may also be affected by the variety seeking behaviour observed in consumers.

IN-STORE STIMULI, STORE IMAGE AND LOYALTY

IN-STORE CHOICE

Consumer store choice results from a process whereby information on various alternatives is evaluated by the consumer prior to the selection of one of these alternatives. In the application of store choice models it is often assumed that the information-processing strategy underlying store choice is a simultaneous one in which all possible alternatives are evaluated by an individual. A competing assumption, increasingly recognized in a spatial choice, is that individuals initially evaluate clusters of alternatives and then only evaluate alternatives within a chosen cluster.

Fierce competition has always been a hallmark of the retail industry. In recent years, it has become even more tough, as innovative new entrants have upset the status quo and existing retailers have become more efficient. But perhaps the greatest challenge faced by retailers is consumers' rising expectations.

Today's consumers have evolved into elusive, finicky targets who have many shopping options and are harder to please. Consumers are more highly informed than ever before and more able to compare prices and products with little time, effort or interaction with a retailer. In addition to being more informed, consumers also shop differently than they have before-often using a combination of going to a physical store and shopping online. It is safe to say that never before have consumers expected more from retailers and exhibited so little loyalty to specific brands.

"Know your customer" is one of the most widely quoted maxims of business- and for good reason. However, companies often talk about the importance of customer knowledge while failing to put action behind their words. Why? Some companies remember the pain involved in failed data warehousing projects or unsuccessful attempts to persuade sales personnel to document customer comments. Other companies engage in modest efforts, such as studying customer profitability or implementing limited CRM software, which may provide some efficiencies, but yield little in the way of deep customer insight.

BEHAVIOUR BASIS

Leading retailers, however, recognize that they must go beyond their historical product-focused operations and become more customer focused if they are to remain successful. But what does customer focused mean? First, retailers need to develop an understanding of the customer that is based on customer behaviour rather than on geography or demographics. Second, they must learn to use this information across the entire organization- including the C-suite-and not just in the marketing department.

The opportunity for retailers to use customer data and information to build more profitable, lasting customer relationships is tremendous. While gathering data can be fairly easy, making sense of it is an entirely different matter. One of the first steps to mastering multi-channel customers is to have the technology needed to serve them, learn about them and make better decisions about how to reach them. The merchants can no longer be satisfied with simple demographics such as gender or age group. They also cannot be content with a good picture of an in-store shopper or an online shopper. Instead, the merchant has to have information about what price levels a customer group reacts to, how discounts on various items affect the impulse to shop and buy, and how a target shopper reacts to various stimuli in all the channels they use. The insight into how a group of customers react to and use different channels can be the piece of information that allows retailers to generate loyalty, improved margins and profitability. Compiling, organizing, analyzing and using this type of complex data takes powerful technology.

TYING THEM TOGETHER

Even more important than computing power, however, is integration. Successful retailers cannot just build better silos of customer information. The greater the number of channels, brands, categories and products involved, the more difficult the task of integrating and analyzing the data. Thus, retailers must create a single view of the customer by combining information from different silos into one complete snapshot of the consumer.

Once retailers have the technology to support and propel their efforts, they must adopt an analytical approach to customer insights. Analytics can take customer information and turn it into information retailers can use across all channels to make effective decisions about pricing, merchandising, advertising, promotions and customer service levels. This approach is based on customer behaviour and differs significantly from traditional retail CRM methods. Specifically, this analytical approach uses methods and associated tools to analyze customer behaviour in three ways:

- Purchasing history, such as frequency of visits and market basket.
- Promotional response to merchandising and marketing levers, such as changes in pricing, promotion and category locations.
- Store (physical and on-line) behaviour, such as the stores at which they shop and the areas of the store in which they shop.

These dynamic behavioural insights help retailers identify and predict which merchandising and marketing levers cause each customer group's behaviour in each store and each channel. This approach is very different from the customer research and demographic segmentation approaches many retailers have depended upon in the past.

It is different because it is driven by actual customer behaviour-not how customers say they will behave-and it predicts the factors that will motivate customers to make future purchases. With this information, retailers are prioritizing customer segments and developing detailed strategies to influence them to buy more products, more often, and in ways that are more profitable to the retailer.

It is worth noting, however, that although purchasing and loyalty card data is extremely valuable in the analysis, it is not absolutely essential. In its absence, retailers can still take a much more fact-based approach to developing customer insights through customer segment and attitudinal analysis using existing data and customer observation.

With the appropriate technology and analytics working for a retailer, what's missing in leveraging the multi-channel customer? What will propel the retailer to the top? Customer insight is necessary, location is still important, ease of access is a differentiator, but the new mantra may well be innovation.

Visual Merchandising (VM) is the art of presentation, which puts the merchandise in focus. It educates the customers, creates desire and finally augments the selling process. This is an area where the Indian textile and clothing industry, particularly, the SMEs lack adequate knowledge and expertise. This inadequacy is best reflected in poor presentation/display and communication in various national and international exhibitions. Organization often tend not to realize that the store image plays a very important role in communication and conveying messages to its customers Marketers are trying to deliver greater value through adopting shelfing techniques. They follow FIFO (first in first out) techniques.

VM helps in:

- Educating the customers about the product/service in an effective and creative way.
- Establishing a creative medium to present merchandise in 3D environment, thereby enabling long lasting impact and recall value.
- Setting the company apart in an exclusive position.

- Establishing linkage between fashion, product design and marketing by keeping the product in prime focus.
- Combining the creative, technical and operational aspects of a product and the business.
- Drawing the attention of the customer to enable him to take purchase decision within shortest possible time, and thus augmenting the selling process.

STORE LOYALTY

According to American Marketing Association - Store Loyalty is defined as-

In context to Consumer Behaviour "The degree to which a consumer consistently patronizes the same store when shopping for particular types of products."

In context to retailing "A condition in which a customer regularly patronizes a specific retailer."

CONSUMERISM

Consumerism is a term used to describe the effects of equating personal happiness with purchasing material possessions and consumption. It is often associated with criticisms of consumption starting with Karl Marx and Thorstein Veblen, but can actually be traced back to the first human civilizations.

In economics, consumerism can also refer to economic policies that place an emphasis on consumption, and, in an abstract sense, the belief that the free choice of consumers should dictate the economic structure of a society (cf. Producerism, especially in the British sense of the term).

HISTORY

Although consumerism is commonly associated with capitalism and the Western world, it is multi-cultural and non-geographical, as seen today in Tokyo, Singapore, Hong Kong, Shanghai, Taipei, Tel Aviv and Dubai, for example. Consumerism, as in people purchasing goods or consuming materials in excess of their basic needs, is as old as the first civilizations (Ancient Egypt, Babylon and Ancient Rome, for example). Since consumerism began, various individuals and groups have consciously sought an alternative lifestyle through simple living.

While consumerism is not a new phenomenon, it has only become widespread over the 20th century and particularly in recent decades, under the influence of neo-liberal capitalism and globalization. Popular media used "Consumerist" as a short-form for "Consumer-Activist". Webster's dictionary added "the promotion of the consumer's interests" alongside "the theory that an increasing consumption of goods is economically desirable" under "Consumerism".

CONSUMERISM IN INDIA

In India, as a developing economy, it is felt that the plight of the consumers are not different from that of the counterparts in the rest of the world. In spite of the fact that not all the Indian consumers are well educated and hence, unable to comprehend and understand the complex methods of marketing, they are also exploited and very often become victims of false claims for products, mislead by deceptive advertisements, misled by packaging, poor after sales service and so on. Because of the above felt abuses, there is observed and seen a growing consumer awareness leading to the growth of consumerism and an increasing demand for consumer protection in India.

Consumerism can be said to be still in its infancy stage. But the consumer movement is slowly gaining momentum. Rapid rise in the consumer earnings, fall in the savings rate resulting in generating increasing amounts of disposable income to be spent on consumer products and services. With the advent of the information age brining with it real time images of the global life style; and thus making high spender and budget shoppers spend lavishly on products and services.

CONSUMER RIGHTS

A perfect example that we would see is as follows:

Manufacturers deliberately set out to fleece consumers by using tactics like misleading or deceptive packaging. Despite the government of India enforcing a law by the name of Standards of Weight and Measures Act, 1977, manufacturers blatantly flout the rules and tamper with the packaging of the products.

The Act requires definite and conspicuous declaration of name and address of the commodity inside, the net quantity in standard unit of weight or measure, the date of manufacture and the maximum retail price and the expiry date. It has laid down the standards of weights and measures or the number for different commodities so that the commodities are packaged in a rationalised standard quantity by weight measures or number to facilitate the purchase transaction as also the price comparison.

Extensive research in several departments reveals the deception in the diminutive print. Packaging of some products do not carry the manufacturing date; some do not have expiry date on them and some brands do not convey the warning like "best before" or "use by". For perishable stuff, such declarations should clearly be conveyed to the consumers.

In reality, if you ask any shopkeeper, you get a curt" "It is a fast-moving item. We don't stock anything stale." Some manufacturers entertain the buyers by incorporating a treasure hunt for the relevant label. They print the information in colours that merge with the plastics, emboss it so you need to run your fingers on it, or hide it under a decorative flap.

The manufacturing date on a toothpaste tube has to be dug out of the crimped tail. As for the expiry date on a battery cell, the number on medium or large ones are visible under a lens, but the script on the seat of a pencil cell is beyond the power of magnifying glass.

A well-known manufacturer gets "20% off" printed in big bold letters and in mini print it says: "On the recommended retail price. Taxes extra as applicable". This is a surreptitious way to dupe consumers in buying the product.

A large number of unidentified consumers do not get what they pay for. Packaging sizes and container shapes for many products deceive and confuse consumers about the amount of product they contain, and some manufacturers have been increasing package size while decreasing content.

It's a common practice for manufacturers to tactically reduce the weight contained in a package while keeping the size of the box, bottle, or container the same, and misrepresent the quantity of good sold. The quantity of the product inside the packet is not consistent with what is specified on it. It is not just a question of grams or a few rupees but an unjust enrichment to manufacturers and a needless loss to consumers.

Very few buyers check if the packed commodities weigh less than weight marked on the panel. If they do so, they don't try to question the malpractice. Shopkeepers often do not have electronic weighing machines that can detect small discrepancies.

As a matter of fact, the packet should weigh more than the marked weight, because the given weight is actually the net weight of the product inside, which is its weight before packaging. On the contrary, the weight of product inside the packet and that of the packet itself is less than marked weight on the panel of packet. The net result is that consumers are taken for a ride, with erring shopkeepers going scot-free. What consumer should do to control such malpractices?

- If you find the product suspicious in case of anomaly weight, get it weighed at the shop itself. And write a short note in the form of complaint to the manufacturer in corporation with the shopkeeper.
- Bring it to the notice of weights and measures department, which is supposed to take the sample and initiate legal proceedings against the manufacturer.
- If manufacturer refuses to fall in line, you ca approach the district-or state-level consumer court for redressal.

Consumer protection is government regulation to protect the interests of consumers, for example by requiring businesses to disclose detailed information about products, particularly in areas where safety or public health is an issue, such as food. Consumer protection is linked to the idea of consumer rights (that consumers have various rights as consumers), and to consumer organizations which help consumers make better choices in the marketplace.

Some of the consumer issues that the Consumer law takes action are on

- Antitrust
- Class action
- Competition policy
- Competition regulator
- Extended warranty
- Fair-trade labelling
- Food safety
- Mandatory labelling
- Product recall
- Predatory mortgage lending
- Transparency (market)

SUMMARY

Let's just remember one thing. India has been a poor country for a long, long while now. Folks below the poverty line have numbered a strong platoon of people. And despite it all, the population has grown, survived and continues to thrive in its sheer numbers. People have found a way to survive. The fittest have survived on high value brands, the less fit have thrived on brands of a lesser calibre in the country. Those even lower in the hierarchy have survived on the fringe of the commodity in every category of want and need. Consumption needs have always found answers. Consumption solutions for all!

There is therefore a pyramid of consumption that lies all over the slopes of Maslow's hierarchy of needs. But then, everybody, rich or poor, has fallen within the confines of this pyramid. And just as long as they do, there is indeed potential for a robust market for commodities, quasi-brands, brands, super-brands and of course at the ultimate level of the self-actualizing folk, no brands at all!

Every one of these segments has a value though. And in value rests the potential for the marketer. The one big true-blue competitive advantage for India of the present and India of the future is indeed its large population base articulating every basic need in consumption of products, services and utilities. Time to change the paradigm of India's population then! Every marketer of whatever origin, be it from within India or outside, will queue up in the consumer markets of the country, trying to woo the wallet of the willing. As traditional source markets reach a plateau in their consumption, nascent markets like the one in India will hold a great deal of allure to the marketing man in his western straitjacket. The competitive advantage of India will rest in both its own shores and in the foreign lands of its source markets. As the WTO regime opens up markets that do not discriminate and markets that don't raise the usual high tariff walls that have been the distinct characteristic of the past that has gone by, the Indian product and the Indian brand has a challenge to seize and exploit to its advantage.

Note:Sheetz is a privately held family owned business that operates convenience stores and gasoline stations. The company operates more than 350 convenience locations throughout Pennsylvania, West Virginia, Maryland, Virginia, Ohio and North Carolina. The company primarily operates in the US. It is headquartered in Altoona, Pennsylvania and employs about 11,000 people. Reader can visit their sitewww.sheetz.com For a detailed study of connected to this chapter.

11

The Borderless Consumer Market and Buying Behaviour

INTRODUCTION

Firms that choose not to understand their customers' purchasing behaviour often lose out. An excellently engineered product may fail just because the customer does not identify himself or herself with it. It is therefore imperative that the firm understands the structural changes taking place in its market and also the long-term impact of these changes on its product and other elements of the marketing mix. The firm must also understand the buyer's purchasing behaviour. Specifically, it must understand how the buyer decides in favour of one brand or product, what motivates him or her to select an alternative, and who influences him or her to buy the brand or product.

The marketer needs to focus on the "how" and "why" of the total experience consumers have with products and services. Unfortunately, most marketers tend to look at only a few aspects of experience and build the complete strategy around it. For example, one of the leading electrical appliances company crafted its strategy around customers' experience at the dealer outlet. Hence the strategy was on developing dealer outlets, enhancing dealer productivity, and loyalty. It failed to understand other dimensions like service, price-performance relationship, and esteem values of the brand which are as important in the consumer's mental space and hence influences his/her attitude towards the brand. Likewise, one of the dotcom companies failed to understand that the consumer valued security of transactions over all other dimensions of web-based transactions. Hence marketers need to focus on discovering the 'why' of an experience. They also need to understand that large samples based survey is no guarantee of having discovered the "truth".

Quantity of data does not guarantee quality. What is needed is a deep understanding of consumer behaviour. Without such an understanding, marketers cannot accurately anticipate consumer responses to product designs, features and marketing ideas.

THE BORDERLESS CONSUMER MARKET

- Seamless Global Society: The internet has today reduced the gap between different societies. This gap, which was on account of physical distance, information and knowledge, has now become redundant. Today we are seeing the emergence of a global society and universal values. One such universal value relates to the concept of time. It is no more perceived as infinite. And hence time is an indicator of opportunity. An organization's competitiveness is greatly determined by its ability to respond within a given time frame determined by market forces and not by its own competencies. The Hindu concept of time, which is eternal and continuing, seems to lose its meaning in this era of information superhighways. Another impact of the Net revolution is the new concept of value. More and more customers have and will come to expect global products and services at local prices. In other words organizations cost structures will have to be globally competitive. Only then will customers get their value for money. Thus, the mere fact that an organization is offering a premium quality product will not be a sufficient reason to motivate customers to buy it. Developments in telecommunications will further contribute to the emergence of these universal concepts, which will affect the customer's definition of time and value. Mobile telephony has altered the concepts of space, time and location.
- Basis for Competitive advantage: The net is also likely to change the concept of nation state. It is not that these states will not exist but their role will change. The governments of these countries will continue to play a role in maintaining their cultural diversity and sovereignty. They will co-operate with other societies like security, taxation, censorship, and ownership. One of the direct outcomes of this seamless global society, therefore, will be the culture of openness and transparency. These technological changes are going to lead to significant shifts in competitive leadership. Future market leaders will use

computers to create new businesses, change existing ones and even restructure many of today's long established marketing practices. The basis for their sustainable competitive advantage will be knowledge management. In the ongoing war for competitive advantage, information technology has become the ultimate weapon. Hence creation, dissemination and protection of knowledge in the organization is perhaps going to be the most crucial armour for competitive survival.

- Business at the speed of thought: Today the internet give very little time to individuals and organizations to react and respond. We have to learn to conduct our business operations at the speed of the human mind. It should be possible for us to offer products and services even as these are conceived in the customer's mind. This obviously means that conventional marketing management will no longer deliver. We are already seeing the emergence of online help, which in many cases, has made conventional forms of service redundant.

Interactive technologies are already eliminating several roles in the marketing of products and services. Fro example, it is perceived that there will be no role for a service centre of a consumer durable firm in the 21st Century if its competitor markets a totally reliable product and, in the extreme case of failure, provides online assistance through its own website or service portal created by a group of service engineers. The product life cycles will be far shorter. Products are further standardized, and hence, the opportunities to differentiate will also no longer exist. From the conventional generic tangible values of performance and reliability, the marketers focus will have to be on tangible and intangible values.

Unfortunately the globalisation of products and markets will provide very little scope for differentiation in regard to these specific product or corporate values. The differentiator, therefore, will be the ability of the marketer to creatively customize them for the buyer. Interactive technologies will come to the marketers rescue. The key issues in these technologies will pertain to continuously updating the customer database and proactively creating research based product solutions and, in turn, moving the customer up the technology path. The marketing challenge lies in enabling customers overcome their resistance to change. It will be the organization's ability to competitively pre-empt others and build volumes that will make it a market leader.

- Virtual enterprise: The above changes, which have already made their presence felt emphatically in the global scene, have led to the creation of virtual enterprises. We have already seen the emergence of an era of Digital Darwinism. Amazon.com, Yahoo! Hotmail and Rediff.com, Indiatimes.com, like many others, are facilitators in the creation of a virtual enterprise. In this era of virtual reality, size and location of an enterprise will have very little or no role to play.
- Customer: Co-producer of products and services: Another dimension of the new millennium, which we can see emerging today, is that the customer will be a co-producer of products and services. No longer will it be the responsibility of the manufacturer to produce the product in its finality as the customer may demand. The producer will take the product up to a certain level in the value chain and then leave it for the buyer to customize it to his/her requirement. A classical case is that of the Asian Paints facility that lets the buyer have his choice of shade customized through the company' outlets, deploying interactive technologies. Similar interactive technologies like the ATM have made the customer a co-producer of products and services.
- Customer: A Warehouse of Information: In the internet age, the customer has access to huge bank of information from various national and global resources. The challenge for the marketer will be how to use this information for developing the marketing mix. In business -to-business marketing, the challenge will be one of integrating organizational operations to the customers environment. e.g., an engineering company will have to tailor its design, engineering and operations to suit the changing requirements of the customer. Hence the era of standardization is today replaced by mass customization.
- The death of Business and consumer marketing: The differentiation between business and consumer marketing, urban and rural marketing, and domestic and global marketing will get more blurred. This will also be the case with product and services marketing. The physical differentiation between the product and service will cease to exist mainly because of the standardization in manufacturing technologies. Hence,

organizations will have to learn from the marketing practices of winning organizations, irrespective of the nature of their products and markets.

- The role of Distribution Channels: The Conventional dealer and distributor will no longer viable. The intermediary's role will no more be that of physical delivery, sharing risks and investment in stock movements. Rather, it will be service and customization of the offer that will make an intermediary succeed.
- The poor as a market segment: Globalization has widened the gap between the rich and the poor. Today poor nations are making an all out effort to bridge the gap. Not only so, poor people all over the world are now a large segment. No marketer can afford to ignore it. So, whether it is customization of products/services, or price reduction or enhancing accessibility, firms will have to come out with creative solutions for this segment. We have to keep in mind that the focus here is on the poor customers who may be located in urban or rural areas. Incidentally, this segment offers a much more attractive opportunity than just the rich.
- Environment Protection: The biggest challenge for the new millennium marketer is protection of the environment. So whether it is in product development, use or disposal, the marketer will have to make a conscious effort to protect and maintain the environment. This has led to the development of eco friendly hotels, watches, food products and packaging material, etc.
- Diversity and Convergence Coexist: Markets are diverse. This diversity is not just based on the demographic & geographical location of the consumers, but also on their response to changes especially to technological changes. While diverse markets are a reality, convergence of needs is also a fact. Given the spread of internet and satellite television, it is not uncommon to see consumers all over the world demanding same products and services.

Thus, the new millennium demands a paradigm shift from marketers to customers who are treated as a resource that has an access to global sources of information and purchase. In this environment, customer's total experience with the brand and the organization will be the differentiator between winners and losers. This total experience is more than just product related. It is based on the organizations culture and systems and hence reflects organizational quality.

BUYER - AN ENIGMA

Although it is important for the firm to understand the buyer and accordingly evolve its marketing strategy, the buyer or consumer continues to be an enigma-sometimes responding the way the marketer wants and on other occasions just refusing to buy the product from the same marketer. For this reason, the buyers' mind has been termed as a black box. The marketer provides stimuli but he is uncertain of the buyer's response. The stimulus is a combination of product, brand name, colour, style, packaging, intangible services, merchandizing, shelf display, advertising, distribution, publicity and so forth. Nothing better illustrates this enigmatic buyer than the failure of a herbal anti-cold balm launched by Warner Hindustan some time back. Though the balm market has grown significantly and Vicks Vaporub had been dominating the anti-cold rub segment for more than two decades now, Warner failed. Was it is the brand name? Did the customer see no significant difference between Vicks and Warner? This has remained an enigma.

Further, today's customer is being greatly influenced by the media especially electronic. Technological developments in the field of information, biotechnology and genetics, and intensive competitions in all products and services are also impacting consumer choices. Consider, for example, the case of consumers who shop on the Internet for books from US-based Amazon.com, music from Sony, banking from HDFC Bank India, airline services from Jet Airways, or order roses from India to be delivered to loved ones in the US on Valentine's day through 1-800 flowers.com. Clearly the Internet has today impacted the customer learning and shopping behaviour. Multiple television channels are also shaping the customer's values. The customer is aware, more than ever before, of the rights and choices available to him/her. Today the Indian customer is at a crossroad-should he/she enjoy the pleasure (arising out of such an act) of buying a consumer durable, service, a holiday or an automobile or defer the experience? Today the customer is demanding more value for the price that he/she pays. Social structures like family, role models, and peer groups are under pressure largely because of the change created by media, technology and competition. As shown in figure, these change drivers are today impacting the customer's awareness, values, social structures and even individual customer personality.

INTERNET USER PROFILE

Indian consumers also have the opportunity to seek out goods and services beyond their local, regional, and national boundaries. This universal access has had a positive impact on the quality of life of some population segments. Typically, an Indian Internet user is young, educated, generally a professional, urban (mostly metro resident), who accesses the Internet either at office/cyber cafés/educational institution. Males/use the Internet more than females. Irrespective of sex, the Internet user generally uses the Net for accessing information. Information products like newspapers and magazines from different countries including India are already on the web. Although most of them are free at the moment, information sellers like the Mumbai-based Centre for Monitoring Indian Economy (CMIE) are running websites which surfers can access for data on the Indian economy. Indian advertising agencies having Websites that open up their detailed information bases and full range of services to paid subscribers are pointing to the future.

E-buying is relatively much less. The International Finance Centre (IFC) reported that Indians bought Rs.93 million (about $2.2m) worth of goods and services over the Net in 1999. This was one sixth of the value of purchases made over the Net by Chinese Internet Users ($13m) in 1999.

INTERNET INFLUENCING THECONSUMER BEHAVIOUR

The Net has virtually become a household name in India. This can be attributed to the growth of the private ISP market in the country, offering the cyber voyage at more and more competitive prices. Internet in India is now one of the most vital mediums for information, entertainment and communication and the sole means for electronic commerce.

According to the India Internet Log Book 2000, India has over 1.8million subscribers (and more than 5.5 million users) and it is estimated to reach a whopping 50 million by December 31, 2003. A closer look at the Internet user profile shows that 41 per cent are large business firms who use the Net for their operations. Corporate India has realized the significance of e-commerce and the Net and has made it a part of its strategic planning exercise. Time and cost savings because of the disintermediation process further motivated large firms to embrace the Internet. SME (Small and Medium firms) accounted for 19 per cent of the user base, while the household segment accounted for 18 per cent. Education/research institutions and the government accounted for 10 per cent and 12 percent respectively. As we had mentioned earlier, access to, rather than ownership of, the communication tool is important. It is not surprising to note that Internet usage is not just restricted to a single individual in a household or business. More than one family member in the Indian house-hold has used the Net for different needs. Research shows that the top Internet user is an adult son/daughter or male head of the family, thus adding up to 42 per cent of Net users in the age group of 15-24 years, 31 per cent in the 25-34 years age group, and the rest above 35 years, with a clear bias in favour of the male bread winner. Cyber cafés are most popular among the younger age groups of 16-20 years. 98 per cent of the times the Net is used for email; 93 per cent users use it for Web browsing, 59 per cent also engage in online chat and 55 per cent use it for information and data transfer. Only 6.5 per cent of net users engage in e-commerce. Figure and table gives details in this regard.

A direct implication of the above changes in consumer lifestyles has been that customer expectations from suppliers have gone up significantly. Today the customer's decision-making parameters are significantly different from those in earlier decades. Though an average Indian customer continues to be price sensitive, he is increasingly moving away from just low-priced product to quality products and services at the lowest prices. In other words, the Internet has created awareness among the Indian consumers about global quality and performance parameters that they can get an affordable price. The fact that an average consumer can buy a newly published book within a week directly from Amazon.com, or a holiday from the best-known tour operator on his (customer's) term through the Net has put pressure on the Indian industry. Industry had to take another look at its costs, distribution models, and even input-output ratios. Competition further aggravated the scenario for most Indian companies, especially the older generation firms. One of the sectors where this change was visible was the banking sector where new generation banks like HDFC and ICICI snatched the lead from nationalized banks, including the State Bank of India. HDFC Bank's leadership today is principally because it redefined banking paradigms for Indian consumers. It was the first to offer Net banking and several other services on the Net. This made banking convenient for the customer. The customer did not have to visit the bank but could do his/her transactions on the Net. Likewise there were developments o the industrial products and commodities front. Disintermediation is now emerging fast in the Indian market. Time and location seem to no longer define customer choices, especially in metros and major urban centres. This is increasingly true for the younger customer group, which, as we saw earlier, is the major Internet user. Also, the younger generation of consumers is less brand loyal, they are shopping for value and it is in this context that the Internet has come as a big boon. There is another interesting paradigm that is shaping the Indian market. Increasingly, information and ownership of products and services is no more concentrated at the top end of the Indian market. The Internet has made it possible for all market segments to have access to the same information and provide equal opportunity to all to buy products and services. Facilities like online chats have increasingly created customer communities which have, in a way, become pressure groups. A company can no more hide poor performance or complaints in one market from its customers in another. It is in this context that the Internet is a great leveller and facilitator that builds relationships between buyers and sellers.

Note: Novelis, a subsidiary of Hindalco (the metals flagship company of India-based Aditya Birla Group), is engaged in the production of aluminum rolled products. Novelis operates in North America, South America, Europe, and Asia. It is headquartered in Atlanta, Georgia and employs about 12,700 people. For a very good study of "The Borderless Consumer Market and Buying Behaviour" see www.novelis.com

12

Consumer Buying Habits and Perceptions of Emerging Non-store Choices

INTRODUCTION

As studied earlier in the chapters perception is the process by which an individual interprets various stimuli received and forms picture of the world. The stimuli are received through the sensory organs namely eyes, ears, nose, mouth and skin and sorted out by the brain and stored as information. While doing so the individuals brain colours and tags the information using its own logic and the previous memory/experience if any. In fact the reality of the world and everything that surrounds is merely the perception of the individual. There is a possibility therefore that different individuals perceive different 'realities' of a single event or object.

IMPORTANCE OF CONSUMER PERCEPTION

Perceptions are being formed by the individual all the time and being stored away for future references. Perceptions so formed will come into play when the individual has to take any consumption decisions. Therefore perceptions about a product or service that are formed in the mind of the consumer are vital factors for the success of the product or service in the market. Astute marketers therefore take extraordinary care to study how perceptions are formed and how they can be changed.

FORMATION OF PERCEPTIONS

Though we have said that the individual constantly receives sensory stimuli throughout his wakeful life, the stimuli do not always register. The stimuli that do get picked up by the sensory organs but do not get registered are in fact the larger portion.

The first reason for non-registration is any monotony and constancy of a given stimulus. As an example we can show that a person may be conscious but not take "notice" of light, sound, touch or movement if any of these stimuli is constant on a time scale and unvaried in strength. The person can notice a light touch on his skin by a feather but does not notice that his feet are touched and pressed by the floor all the time. Similarly if a person is driving through a street that has billboards of identical style and positioned all along the road, only the first one may be noticed and later on eve that image may erased as the drive continues.

The second reason for non-registration is that even if the stimulus increases or decreases, the change or difference may not be substantial to merit notice. We will examine this phenomenon in a little more detail later in the chapter under the head JND (Just Noticeable Difference). The third reason for non-registration is the "shut-out" or rejection by the individual. This shut out or turn-off occurs automatically in the individual who is exposed to an overdose of any sensation for a length of time. As an example, an individual who is shown a TV commercial over and over may mentally block it and may not notice it any longer. If such individual is forced to notice it by mere changes in the strengths of stimuli like its sound or light without any change in its content, may even develop an unfavourable perception about it. Marketers can learn important lessons by observing the above phenomenon and avoid counter productive communications and wasted efforts in advertisements.

MARKETER'S CONCERN

A company marketing its products constantly strives to make the consumers form a positive and favourable perception about the company and its products. For this the stimuli sent out by the company through its messages, the packaging, advertisements and the very products themselves should stand out. They should be designed to be noticeable among the din of other stimuli. Some strategies to make the stimuli stand out are:

By contrasting: Inviting attention to an advertisement by employing contrast with the surroundings in size, colour, colour-reversal, or style is common. Newer methods of contrasting are being found all the time. A short silence in an audio commercial or a blank space in a closely printed page or a colour spot in black and white visual create contrast and can be used with advantage. Printing a message upside down, using different language and symbols, printing a teasing message, etc., are some of the others methods which fall broadly in this category.

By Projecting the unexpected: Delivering the blow where and when it is least expected is another strategy to grab attention. Advertisements cleverly using phrases such as "do not buy...." Or "we are sorry..." "why we cannot...." Do grab attention. They succeed in making the target audience read the message fully to solve the intrigue.

Stimuli that demolish certain prevailing myths or certain preconceived notions are always better noticed. In fact one would tend to notice a message that contradicts a belief than another message which goes along with the belief. For example, if you notice a commercial that depicts Dubai as a cool and green place or Bangkok as a place for family holiday a religious pilgrimage, you are tempted to read the message fully.

By Motivating: In the separate chapter on motivation it has been explained how the highlighting of dissatisfaction and projecting of solutions can motivating a person. By a proper design of the messages, the advertiser can grab the attention of the person who are dissatisfied with a particular situation. Their perception of the cause of dissatisfaction can be moulded and a positive perception about the solution created.

As an example, we can mention the advertisements for Horlicks, which points the dissatisfactory condition of a convalescing patient and how the patient can find a solution in Horlicks. The promotional campaigns for soft drinks in the tropical countries have always projected how one gets thirsty and how thirst can be quenched by the soft drink.

CONSUMER PERCEPTIONS IN THE SERVICE SECTOR

The understanding and the handling of consumer perception become more complex as one moves from the arena of goods to services. It is universally accepted that consumers have more difficulty in evaluating "quality" when it comes to service. Since services are intangible, perishable, and have no preset physical standards, the customer may form perceptions based on ideal expectations. The supplier too forms a perception of what is adequate. Often there is no meting point even to start with Worse still is the fact that the supplier and the consumer never sat together and created a common agreed perception. The result is that after the service is actually delivered the consumer gets a disappointment or shock - a wholly avoidable thing.

As an example we can talk about a package holiday sold by a tour operator to a first time consumer. The supplier did not inform the consumer of certain exclusions and limitations in the specification of the package in the intervening time before the tour commenced. The consumer in the meantime built his own high expectations. He thought that,

- Accommodation in hotels was single bedded.
- Free bed tea and breakfast were included.
- Visa charges and entrance tickets to museums were included in the fare.

None of the above were met. By the negation of the above three minor expectations, the entire tour was perceived as lousy and unsatisfactory. Tourists who had earlier experiences along these lines however did not have such expectations and their perceptions were positive.

Perceptions and Brand: Brand identity helps in making the consumer remember the association of the brand with quality and speeds up the purchase decision. However, the consumer presupposes that brand ensures an earlier perceived quality. In fact the expectation in a brand purchase situation is higher and shortcomings are not easily forgiven or forgotten. The golden principle in this for marketers is that they should offer only quality products when a brand is invoked.

Consumer Perception of Risks: Every consumer perceives some possible risks even with purchase decisions already taken. Apprehensions about these risks are not openly expressed. Even after a transaction is completed without any risks materializing, the consumer may carry the perception that there were risks. These perceived risks are:

- Functional risk of the product not performing as expected.
- Financial risk of having paid a higher price than necessary.
- Risk of effort and time being wasted consequent to a possible product failure.

Marketers can do a lot to reassure the consumers post-purchase, on the correctness of the choice. More importantly they should follow up every successful transaction and lay the foundation for repeat purchases and erase perception of risks.

Playing Trumps: At the store or on the Net or a home, you are bound to find consumers who are having difficulty in making choices due to the risks they perceive. In such cases the sales executive has the duty to guide the consumer. He could:

- Ascertain their real needs and suggest products that can meet these needs.

- Encourage consumer to rely on the brand.
- Give honest brand comparisons.
- Explain the scope and limitations of after-sales-service and warranties.
- When in doubt, play trumps. Recommend only the best, setting aside the cost factors.

Note: ArvinMeritor is a global supplier of a broad range of integrated systems, modules and components serving commercial truck, light vehicle, trailer and specialty original equipment manufacturers and certain aftermarkets. The company primarily operates in the US, Canada, and Europe. It is headquartered in Troy, Michigan and employed about 19,800 people as on September 30, 2008. For further knowledge regarding this chapter reader can visit www.arvinmeritor.com

13

Research and Applications of Responses to Direct Marketing Approaches

INTRODUCTION

Research is a key to the evolution of successful marketing strategies and programmes. It is an important tool to study buyer behaviours, changes in consumer lifestyles, consumption patterns, brand loyalty, and also forecast market changes. Research is also used to study competition and analyze the competitor's product positioning and how to gain competitive advantage. Of late, Marketing Research is also being used to help create and enhance brand equity. This is a new role and decidedly different from the conventional one where it was used for just studying buyer behaviour or for conducting feasibility studies. In fact, because of this conventional role, Marketing Research, until the mid 1980s, was considered a luxury, which only multinationals like Lever and Procter & Gamble and their like could afford. However, it is not so now. This is because competition has increased manifold in all sectors since 1985, and especially after 1991.

Following liberalization and decontrol, most firms today find that the government does not take strategy decisions for them any more. Rather, the arena has now shifted to their boardrooms, and they do not have answers to several questions. More specifically, they do not have the answer to the question: "How to gain and retain competitive advantage?" This is where MR plays an important role. Realizing the contribution that MR makes, more and more companies are now turning towards it. FMCG firms have now realized the futility of product research without understanding the dynamics of customer decision-making. Marketing research has often been delinked from business strategy. When that happens, most research reports become "academic" in nature and are "filed".

Many a time, research or respondent bias makes the MR exercise a waste of resources. Often the researcher has the temptation to conclude what the top management may like to hear. For example, most chief executive and marketing chiefs would like to believe that everything about their operations is good. The researcher may find just the opposite. For example, he may find that the firm's distribution plan and strategy is not competitive and channel members do not have faith in company's policies. The trade has switched loyalties and the company's penetration is now reduced to only a few select outlets who are also with the company due to their long-term association only.

Should the researcher choose to present these facts? If he or she does the management and, more so, the marketing chief may not appreciate the facts and that may mean an end to any other subsequent assignment or being relegated in the organization, a dilemma that most researchers face. But a good researcher, like a good doctor, knows that it is better to present facts and let the company decide the strategy, rather than hide it, which subsequently may even affect its survival. Therefore to make Research effective, it is important that it has a linkage wit business strategy and should respond to future or emerging scenarios in the market place. To understand the research and applications of responses to direct marketing approaches one has to first understand what direct marketing is?

DIRECT MARKETING

Direct marketing is an interactive mode of marketing through which the marketer reaches out his target market at any location. The Direct Marketing Association of USA has defined direct marketing as "an interactive system of marketing which uses one or more advertising media to effect a measurable response and/or transaction at any location". An analysis of this definition brings out three key elements, namely:

- It is an interactive system in the sense that there is a two-way communication between the marketer and his/her target market; the response or non-response of the customer completes the communication loop in the direct marketing programme. For example, when the customer fills in the response coupon in an advertisement or a catalogue and mails it, he/she communicates to the marketer and hence completes the communication loop.

- Another element is measurability of response - a mentioned above the number of coupons received indicates the response rate to the marketer's communication.
- Direct marketing activities are not location specific; it is not necessary for the customer to physically interact with the marketer; he/she can establish a contact through mail, phone, fax or the internet.

As mentioned above, direct marketing is an efficient way to promote and sell products and services in a highly competitive market. The goal of direct marketing is to always get a response from the customer. Direct marketing has also been known by other terms like direct selling, mail order selling or catalogue selling. Today direct marketing uses all these tools and is based on a customer database. In fact, the key to successful direct marketing is the development of this database.

RESEARCH AND DATABASE DEVELOPMENT

Database marketing is the most effective way to customize the marketing mix to suit target market. This helps not only in customizing the offering but also its delivery. Given the developments in the area of information technology (Software like geographical information system - GIS), today it is possible to deliver the right product with the right message, at the right time to the right person. This presupposes the creation of customer's purchase and other related information. It also includes the development of a database of potential customers. Database marketing, therefore, is an interactive approach to marketing that uses all communication tools and media vehicles through research to reach to the target market. It is also the basis of all relationship marketing efforts of the company. The information stored in the database is used to develop customer loyalty and to identify all potential buyers for any new product or service. It also helps in identifying the most cost effective media and delivery vehicles.

CHARACTERISTICS OF A GOOD DATABASE

Although each firm may decide to develop its own database, there are certain characteristics that help enrich it. These are:

- Each customer or prospect should be treated as an individual entity and hence a separate record for him/her should exist in the marketing database. Market segments are an agglomeration of such individual customers.

- Each such marketing record should contain all the relevant information and access details like name, address, telephone numbers, frequency of product use, experience with the product, industry and decision making units for organizational customer, response to any earlier direct marketing campaign, and soon.
- This information should be available to all departments and employees of the company involved in the direct marketing programme to enable them to be customer friendly.
- The aim of the organization should be to replace routine usage surveys with this database.
- Information technology tools should be used to strengthen this database and also develop corporate responses to the customer. These tools can also be used to identify opportunities and threats in the customer environment and craft appropriate responses which will help the marketer to exploit opportunities and neutralize threats. The use of these tools should also help in optimum resource utilization.

Increasingly, firms are realizing the importance of database in targeting and creating competitive advantage. Today several organizations are also using this database for their customer relationship management programmes. Cross-selling can also be effectively managed through database marketing. This is especially true for firms operating in several products/businesses that require the same database. Citibank, for example, uses its credit card customers database to market several other financial products, including banking services. Once again, information technology has further augmented these strengths. Database management, therefore, is a key to the development of an effective direct marketing programme.

DIRECT MARKETING MIX

Marketing mix in the direct marketing mode, by and large, remains the same except for communication programme and customer service, which have acquired a new meaning. For example, if the marketer guarantees delivery of the product within a defined time frame and promises to take it back in case it fails to live up to customer expectations and return his/her money, then the customer service executive cannot refuse a claim. This is opposed to general marketing practices where marketing can put several disclaimer and refuse to without any question may cost the marketer significant losses as he not only loses that customer but subsequent prospects as well. In general marketing the loss can be contained through other elements of the marketing mix. In addition to marketing mix decisions, the direct marketer has to pay special attention to the following factors in decision making.

COMMUNICATION PROGRAMME

This involves (both) creative and media decisions. The creative decisions centre around the copy platform, graphic design elements, mailers, stickers, and so forth. Consider, for example, the campaigns of Orange (Hutchison Max Telecom), a cellular phone service provider in the country. These were not only crisp but also helped in positioning. Orange as one of the most customer friendly cellular services in India. The communication of its various products like the prepaid Sim card (just talk), roaming facilities and various air time packages shared the same colours and motivate customer to buy the service. The media used by direct marketers are mailers, telephone, television and the Internet. Direct response print and television advertising are particularly effective in generating response to the offer, especially if it is complex to understand. Also, the direct marketer today uses various outdoor retail panels (Just Talk and BPL MOTS brands of prepaid Sim card in Mumbai) and even stickers to retain the brand at the top of customer's mind. These also serve the purpose of a remainder.

CUSTOMER SERVICE

As mentioned earlier, customer service is a key input in direct marketing. In direct marketing physical contact with the customer is low and it is the quality of service that facilitates customer decision-making. Service, therefore, is an investment and cannot be ignored. The customer service mix today involves the following:

- Speed and Accuracy of Order fulfilment: This includes the speed at which the customer is able to complete order form and the organization's ability to acknowledge and execute the order. This involves the development of an appropriate order fulfilment process in which speed and accuracy hold the key to purchase and retention. In online order procurement, the company will have to pay special attention to its bandwidth and server capacity. The same holds true for marketers who use call centres to book, deliver, and service customers' orders.
- Immediate customer complaint resolution: Today, customers demand on-the-pot resolution of complaints. Given the Internet

and call centres, customers look for seamless complaint management.

- Other important elements of customer service: Toll free telephone numbers (1-600), money back guarantee, multiple modes of payment (credit cards, cheque, money order, VPP and so on) are giving customers flexibility.

The Jet Airways in-flight shopping mall (now withdrawn) offered all these modes thereby making it easy for customer to buy a product. Dettol, a brand of Reckitt Benckiser of India, ahs launched the 'Healthy Home Careline'. Consumers can reach the company by dialling a toll free number and their queries are answered instantly. This, in turn, builds the image of RB as a caring company, increases the company's interaction with customers, and also gives it access to the name and phone numbers of consumers, thus expanding its consumer database.

TIMING AND SEQUENCING

This factor involves determination of whether the product or service is offered once, as a part of the campaign, or continuously. This will obviously involve campaign decisions like whether to have bursts, pulsing, or a continuous campaign.

THE RESEARCH PROCESS

Having known the concept of direct marketing, we also have to scan through the marketing research process itself to know how this research is applied in the direct marketing approach. This process, has seven stages as mentioned below:

1. Problem definition related to direct marketing
2. Defining research objectives
3. Working out a research design
4. Deciding on the sources of data
5. Planning and deciding on data collection techniques and tools
6. Analyzing data
7. Making a report and presenting it to the decision maker/s

Direct marketing approach through Marketing Intelligence system:

The purpose of any marketing research is to provide information at a specific time on customers, trade, competition and future trends in each of these segments. Most of these research exercises help strengthen an enterprise and assist it in strategic decision making. But marketing is a war that requires continuous surveillance of markets (customers), competition, and other structural components like government policy. Based on this continuous surveillance, successful enterprises evolve their tactics to win smaller battles which help it win the war of market shares. The entire concept of market intelligence is similar to military sciences, where it is a known fact that no army can win a war without good, effective and timely information on enemy forces and the terrain on which the war is going to be fought.

Components of Intelligence System

In marketing the intelligence system has two components:

Customer intelligence

Competitor intelligence

Customer Intelligence: This provides useful information on a customer's business, preferences or loyalties, personal demographic details, and also "whims and fancies". A good intelligence system will even tell a marketer what to do and not do when he or she is with the customer. Like what words to use and which ones to avoid, the proper dress code, habits or tendencies to watch out for, and so on. This information becomes useful in planning sales calls on customers. It is also useful in evolving advertising and promotion programmes. Most often this data is collected by sales people either as a separate stand-alone exercise or as a part of their regular sales call.

Competitor Intelligence: This gives information on strengths and weaknesses of each competitor in the territory, the strategy and tactics being used by them, and how the customer procures competitor brands. This also provides inputs on the key persons in competitor firms. This information is collected on a regular basis by sales people and I continuously updated.

Most marketing researches involve studying consumer's perceptions, beliefs, preferences, and motivations. Some may involve studying the psychological dimensions of the dealer, retailer, or sales person's behaviour. In a way, most research exercises measure attitudes of individuals. An attitudinal study involves specifying:

- The class of persons, objects, events, or states to be observed.
- The environmental conditions under which the observation takes place.

- The operations to be performed in making the observations.
- The instruments to be used to perform the operations and
- The observations to be made.

Extending this concept to marketing, the attitude of a consumer towards a particular brand of a product or service can be understood as a function of:

- The number of consumers of that brand.
- At a specific time and in a given geographical area, who are
- Personally interviewed, using a
- Specified attitudinal scale, to obtain
- The response information provided by the attitude scale.

In other words, consumer attitudes towards a brand, product, or service may be understood as numerical ratings on a like-dislike scale.

SCALES USED TO MEASURE THE ATTITUDE OF THE CUSTOMERS IN THE CUSTOMER INTELLIGENCE SYSTEM

To measure the attitudes of a consumer, a researcher has to understand different scales, situations in which they may be used, or the analytical tools that can be used to analyze the responses. Scales are of four types: (a) nominal, (b) ordinal, (c) interval, and (d) ratio.

Nominal Scales: These are the least restrictive of all the scales. Here numbers are used for identification purposes only. A typical example of this scale is telephone numbers allotted to subscribers. An other illustration is classification of retail outlets "carrying brand X" and those "not carrying brand X". These scales permit only the most elementary mathematical analysis. For example, mode is a common statistical tool used here. Let us consider the example of different brands of toilet soaps being marketed in a given area. On the basis of the number of shops keeping different brands of toilet soaps, we can find out the most popular brand of soap in a particular geographical area, or the brand sold by maximum number of shops in that area.

Ordinal Scales:

These are the ranking scales. These scales require the customer's ability to distinguish between elements according to a single attribute and direction. Consider, for example, a person who may be asked to rank different brands of cars on fuel efficiency.

Suppose the response is:

Maruti 800 CC -1

Indica -2

Santro -2

Zen -3

Esteem -4

Accent -5

In this situation an ordinal scale has been used. It may be understood that mere ranking of different brands in a product class (in the above case, car brands) does not permit the researcher to conclude about the differences separating brands on a specific attribute. In the above example, the only conclusion that can be drawn is that Maruti 800 is the most fuel efficient car in this area. But by how much and how different it is from others on fuel efficiency cannot be assessed by this scale.

An ordinal scale contains all the information of a nominal scale, as equivalent entities receive the same rank. Ordinal scales lend themselves to statistical analysis like median, quartile, percentile, and other summary statistics.

Interval Scales: These scales allow an individual to make meaningful statements about differences separating two objects. However, it may be noted that the zero point of this scale is arbitrary. The most common example of this scale is a thermometer measuring temperatures in Fahrenheit and centigrade scales. While an arbitrary zero is assigned to each scale, equal temperature differences are found by 'scaling' equal volumes of expansion of mercury. A typical example of interval scale is the preference for a brand of perfume exhibited by a consumer on the following scale

- I like it the most
- I like it
- I neither like nor dislike it
- I dislike it
- I dislike it the most

Here, each response refers to specific degree of consumer preference. Responses measured on these scales can be analyzed using statistical tools like mean, standard deviation, and correlation coefficient. Advanced statistical analyses using t-test and f-test can also be done on responses measured on this scale.

Ratio Scales: These are at the top end of scaling techniques as all arithmetical operations are possible here. A ratio scale possesses a unique zero point. It contains all the information of earlier-mentioned scales. Having considered the choice of scales, the researcher should now understand that all attitude measurement procedures are concerned with having people respond to a specific stimuli according to a certain set of instructions. These stimuli may be advertising copy, themes, packaging, shelf display, or even a sales person's presentation. The response may involve assessing attractiveness of an advertisement, appeal of a package, or credibility of presentation. The respondent's task is to express his/her response on a scale (could be any, chosen by the researcher). An important point to be considered by the researcher is whether the emphasis in the analysis is to be on the respondents or the stimuli, or both. Suppose the marketing research is on detergent powders (stimuli) and the housewives have been asked to evaluate different brands on one attribute "gentleness on hands". Now three types of scaling might be identical.

i. Respondent-centred approach: Here the researcher examines systematic variation across respondents.

ii. Response approach: Here the researcher examines both (i) and (ii).Most marketing researches have scales and analysis that measure based on response approach.

In measuring attitudes, several scaling techniques are used. Some of these are Thurstones Case V, Osgood's Semantic Differential, Likert's Summated Scale, and the Q-Soct. Among these, the most common are the Semantic Differential and Likert's Summated scales. "The semantic differential is a type of quantitative judgement method that results in (assumed interval) scales that are often further analyzed by such techniques as factor analysis; (the procedure) enables the researcher to probe both the direction and the intensity of respondents' attitudes towards such concepts as corporate image, advertising image and brand image". The most common approach is to ask respondents to describe a firm on bipolar adjectives on a seven point scale, as shown in table.

Table: Customer's Perception of Company X

Progressive	--	--	--	--	X	--	--	Traditionalist
Reliable	--	--	--	--	--	--	X	Unreliable
Strong	--	X	--	--	--	--	--	Weak
Customer focused	--	--	--	--	--	X	--	Non-customer focused
Responsive	--	--	--	--	--	X	--	Non-responsive

These seven points on the scale represent equal intervals. Each point measures the intensity of the respondent's perception or feeling and the more the respondent moves towards a particular pole, the more positive or negative he or she feels. Specifically, the two ends of the scale represent strong feelings, while the middle or the 4th point reflects indifference. The scale is quantified as being +3, +2, +1, 0, -1, -2, -3. In this example, the firm is perceived as being traditionalist, highly unreliable, strong but non-customer focused, and nonresponsive. Likewise, a firm may measure its competitive image against its major competitors. Figure shows a customer's perception of firm X vis-à-vis firms Y and Z. Here, we note that customers have a highly negative image of firm X and a highly positive image of firm Y.

Today semantic differential scales are being used in image measurement, comparing competitive brands and services, analyzing effectiveness of advertising and other promotional inputs, and to determine the attitudinal characteristics of buyers of a particular product class or brands within a product class. These scales are most popular in marketing research.

Interview Schedule: At times a questionnaire is not able to give an insight into the rationale of a customer's feeling, or factors that will lead to the success of a new technology like e-mail and voice-mail or new products that a firm may consider introducing. It is for these and several similar reasons that an interview schedule is developed. The purpose of this schedule is to study in depth an object, event, or a group of people. Unlike a questionnaire the responses here are unstructured. The limitation of an interview schedule is that it does not lend itself to tabulation and, generally, analysis of responses is difficult. It is for this reason that its use is limited and the sample size, too, is much smaller than the one in a market survey using questionnaires.

Association Tests: Of late, the researcher's focus has been on qualitative research, or researching the psychological dimension of consumer behaviour. We mentioned earlier that in most direct questioning, using a questionnaire or an interview schedule, the respondent is generally guarded and gives responses more from the conscious part of his or her psyche.

To get to the subconscious mind, marketing researchers are using several psychological instruments like association tests, sentence completion tests, and thematic appreciation tests (TAT). These tests are believed to reveal the customer's perception of a product, brand, or firm's image. These tests can also give information on the customer's perception of brand personality as also the personality and lifestyle of the target customer group.

Some of the other commonly used tools in qualitative research, aimed at discovering consumers hidden thoughts, are the use of metaphors and stories and even asking them to recall their experiences with a brand or any other event. Memories of experiences are often told through a story. Consumer reconstruct them each time use them to communicate their earlier experiences. But memories are also communicated in a metaphoric manner. The overload of memories, metaphors and storytelling strongly influence consumers' consumption experience and behaviours. By providing particular metaphors, researchers can guide customers in weaving their stories of past, current and future experiences in the market-place. Consumers, in turn, use their own metaphors to express their thoughts, feelings, and emotions. Stories about brands demonstrate how brands are represented in the consumer's mind.

TOOLS FOR DATA COLLECTION

The researcher has to decide on the appropriate tool for data collection. These tools are:

- Questionnaire: This is the most popular tool for data collection. A questionnaire contains questions that a researcher wishes to ask his respondents. It is important that these questions be put in a language the customer understands and finds easy to answer. As far as possible, all technical terms or words that can have multiple meanings and interpretations should be explained. This is essential so as to have consistency in responses from all sample respondents. For example, words like "regularly", "frequently", "occasionally", need to be explained. A question like "How regularly do you buy a detergent powder?" and having the choices "always, frequently, occasionally, sometimes, and never", will not get the desired response if not explained. So the researcher may explain these words in the following manner:
- Always: every shopping cycle
- Frequently: every alternate shopping cycle
- Occasionally: Once in six shopping cycles
- Sometimes: not very often; once in a while
- Never: never buy in any of the shopping cycles

The shopping cycle means every time you go to buy groceries for your house.

This could be weekly, fortnightly, or monthly.

Steps in Questionnaire Design: It is important that the questions are unloaded, to avoid any researcher bias. It is also important that the information collected must be believable and unbiased. Just as researcher bias has to be avoided, respondent bias must also be avoided. Further, there must be a flow in a questionnaire. For example, "How many children do you have?" and then asking "your marital status" is improper. The question on marital status should logically precede the one of the number of children.

A questionnaire should be pre-tested before final printing. The pre-testing should be for the following:

- Are the questions clear to the respondents?
- Is the researcher getting answers to the questions? Or does the respondent understand questions in the same way as the researcher does?
- Are there any terms or words requiring explanation?
- Are there any sensitive "spots" or "questions" which respondents would feel uncomfortable with and would not want to respond to? Typically, these could be questions relating to respondent's income, age, or personal particulars. To avoid such drawbacks, put these questions with multiple choices in different ranges. Also, with regard to income, it is best to ask annual family income as it is less threatening.
- What is the time that an average respondent is taking to complete the questionnaire? It is important to remember long questionnaires lead to fatigue and also puts off the respondent. Non-response or inappropriate response is very common in a long questionnaire. So the key is in avoiding respondent fatigue by having a short questionnaire.
- Does the customer feel interested in the research project? Is his/her interest sustained while responding to the questionnaire?
- Is there a logical flow among the questions?
- Are the investigators able to explain the purpose and questions, if required?

Thus through questionnaires the data are collected and analysed with the help of the statistical tools and then the interpretations are reported.

FUTURE OF DIRECT MARKETING IN INDIA AND THE CONSUMER BEHAVIOUR

The future of direct marketing in India is dependent on the following:

- Reaching out to non-metro/non-urban markets: As metro and urban markets get saturated by products and services promoted in both general and direct marketing models, the key to any direct marketing campaign lies in expanding its reach to rural and semi-rural markets. Infrastructural constraints have so far come in the way of the direct marketer. But with rural cyber cafes, satellite television reaching rural areas, telecom booths, and mobile telephony gaining popularity, it should be possible for marketers to reach out to their target market in these areas. Post offices are located in the farthest corner of India and service village with a population as low as 20 households. These offices can be used as an effective medium to communicate, deliver and even service the rural customer. IDBI, ICICI, SBI and other financial institutions are today directly marketing their mutual funds and other financial products through the Indian postal system. Thus, the key to success in the Indian market lies in the firm's ability to access rural markets.
- Enhancing Credibility of the Offer: The Indian customer generally does not buy a product or service until he/she has seen it, touched it, and experienced it. Therefore, these are key ingredients in the customer's selection process and the direct marketer has to enhance his credibility as he cannot offer these benefits. He thus needs to pay special attention to ensuring that the customer's experience with the product exceeds his/her expectations. Also, he needs to focus on service to ensure speedy settlement of any claims. Credibility is the key to success in direct marketing.
- Wider use of debit and credit card: Direct marketing's success in India will be dependent on the wider use of debit and credit cards as mode of payment by both the customer and the marketer. This involves a shift of transactions from cash to non-cash modes and hence a change in the customers' and sellers' mindset.

- Emergence of specialized database firms: Another key factor in the success of direct marketing is the evolution of specialized database firms. It is an expensive proposition both in terms of money and time to create customer database. This makes direct marketing feasible only for large firms. A very large component of the Indian economy consists of small-and medium-sized firms vho cannot afford to create this database. Hence the emergence and evolution of firms specialized in database management will contribute to the success of direct marketing in India. To conclude, direct marketing has arrived in India, but is still an urban and metro phenomenon. It is gradually widening out to non-urban areas too. It is important to remember that competitive marketing strategies involve using a combination of general and direct marketing approaches.

Note: Packaging Corporation of America (PCA) is a producer of containerboard and corrugated packaging products. It also produces special design application boxes used in the food and agriculture industry. The company operates primarily in the US. It is headquartered in Lake Forest, Illinois and employed 8,100 people. For a very good case study regarding this topic, reader can visit company's website www.packagingcorp.com

14

Issues of Privacy and Ethics

CONSUMER PRIVACY

The word "Consumerism" has many connotations, depending on who is using the term. Business, government, consumer groups and academic researchers have each developed their own definition of the term. These definitions span the gamut from challenging society's goals for material goods to reflecting peoples desire for better values. One succinct definition is that "Consumerism is a social movement of citizens and government to enhance the rights and powers of buyers in relation to sellers.

One of the consumer rights relates to privacy, information, data banks, and similar emerging issues. Consumer information collected, merged, and exchanged through computer and communication technologies has become the main resource that business and government use to facilitate the millions of daily transactions engaged in by consumers. Timely, accurate, and complete consumer information is needed by a variety of organizations, direct response marketers, advertising agencies, insurance companies, and private utilities. The purposes of consumer information may include such things as approving or denying credit, issuing credit cards, writing insurance policies, selecting people for direct mail solicitation, preventing fraud, determining eligibility for government aid, investigating and law enforcement purposes and many other activities.

To obtain the benefits of technology without losing basic privacy rights, six basic computer -age privacy rules were formulated:

1. Only relevant and socially approved personal information should be collected by private or public organizations to determine people's access to rights, benefits and opportunities.

2. Individuals should be informed what information about them is to be collected and how it will be used.
3. Individuals should have practical procedures for inspecting their records and for raising issues as to the accuracy, completeness, and propriety of information used to make evaluative decisions about them.
4. Sensitive personal information should be circulated within the collecting organization only to those with a need to see it for legitimate purposes.
5. Disclosures of identified personal information should not be made by collecting organizations to others outside the original area of activity unless agreed to by the individual or required by legal process.
6. Organizations must create and apply effective data security measures so that they can keep the promises of confidentiality that they have made to individuals whose information they are holding in a trustee relationship. But new consumer privacy issues have surfaced recently. For instance:
   - Feature stories in magazines, newspapers, and on TV informed the public that information given for one purpose - credit, insurance, employment, organizational memberships, publication subscriptions, charitable donations, etc., -was being widely used for other commercial purposes without the individual's knowledge or consent.
   - When the Society of Consumer Affairs Professionals in industry polled ten leading consumer advocacy organizations in 1989 as to the issues they believed would be consumer action priorities in the '90's, a majority cited better "Consumer privacy protection".

A major survey of consumers and industry leaders in the privacy - intensive sector (e.g., banks and thrifts, insurance companies, direct marketers, credit bureaus, etc.,) made the following conclusions regarding consumer privacy in the information age:

- The general concern over threats to privacy by 79 percent of the public reflects the low trust in institutions that has become a hall mark.
- Despite these high general concerns over privacy invasion, the public is prepared to provide personal information for consumer

services when convinced that fair information practices are observed.

- Concern about privacy varies by race, religion, political philosophy, information level, age and computer use. For instance blacks, Jews, liberals and those aged 30 - 49 are most pro-privacy.
- Lowering general public concern over threats to privacy will not be easy but there

Are three important ways to enhance consumer privacy interests:

- Update consumer privacy laws such as the Fair Credit Reporting Act.
- Create new information property rights for consumers whereby they could opt in or out of particular consumer-profile information systems and receive some kind of compensation if they participate.
- Develop more proactive consumer privacy protection policies by business and consumer advocacy groups.

This topic would be of continuing concern to the marketers because of the potential for a consumer backlash on privacy issues. More education of consumers will be required about why certain information is being collected and about their consumer rights.

ETHICS IN BUSINESS AND ITS RELEVANCE TO CONSUMER BEHAVIOUR

Understanding of consumer Behaviour gives a clear advantage to the marketer who would know all that is there to know about the target consumers personality and choices. In fact almost all companies producing or marketing continuously gather and update their information about their target consumers and form strategies. In many circles it is felt that in depth understanding about the behaviour of the consumers gives scope to the marketer to manipulate the market itself and that strategies are formed without regard to fundamental ethics of being honest, truthful and fare. The principal aim of the strategies is to somehow overcome the resistance of the consumers and sell more. This leads to a situation where cleverness in the market place and selling success become prized qualities of a market man when viewed from the angle of his employer or the company. Unless the company draws the line and encourages the employees to be within certain limits, ethics becomes the first casualty.

In the long run it does immense damage to the relationship between the company and its customers. Therefore, more than anyone else companies doing marketing have to make ethics their way of life not be compromised even under grave provocation or threat from competition. Without ethics there can be no business.

ETHICS IS NOT A MATTER OF CHOICE

It is difficult to precisely define what ethics is. However most people have no difficulty in understanding the spirit of ethics. Most people do not question or argue about the axiom that ethics is not a matter of choice. Just as you do not question the right of other people to live you do not question their right to expect ethical behaviour from you. Having said that we must however admit that unethical practices are seen and put up within every area including marketing. In marketing-be it product design, packaging, pricing, promotion, distribution or quality assurance, ethics gets a go-by many times. Seemingly honest business persons educated and respectable sometimes allow unethical practices by the companies to go on. Common explanations that they are caught up in a competitive situation and therefore helpless is not acceptable. The real reason could be that in their quest for commercial superiority they are closing an eye and allowing unethical practices to continue. In short they are subverting what should have been their fundamental principal and philosophy. The society cannot accept such business because it affects the very fabric of life.

ETHICS FROM THE TOP

A business place dishonesty or rot has described above could not be taking place without some knowledge of the management. Management are in any case expected to be constantly on the alert to detect and stem any rot at the first instance. They are to educate their employees and pro actively install all policies that would prevent unethical practices. Ethical practices should be instituted by the companies to flow from the top and percolating to all levels below. Including lofty statements about ethics in the company's vision statement is good but not enough. The corporate management should understand that Junior executives constantly look upward their supervisors and top management for moral guidance. Absence of guidance is taken by the working levels as a signal that the company is not serious about ethics. In such company's commercial success becomes the paramount policy. All means, fare or foul, that brings success will be viewed as strategies. One company's unethical practices will induce the other company's to follow suit in the name of the competition. Using trick for trick, fighting fire with fire, the competitors bring down the general image of the industry. All because few managements did not have the foresight or guts to stand up and stick to ethics even at the cost of some short term set backs. However history has shown that those company's stand erect and instil ethics in their employees get notices by consumers and become leaders.

ETHICS: A JOURNEY

Ethics is not a destination. It is a journey. Company's and persons should continuously practice it, question themselves periodically and take course corrections to travel in correct directions. Induction of the code of ethics and their maintenance should be proactively supervised by the entire organization be it a government, business or a group on a continuous basis. Appreciation and reward for followers of ethical codes is important and so also punishments for breaking these codes.

ETHICAL PURCHASING

Ethical purchasing put simply is buying things that are made ethically by companies that act ethically. Ethical can be a subjective term both for companies and consumers, but in its truest sense means without harm to or exploitation of humans, animals or the environment.

UNDERSTANDING BUYING ETHICALLY

The ways in which you can act as an 'ethical consumer' can take on a number of often subtle forms. Positive buying is favouring ethical products, be they fair trade, organic or cruelty free. This option is arguably the most important since it directly supports progressive companies. Negative purchasing means avoiding products you disapprove of such as battery eggs or polluting cars.

Company-based purchasing involves targeting a business as a whole. For example, the Nestlé boycott targets all its brands and subsidiaries in a bid to force the company to change its marketing of baby milk formula in the Third World.

The fully screened approach is a combination of all three and means looking at all the companies and products together and evaluating which brand are the most ethical...

SHOPPING TIPS FOR THE ETHICAL SHOPPER

1. Local shops
2. Health food shops

3. Fair trade
4. Products not tested on animals
5. Vegetarian products
6. Organic produce
7. Non-genetically altered food
8. Ethical money
9. Recycling & second hand
10. Wood Products

DEVIANT CONSUMER BEHAVIOUR

The deviant consumer behaviours include negligent and fraudulent behaviours.

Negligent Consumer Behaviour: Compulsive Buying

Most consumers engage in buying as a normal and routine part of their everyday lives. But when the buying becomes compulsive the goal shifts from obtaining utility from the purchased item to achieving gratification from the purchasing process itself. Compulsive buying is chronic. Repetitive purchasing that becomes a primary response to negative events or feelings. It becomes very difficulty to stop and ultimately results in harmful consequences to individuals or others. Compulsive buying is undesirable because it has sever consequences such as amassing huge amounts of debt that are difficult to retire and feelings of remorse, lowered self esteem, and weekend inter personal relationships. Shopaholics are addicted to purchasing and use it as a fix to offset emotional deprivation. And when they are confronted over their spending habits they will often switch to another type of chronic destructive habits such as over eating, work holism or over exercising.

Studies show that as much as 10 percent of the American population can be classified as hard core shoppers who shop for shopping sake rather that to fill real needs. One factor facilitating the process is the easy availability of the credit cards. It is probably no coincidence that there has been a rapid growth in the bank cards issued during the rise in the problem of compulsive consumption. One consumer was even able to obtain 1199 different types of credit cards to win a bet with a friend. The result of easy credit can be staggering debt. Support groups have been established to fight this type of addiction by helping people who are trying to stop their compulsion to spend beyond their means for things they don't need.

FRAUDULENT CONSUMER BEHAVIOUR

Shop lifting is an example of fraudulent or a criminal type of deviant consumer behaviour that involves the theft of retail merchandise during the store hours by someone who is shopping or pretending to shop. Shop lifting rose 35 per cent between the mid - 1980's - 1990 and equals about two per cent of all retail sales excluding gas and car purchases.

Thus, it must be emphasized that consumers, just as business and other organizations, have an obligation to act responsibly in the marketplace in exchange relationships.

Ethical shopping and ethical trade initiatives:

Every day we choose between different products. Our purchase decisions do not only affect us ourselves. The way the products have been produced can make a big difference to other people, to nature, the environment and to animals. Ethical purchase behaviour is about taking responsibility for the influence which we control ourselves.

ETHICALLY QUESTIONABLE CONSUMER BEHAVIOUR

The more one equals ethics with moral criticism and moral self-criticism, the more natural it is to start with looking at unethical rather than ethical consumer behaviour. In addition to potential theory-traditional reasons, there are good practical and economic reasons for explaining, influencing and prohibiting ethically questionable consumer behaviour. A red thread in this consumer ethics research tradition has been it's the development, validation and frequent replication of the "consumer ethics scale" (often referred to as CES. This CES scale offers a list of more or less ethically questionable consumer activities for a vote. The activities can be grouped into four categories, ranging from clearly questionable to little controversial categories:

BENEFITING FROM ILLEGAL ACTIVITY

- Changing price tags on merchandise in a retail store.
- Drinking a can of soda in a supermarket without paying for it.
- Reporting a lost item as "stolen" to an insurance company in order to collect the money.
- Giving misleading price information to a clerk for an un-priced item.
- Returning damaged merchandise when the damage is your own fault passively benefiting at the expense of others.

- Getting too much change and not saying anything.
- Lying about a child's age in order to get a lower price.
- Not saying anything when the server miscalculates the bill in your favour actively benefiting from questionable behaviour
- Breaking a bottle of salad dressing in a supermarket and doing nothing about it.
- Stretching the truth on an income tax return.
- Using an expired coupon for merchandise.
- Using a coupon for merchandise that you did not buy.
- Not telling the truth when negotiating the price of a new automobile. No harm/no foul.
- Tasting grapes in a supermarket and not buying any.
- Using computer software or games that you did not buy.
- Recording an album instead of buying it.
- Spending over an hour trying on different dresses and not purchasing any.
- Taping a movie off the television.
- Returning merchandise after trying it and not liking it.

Note: Chevron Corporation (Chevron) is one of the largest integrated energy companies in the world. The company is engaged in every aspect of the oil and natural gas industry, including exploration and production, refining, marketing and transportation, chemicals manufacturing and sales, geothermal, mining operations, and power generation. It has operations in more than 100 countries including the US. Chevron is headquartered in San Ramon, California and employs about 67,000 people. For a case study visit company's site www.chevron.com

15

The Psychology of Marketing

INTRODUCTION

The study of consumers helps firms and organizations improve their marketing strategies by understanding issues such as how:

- The psychology of how consumers think, feel, reason, and select between different alternatives (e.g., brands, products);
- The psychology of how the consumer is influenced by his or her environment (e.g., culture, family, signs, media);
- The behaviour of consumers while shopping or making other marketing decisions;
- Limitations in consumer knowledge or information processing abilities influence decisions and marketing outcome;
- How consumer motivation and decision strategies differ between products that differ in their level of importance or interest that they entail for the consumer; and
- How marketers can adapt and improve their marketing campaigns and marketing strategies to more effectively reach the consumer.

One "official" definition of consumer behaviour is "The study of individuals, groups, or organizations and the processes they use to select, secure, use, and dispose of products, services, experiences, or ideas to satisfy needs and the impacts that these processes have on the consumer and society." Although it is not necessary to memorize this definition, it brings up some useful points:

- Behaviour occurs either for the individual, or in the context of a group (e.g., friends influence what kinds of clothes a person wears) or an organization (people on the job make decisions as to which products the firm should use).

- Consumer behaviour involves the use and disposal of products as well as the study of how they are purchased. Product use is often of great interest to the marketer, because this may influence how a product is best positioned or how we can encourage increased consumption. Since many environmental problems result from product disposal (e.g., motor oil being sent into sewage systems to save the recycling fee, or garbage piling up at landfills) this is also an area of interest.
- Consumer behaviour involves services and ideas as well as tangible products.
- The impact of consumer behaviour on society is also of relevance. For example, aggressive marketing of high fat foods, or aggressive marketing of easy credit, may have serious repercussions for the national health and economy.

There are four main applications of consumer behaviour:

- The most obvious is for marketing strategy-i.e., for making better marketing campaigns. For example, by understanding that consumers are more receptive to food advertising when they are hungry, we learn to schedule snack advertisements late in the afternoon. By understanding that new products are usually initially adopted by a few consumers and only spread later, and then only gradually, to the rest of the population, we learn that (1) companies that introduce new products must be well financed so that they can stay afloat until their products become a commercial success and (2) it is important to please initial customers, since they will in turn influence many subsequent customers' brand choices.
- A second application is public policy. In the 1980s, Accutane, a near miracle cure for acne, was introduced. Unfortunately, Accutane resulted in severe birth defects if taken by pregnant women. Although physicians were instructed to warn their female patients of this, a number still became pregnant while taking the drug. To get consumers' attention, the Federal Drug Administration (FDA) took the step of requiring that very graphic pictures of deformed babies be shown on the medicine containers.

- Social marketing involves getting ideas across to consumers rather than selling something. Marty Fishbein, a marketing professor, went on sabbatical to work for the Centres for Disease Control trying to reduce the incidence of transmission of diseases through illegal drug use. The best solution, obviously, would be if we could get illegal drug users to stop. This, however, was deemed to be infeasible. It was also determined that the practice of sharing needles was too ingrained in the drug culture to be stopped. As a result, using knowledge of consumer attitudes, Dr. Fishbein created a campaign that encouraged the cleaning of needles in bleach before sharing them, a goal that was believed to be more realistic.
- As a final benefit, studying consumer behaviour should make us better consumers. Common sense suggests, for example, that if you buy a 64 liquid ounce bottle of laundry detergent, you should pay less per ounce than if you bought two 32 ounce bottles. In practice, however, you often pay a size premium by buying the larger quantity. In other words, in this case, knowing this fact will sensitize you to the need to check the unit cost labels to determine if you are really getting a bargain.

There are several units in the market that can be analyzed. Our main thrust in this course is the consumer. However, we will also need to analyze our own firm's strengths and weaknesses and those of competing firms. Suppose, for example, that we make a product aimed at older consumers, a growing segment. A competing firm that targets babies, a shrinking market, is likely to consider repositioning toward our market. To assess a competing firm's potential threat, we need to examine its assets (e.g., technology, patents, market knowledge, awareness of its brands) against pressures it faces from the market. Finally, we need to assess conditions (the marketing environment). For example, although we may have developed a product that offers great appeal for consumers, a recession may cut demand dramatically.

METHODS IN CONSUMER RESEARCH

Market research is often needed to ensure that we produce what customers really want and not what we think they want.

Primary vs. secondary research methods. There are two main approaches to marketing. Secondary research involves using information that others have already put together. For example, if you are thinking about starting a business making clothes for tall people, you don't need to question people about how tall they are to find out how many tall people exist-that information has already been published. Primary research, in contrast, is research that you design and conduct yourself. For example, you may need to find out whether consumers would prefer that your soft drinks be sweater or tarter.

Research will often help us reduce risks associated with a new product, but it cannot take the risk away entirely. It is also important to ascertain whether the research has been complete. For example, Coca Cola did a great deal of research prior to releasing the New Coke, and consumers seemed to prefer the taste. However, consumers were not prepared to have this drink replace traditional Coke. Several tools are available to the market researcher-e.g., mail questionnaires, phone surveys, observation, and focus groups.

Surveys are useful for getting a great deal of specific information. Surveys can contain open-ended questions (e.g., "In which city and state were you born?") or closed-ended, where the respondent is asked to select answers from a brief list (e.g., "Male- Female." Open ended questions have the advantage that the respondent is not limited to the options listed, and that the respondent is not being influenced by seeing a list of responses. However, open-ended questions are often skipped by respondents, and coding them can be quite a challenge. In general, for surveys to yield meaningful responses, sample sizes of over 100 are usually required because precision is essential. For example, if a market share of twenty percent would result in a loss while thirty percent would be profitable, a confidence interval of 20-35% is too wide to be useful.

Surveys come in several different forms. Mail surveys are relatively inexpensive, but response rates are typically quite low-typically from 5-20%. Phone-surveys get somewhat higher response rates, but not many questions can be asked because many answer options have to be repeated and few people are willing to stay on the phone for more than five minutes. Mall intercepts are a convenient way to reach consumers, but respondents may be reluctant to discuss anything sensitive face-to-face with an interviewer.

Surveys, as any kind of research, are vulnerable to bias. The wording of a question can influence the outcome a great deal. For example, more people answered no to the question "Should speeches against democracy be allowed?" than answered yes to "Should speeches against democracy be forbidden?" For face-to-face interviews, interviewer bias is a danger, too. Interviewer bias occurs when the interviewer influences the way the respondent answers. For example, unconsciously an interviewer that works for the firm manufacturing the product in question may smile a little when something good is being said about the product and frown a little when something negative is being said. The respondent may catch on and say something more positive than his or her real opinion. Finally, a response bias may occur-if only part of the sample responds to a survey, the respondents' answers may not be representative of the population.

Focus groups are useful when the marketer wants to launch a new product or modify an existing one. A focus group usually involves having some 8-12 people come together in a room to discuss their consumption preferences and experiences. The group is usually led by a moderator, who will start out talking broadly about topics related broadly to the product without mentioning the product itself. For example, a focus group aimed at sugar-free cookies might first address consumers' snacking preferences, only gradually moving toward the specific product of sugar-free cookies.

By not mentioning the product up front, we avoid biasing the participants into thinking only in terms of the specific product brought out. Thus, instead of having consumers think primarily in terms of what might be good or bad about the product, we can ask them to discuss more broadly the ultimate benefits they really seek. For example, instead of having consumers merely discuss what they think about some sugar-free cookies that we are considering releasing to the market, we can have consumers speak about their motivations for using snacks and what general kinds of benefits they seek.

Such a discussion might reveal a concern about healthfulness and a desire for wholesome foods. Probing on the meaning of wholesomeness, consumers might indicate a desire to avoid artificial ingredients. This would be an important concern in the marketing of sugar-free cookies, but might not have come up if consumers were asked to comment directly on the product where the use of artificial ingredients is, by virtue of the nature of the product, necessary.

Focus groups are well suited for some purposes, but poorly suited for others. In general, focus groups are very good for getting breadth-i.e., finding out what kinds of issues are important for consumers in a given product category. Here, it is helpful that focus groups are completely "open-ended:" The consumer mentions his or her preferences and opinions, and the focus group moderator can ask the consumer to elaborate. In a questionnaire, if one did not think to ask about something, chances are that few consumers would take the time to write out an elaborate answer. Focus groups also have some drawbacks, for example:

- They represent small sample sizes. Because of the cost of running focus groups, only a few groups can be run. Suppose you run four focus groups with ten members each. This will result in an n of 4(10)=40, which is too small to generalize from. Therefore, focus groups cannot give us a good idea of:
- What proportion of the population is likely to buy the product.
- What price consumers are willing to pay.
- The groups are inherently social. This means that:
- Consumers will often say things that may make them look good (i.e., they watch public television rather than soap operas or cook fresh meals for their families daily) even if that is not true.
- Consumers may be reluctant to speak about embarrassing issues (e.g., weight control, birth control).

Personal interviews involve in-depth questioning of an individual about his or her interest in or experiences with a product. The benefit here is that we can get really into depth (when the respondent says something interesting, we can ask him or her to elaborate), but this method of research is costly and can be extremely vulnerable to interviewer bias.

To get a person to elaborate, it may help to try a common tool of psychologists and psychiatrists-simply repeating what the person said. He or she will often become uncomfortable with the silence that follows and will then tend to elaborate. This approach has the benefit that it minimizes the interference with the respondent's own ideas and thoughts. He or she is not influenced by a new question but will, instead, go more in depth on what he or she was saying.

Personal interviews are highly susceptible to inadvertent "signalling" to the respondent. Although an interviewer is looking to get at the truth, he or she may have a significant interest in a positive consumer response. Unconsciously, then, he or she may inadvertently smile a little when something positive is said and frown a little when something negative is said. Consciously, this will often not be noticeable, and the respondent often will not consciously be aware that he or she is being "reinforced" and "punished" for saying positive or negative things, but at an unconscious level, the cumulative effect of several facial expressions are likely to be felt. Although this type of conditioning will not get a completely negative respondent to say all positive things, it may "swing" the balance a bit so that respondents are more likely to say positive thoughts and withhold, or limit the duration of, negative thoughts.

Projective techniques are used when a consumer may feel embarrassed to admit to certain opinions, feelings, or preferences. For example, many older executives may not be comfortable admitting to being intimidated by computers. It has been found that in such cases, people will tend to respond more openly about "someone else." Thus, we may ask them to explain reasons why a friend has not yet bought a computer, or to tell a story about a person in a picture who is or is not using a product. The main problem with this method is that it is difficult to analyze responses.

Projective techniques are inherently inefficient to use. The elaborate context that has to be put into place takes time and energy away from the main question. There may also be real differences between the respondent and the third party. Saying or thinking about something that "hits too close to home" may also influence the respondent, who may or may not be able to see through the ruse.

Observation of consumers is often a powerful tool. Looking at how consumers select products may yield insights into how they make decisions and what they look for. For example, some American manufacturers were concerned about low sales of their products in Japan.

Observing Japanese consumers, it was found that many of these Japanese consumers scrutinized packages looking for a name of a major manufacturer-the product specific-brands that are common in the U.S. (e.g., Tide) were not impressive to the Japanese, who wanted a name of a major firm like Mitsubishi or Proctor & Gamble. Observation may help us determine how much time consumers spend comparing prices, or whether nutritional labels are being consulted.

A question arises as to whether this type of "spying" inappropriately invades the privacy of consumers. Although there may be cause for some concern in that the particular individuals have not consented to be part of this research, it should be noted that there is no particular interest in what the individual customer being watched does.

The question is what consumers-either as an entire group or as segments-do. Consumers benefit, for example, from stores that are designed effectively to promote efficient shopping. If it is found that women are more uncomfortable than men about others standing too close, the areas of the store heavily trafficked by women can be designed accordingly. What is being reported here, then, are averages and tendencies in response. The intent is not to find "juicy" observations specific to one customer.

The video clip with Paco Underhill that we saw in class demonstrated the application of observation research to the retail setting. By understanding the phenomena such as the tendency toward a right turn, the location of merchandise can be observed.

It is also possible to identify problem areas where customers may be overly vulnerable to the "but brush," or overly close encounter with others. This method can be used to identify problems that the customer experiences, such as difficulty finding a product, a mirror, a changing room, or a store employee for help.

Online research methods. The Internet now reaches the great majority of households in the U.S., and thus, online research provides new opportunity and has increased in use.

One potential benefit of online surveys is the use of "conditional branching." In conventional paper and pencil surveys, one question might ask if the respondent has shopped for a new car during the last eight months. If the respondent answers "no," he or she will be asked to skip ahead several questions-e.g., going straight to question 17 instead of proceeding to number 9.

If the respondent answered "yes," he or she would be instructed to go to the next question which, along with the next several ones, would address issues related to this shopping experience. Conditional branching allows the computer to skip directly to the appropriate question.

If a respondent is asked which brands he or she considered, it is also possible to customize brand comparison questions to those listed. Suppose, for example, that the respondent considered Ford, Toyota, and Hyundai, it would be possible to ask the subject questions about his or her view of the relative quality of each respective pair-in this case, Ford vs. Toyota, Ford vs. Hyundai, and Toyota vs. Hyundai.

There are certain drawbacks to online surveys. Some consumers may be more comfortable with online activities than others-and not all households will have access. Today, however, this type of response bias is probably not significantly greater than that associated with other types of research methods.

A more serious problem is that it has consistently been found in online research that it is very difficult-if not impossible-to get respondents to carefully read instructions and other information online-there is a tendency to move quickly. This makes it difficult to perform research that depends on the respondent's reading of a situation or product description.

Online search data and page visit logs provides valuable ground for analysis. It is possible to see how frequently various terms are used by those who use a firm's web site search feature or to see the route taken by most consumers to get to the page with the information they ultimately want.

If consumers use a certain term frequently that is not used by the firm in its product descriptions, the need to include this term in online content can be seen in search logs. If consumers take a long, "torturous" route to information frequently accessed, it may be appropriate to redesign the menu structure and/or insert hyperlinks in "intermediate" pages that are found in many users' routes.

Scanner data. Many consumers are members of supermarket "clubs." In return for signing p for a card and presenting this when making purchases, consumers are often eligible for considerable discounts on selected products.

Researchers use a more elaborate version of this type of program in some communities. Here, a number of consumers receive small payments and/or other incentives to sign up to be part of a research panel. They then receive a card that they are asked to present any time they go shopping. Nearly all retailers in the area usually cooperate. It is now possible to track what the consumer bought in all stores and to have a historical record.

The consumer's shopping record is usually combined with demographic information (e.g., income, educational level of adults in the household, occupations of adults, ages of children, and whether the family owns and rents) and the family's television watching habits. (Electronic equipment run by firms such as A. C. Nielsen will actually recognize the face of each family member when he or she sits down to watch).

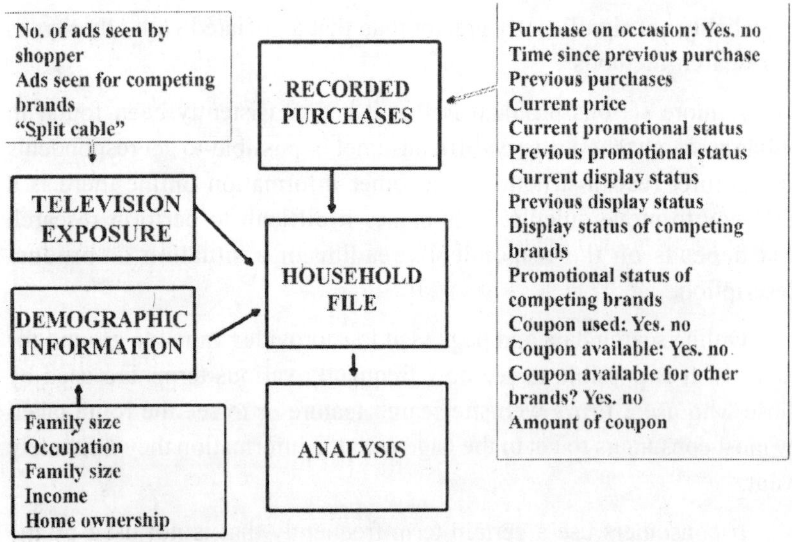

It is now possible to assess the relative impact of a number of factors on the consumer's choice-e.g.,

- What brand in a given product category was bought during the last, or a series of past, purchase occasions;
- Whether, and if so, how many times a consumer has seen an ad for the brand in question or a competing one;
- Whether the target brand (and/or a competing one) is on sale during the store visit;
- Whether any brand had preferential display space;
- The impact of income and/or family size on purchase patterns; and
- Whether a coupon was used for the purchase and, if so, its value.

A "split cable" technology allows the researchers to randomly select half the panel members in a given community to receive one advertising treatment and the other half another. The selection is truly random since each household, as opposed to neighbourhood, is selected to get one treatment or the other. Thus, observed differences should, allowing for sampling error, to be result of advertising exposure since there are no other systematic differences between groups.

Interestingly, it has been found that consumers tend to be more influenced by commercials that they "zap" through while channel surfing even if they only see part of the commercial. This most likely results from the reality that one must pay greater attention while channel surfing than when watching a commercial in order to determine which program is worth watching.

Scanner data is, at the present time, only available for certain grocery item product categories-e.g., food items, beverages, cleaning items, laundry detergent, paper towels, and toilet paper. It is not available for most non-grocery product items. Scanner data analysis is most useful for frequently purchased items (e.g., drinks, food items, snacks, and toilet paper) since a series of purchases in the same product category yield more information with greater precision than would a record of one purchase at one point in time. Even if scanner data were available for electronic products such as printers, computers, and MP3 players, for example, these products would be purchased quite infrequently.

A single purchase, then, would not be as effective in effectively distinguishing the effects of different factors-e.g., advertising, shelf space, pricing of the product and competitors, and availability of a coupon-since we have at most one purchase instance during a long period of time during which several of these factors would apply at the same time. In the case of items that are purchased frequently, the consumer has the opportunity to buy a product, buy a competing product, or buy nothing at all depending on the status of the brand of interest and competing brands.

In the case of the purchase of an MP3 player, in contrast, there may be promotions associated with several brands going on at the same time, and each may advertise. It may also be that the purchase was motivated by the breakdown of an existing product or dissatisfaction or a desire to add more capabilities.

Physiological measures are occasionally used to examine consumer response. For example, advertisers may want to measure a consumer's level of arousal during various parts of an advertisement. This can be used to assess possible discomfort on the negative side and level of attention on the positive side.

By attaching a tiny camera to plain eye glasses worn by the subject while watching an advertisement, it is possible to determine where on screen or other ad display the subject focuses at any one time. If the focus remains fixed throughout an ad sequence where the interesting and active part area changes, we can track whether the respondent is following the sequence intended. If he or she is not, he or she is likely either not to be paying as much attention as desired or to be confused by an overly complex sequence. In situations where the subject's eyes do move, we can assess whether this movement is going in the intended direction.

Mind-reading would clearly not be ethical and is, at the present time, not possible in any event. However, it is possible to measure brain waves by attaching electrodes. These readings will not reveal what the subject actually thinks, but it is possible to distinguish between beta waves-indicating active thought and analysis-and alpha waves, indicating lower levels of attention.

An important feature of physiological measures is that we can often track performance over time. A subject may, for example, be demonstrating good characteristics-such as appropriate level of arousal and eye movement-during some of the ad sequence and not during other parts. This, then, gives some guidance as to which parts of the ad are effective and which ones need to be reworked.

In a variation of direct physiological measures, a subject may be asked, at various points during an advertisement, to indicate his or her level of interest, liking, comfort, and approval by moving a lever or some instrument (much like one would adjust the volume on a radio or MP3 player). Republican strategist used this technique during the impeachment and trial of Bill Clinton in the late 1990s. By watching approval during various phases of a speech by the former President, it was found that viewers tended to respond negatively when he referred to "speaking truthfully" but favourably when the President referred to the issues in controversy as part of his "private life." The Republican researchers were able to separate average results from Democrats, Independents, and Republicans, effectively looking at different segments to make sure that differences between each did not cancel out effects of the different segments. (For example, if at one point Democrats reacted positively and Republicans responded negatively with the same intensity, the average result of apparent indifference would have been very misleading).

Research sequence. In general, if more than one type of research is to be used, the more flexible and less precise method-such as focus groups and/or individual interviews-should generally be used before the less flexible but more precise methods (e.g., surveys and scanner data) are used. Focus groups and interviews are flexible and allow the researcher to follow up on interesting issues raised by participants who can be probed. However, because the sample sizes are small and because participants in a focus group are influenced by each other, few data points are collected.

If we run five focus groups with eight people each, for example, we would have a total of forty responses. Even if we assume that these are independent, a sample size of forty would give very imprecise results. We might conclude, for example, that somewhere between 5% and 40% of the target market would be interested in the product we have to offer. This is usually no more precise than what we already reasonably new. Questionnaires, in contrast, are highly inflexible. It is not possible to ask follow-up questions.

Therefore, we can use our insights from focus groups and interviews to develop questionnaires that contain specific questions that can be asked to a larger number of people. There will still be some sampling error, but with a sample size of 1,000+ responses, we may be able to narrow the 95% confidence interval for the percentage of the target market that is seriously interested in our product to, say, 17-21%, a range that is much more meaningful.

Cautions. Some cautions should be heeded in marketing research. First, in general, research should only be commissioned when it is worth the cost. Thus, research should normally be useful in making specific decisions (what size should the product be? Should the product be launched? Should we charge $1.75 or $2.25?)

Secondly, marketing research can be, and often is, abused. Managers frequently have their own "agendas" (e.g., they either would like a product to be launched or would prefer that it not be launched so that the firm will have more resources left over to tackle their favourite products). Often, a way to get your way is to demonstrate through "objective" research that your opinions make economic sense. One example of misleading research, which was reported nationwide in the media, involved the case of "The Pentagon Declares War on Rush Limbaugh." The Pentagon, within a year of the election of Democrat Bill Clinton, reported that only 4.2% of soldiers listening to the Armed Forces Network wanted to hear Rush Limbaugh. However, although this finding was reported without question in the media, it was later found that the conclusion was based on the question "What single thing can we do to improve programming?" If you did not write in something like "Carry Rush Limbaugh," you were counted as not wanting to hear him.

CULTURE AND SUBCULTURE

Culture is part of the external influences that impact the consumer. That is, culture represents influences that are imposed on the consumer by other individuals.

The definition of culture offered in one textbook is "That complex whole which includes knowledge, belief, art, morals, custom, and any other capabilities and habits acquired by man person as a member of society." From this definition, we make the following observations:

- Culture, as a "complex whole," is a system of interdependent components.
- Knowledge and beliefs are important parts. In the U.S., we know and believe that a person who is skilled and works hard will get ahead. In other countries, it may be believed that differences in outcome result more from luck. "Chunking," the name for China in Chinese, literally means "The Middle Kingdom." The belief among ancient Chinese that they were in the centre of the universe greatly influenced their thinking.
- Other issues are relevant. Art, for example, may be reflected in the rather arbitrary practice of wearing ties in some countries and wearing turbans in others. Morality may be exhibited in the view in the United States that one should not be naked in public. In Japan, on the other hand, groups of men and women may take steam baths together without perceived as improper. On the other extreme, women in some Arab countries are not even allowed to reveal their faces. Notice, by the way, that what at least some countries view as moral may in fact be highly immoral by the standards of another country. For example, the law that once banned interracial marriages in South Africa was named the "Immorality Act," even though in most civilized countries this law, and any degree of explicit racial prejudice, would itself be considered highly immoral.

Culture has several important characteristics:

1. Culture is comprehensive. This means that all parts must fit together in some logical fashion. For example, bowing and a strong desire to avoid the loss of face are unified in their manifestation of the importance of respect.
2. Culture is learned rather than being something we are born with.
3. Culture is manifested within boundaries of acceptable behaviour. For example, in American society, one cannot show up to class naked, but wearing anything from a suit and tie to shorts and a T-shirt would usually be acceptable. Failure to behave within the prescribed norms may lead to sanctions, ranging

from being hauled off by the police for indecent exposure to being laughed at by others for wearing a suit at the beach.

4. Conscious awareness of cultural standards is limited. One American spy was intercepted by the Germans during World War II simply because of the way he held his knife and fork while eating.
5. Cultures fall somewhere on a continuum between static and dynamic depending on how quickly they accept change. For example, American culture has changed a great deal since the 1950s, while the culture of Saudi Arabia has changed much less.

Dealing with culture. Culture is a problematic issue for many marketers since it is inherently nebulous and often difficult to understand. One may violate the cultural norms of another country without being informed of this, and people from different cultures may feel uncomfortable in each other's presence without knowing exactly why (for example, two speakers may unconsciously continue to attempt to adjust to reach an incompatible preferred interpersonal distance).

Warning about stereotyping. When observing a culture, one must be careful not to over-generalize about traits that one sees. Research in social psychology has suggested a strong tendency for people to perceive an "outgroup" as more homogenous than an "ingroup," even when they knew what members had been assigned to each group purely by chance. When there is often a "grain of truth" to some of the perceived differences, the temptation to over-generalize is often strong. Note that there are often significant individual differences within cultures.

Cultural lessons. We considered several cultural lessons in class; the important thing here is the big picture. For example, within the Muslim tradition, the dog is considered a "dirty" animal, so portraying it as "man's best friend" in an advertisement is counter-productive. Packaging, seen as a reflection of the quality of the "real" product, is considerably more important in Asia than in the U.S., where there is a tendency to focus on the contents which "really count." Many cultures observe significantly greater levels of formality than that typical in the U.S., and Japanese negotiator tend to observe long silent pauses as a speaker's point is considered.

Cultural characteristics as a continuum. There is a tendency to stereotype cultures as being one way or another (e.g., individualistic rather than collectivistic). Note, however, countries fall on a continuum of cultural traits. Hofstede's research demonstrates a wide range between the most individualistic and collectivistic countries, for example-some fall in the middle.

Hofstede's Dimensions. Gert Hofstede, a Dutch researcher, was able to interview a large number of IBM executives in various countries, and found that cultural differences tended to centre around four key dimensions:

- Individualism vs. collectivism: To what extent do people believe in individual responsibility and reward rather than having these measures aimed at the larger group? Contrary to the stereotype, Japan actually ranks in the middle of this dimension, while Indonesia and West Africa rank toward the collectivistic side. The U.S., Britain, and the Netherlands rate toward individualism.
- Power distance: To what extent is there a strong separation of individuals based on rank? Power distance tends to be particularly high in Arab countries and some Latin American ones, while it is more modest in Northern Europe and the U.S.
- Masculinity vs. femininity involves a somewhat more nebulous concept. "Masculine" values involve competition and "conquering" nature by means such as large construction projects, while "feminine" values involve harmony and environmental protection. Japan is one of the more masculine countries, while the Netherlands rank relatively low. The U.S. is close to the middle, slightly toward the masculine side. (The fact that these values are thought of as "masculine" or "feminine" does not mean that they are consistently held by members of each respective gender-there are very large "within-group" differences. There is, however, often a large correlation of these cultural values with the status of women.)
- Uncertainty avoidance involves the extent to which a "structured" situation with clear rules is preferred to a more ambiguous one; in general, countries with lower uncertainty avoidance tend to be more tolerant of risk. Japan ranks very high. Few countries are very low in any absolute sense, but relatively speaking, Britain and Hong Kong are lower, and the U.S. is in the lower range of the distribution.

Although Hofstede's original work did not address this, a fifth dimension of long term vs. short term orientation has been proposed. In the U.S., managers like to see quick results, while Japanese managers are known for take a long term view, often accepting long periods before profitability is obtained.

High vs. low context cultures: In some cultures, "what you see is what you get"-the speaker is expected to make his or her points clear and limit ambiguity. This is the case in the U.S.-if you have something on your mind, you are expected to say it directly, subject to some reasonable standards of diplomacy. In Japan, in contrast, facial expressions and what is not said may be an important clue to understanding a speaker's meaning. Thus, it may be very difficult for Japanese speakers to understand another's written communication. The nature of languages may exacerbate this phenomenon-while the German language is very precise, Chinese lacks many grammatical features, and the meaning of words may be somewhat less precise. English ranks somewhere in the middle of this continuum.

Ethnocentrism and the self-reference criterion. The self-reference criterion refers to the tendency of individuals, often unconsciously, to use the standards of one's own culture to evaluate others. For example, Americans may perceive more traditional societies to be "backward" and "unmotivated" because they fail to adopt new technologies or social customs, seeking instead to preserve traditional values. In the 1960s, a supposedly well read American psychology professor referred to India's culture of "sick" because, despite severe food shortages, the Hindu religion did not allow the eating of cows. The psychologist expressed disgust that the cows were allowed to roam free in villages, although it turns out that they provided valuable functions by offering milk and fertilizing fields. Ethnocentrism is the tendency to view one's culture to be superior to others. The important thing here is to consider how these biases may come in the way in dealing with members of other cultures.

It should be noted that there is a tendency of outsiders to a culture to overstate the similarity of members of that culture to each other. In the United States, we are well aware that there is a great deal of heterogeneity within our culture; however, we often underestimate the diversity within other cultures. For example, in Latin America, there are great differences between people who live in coastal and mountainous areas; there are also great differences between social classes.

Language issues. Language is an important element of culture. It should be realized that regional differences may be subtle. For example, one word may mean one thing in one Latin American country, but something off-colour in another. It should also be kept in mind that much information is carried in non-verbal communication. In some cultures, we nod to signify "yes" and shake our heads to signify "no;" in other cultures, the practice is reversed. Within the context of language:

- There are often large variations in regional dialects of a given language. The differences between U.S., Australian, and British English are actually modest compared to differences between dialects of Spanish and German.
- Idioms involve "figures of speech" that may not be used, literally translated, in other languages. For example, baseball is a predominantly North and South American sport, so the notion of "in the ball park" makes sense here, but the term does not carry the same meaning in cultures where the sport is less popular.
- Neologisms involve terms that have come into language relatively recently as technology or society involved. With the proliferation of computer technology, for example, the idea of an "add-on" became widely known. It may take longer for such terms to "diffuse" into other regions of the world. In parts of the World where English is heavily studied in schools, the emphasis is often on grammar and traditional language rather than on current terminology, so neologisms have a wide potential not to be understood.
- Slang exists within most languages. Again, regional variations are common and not all people in a region where slang is used will necessarily understand this. There are often significant generation gaps in the use of slang.

Writing patterns, or the socially accepted ways of writing, will differs significantly between cultures.

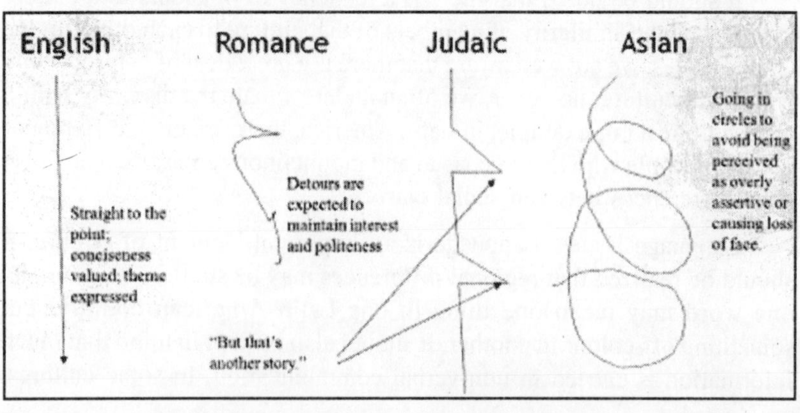

In English and Northern European languages, there is an emphasis on organization and conciseness. Here, a point is made by building up to it through background. An introduction will often foreshadow what is to be said. In Romance languages such as Spanish, French, and Portuguese, this style is often considered "boring" and "inelegant." Detours are expected and are considered a sign of class, not of poor organization. In Asian languages, there is often a great deal of circularity. Because of concerns about potential loss of face, opinions may not be expressed directly. Instead, speakers may hint at ideas or indicate what others have said, waiting for feedback from the other speaker before committing to a point of view.

Because of differences in values, assumptions, and language structure, it is not possible to meaningfully translate "word-for-word" from one language to another. A translator must keep "unspoken understandings" and assumptions in mind in translating. The intended meaning of a word may also differ from its literal translation. For example, the Japanese word hai is literally translated as "yes." To Americans, that would imply "Yes, I agree." To the Japanese speaker, however, the word may mean "Yes, I hear what you are saying" (without any agreement expressed) or even "Yes, I hear you are saying something even though I am not sure exactly what you are saying."

Differences in cultural values result in different preferred methods of speech. In American English, where the individual is assumed to be more in control of his or her destiny than is the case in many other cultures, there is a preference for the "active" tense (e.g., "I wrote the marketing plan") as opposed to the passive (e.g., "The marketing plan was written by me.")

Because of the potential for misunderstandings in translations, it is dangerous to rely on a translation from one language to another made by one person. In the "decentring" method, multiple translators are used.

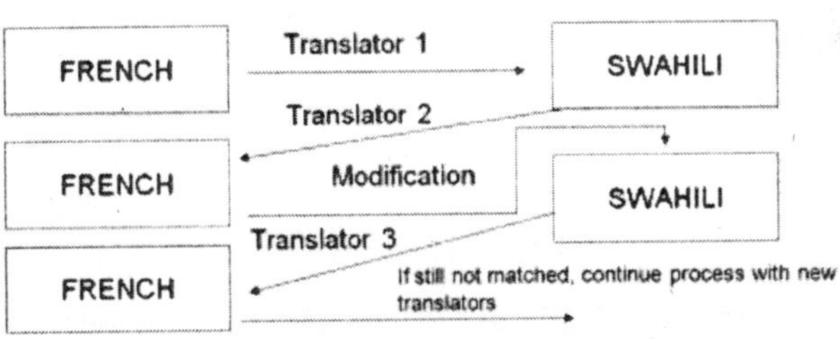

The text is first translated by one translator-say, from German to Mandarin Chinese. A second translator, who does not know what the original German text said, will then translate back to German from Mandarin Chinese translation. The text is then compared. If the meaning is not similar, a third translator, keeping in mind this feedback, will then translate from German to Mandarin. The process is continued until the translated meaning appears to be satisfactory.

Different perspectives exist in different cultures on several issues; e.g.:

- Monochronic cultures tend to value precise scheduling and doing one thing at a time; in polychronic cultures, in contrast, promptness is valued less, and multiple tasks may be performed simultaneously.
- Space is perceived differently. Americans will feel crowded where people from more densely populated countries will be comfortable.
- Symbols differ in meaning. For example, while white symbols purity in the U.S., it is a symbol of death in China. Colours that are considered masculine and feminine also differ by culture.
- Americans have a lot of quite shallow friends toward whom little obligation is felt; people in European and some Asian cultures have fewer, but more significant friends. For example, one Ph.D. student from India, with limited income, felt obligated to try buy an airline ticket for a friend to go back to India when a relative had died.
- In the U.S. and much of Europe, agreements are typically rather precise and contractual in nature; in Asia, there is a greater tendency to settle issues as they come up. As a result, building a relationship of trust is more important in Asia, since you must be able to count on your partner being reasonable.
- In terms of etiquette, some cultures have more rigid procedures than others. In some countries, for example, there are explicit standards as to how a gift should be presented. In some cultures, gifts should be presented in private to avoid embarrassing the recipient; in others, the gift should be made publicly to ensure that no perception of secret bribery could be made.

DEMOGRAPHICS

Demographics are clearly tied to subculture and segmentation. Here, however, we shift our focus from analyzing specific subcultures to trying to understand the implications for an entire population of its makeup.

Several issues are useful in the structure of a population. For example, in some rapidly growing countries, a large percentage of the population is concentrated among younger generations. In countries such as Korea, China, and Taiwan, this has helped stimulate economic growth, while in certain poorer countries, it puts pressures on society to accommodate an increasing number of people on a fixed amount of land. Other countries such as Japan and Germany, in contrast, experience problems with a "graying" society, where fewer non-retired people are around to support an increasing number of aging seniors. Because Germany actually hovers around negative population growth, the German government has issued large financial incentives, in the forms of subsidies, for women who have children. In the United States, population growth occurs both through births and immigration. Since the number of births is not growing, problems occur for firms that are dependent on population growth (e.g., Gerber, a manufacturer of baby food).

Social class is a somewhat nebulous subject that involves stratifying people into groups with various amounts of prestige, power, and privilege. In part because of the pioneering influence in American history, status differentiations here are quite vague. We cannot, for example, associate social class with income, because a traditionally low status job as a plumber may today come with as much income as a traditionally more prestigious job as a school teacher. In certain other cultures, however, stratification is more clear-cut. Although the caste system in India is now illegal, it still maintains a tremendous influence on that society. While some mobility exists today, social class awareness is also somewhat greater in Britain, where social status is in part reinforced by the class connotations of the accent with which one speaks.

Textbooks speak of several indices that have been used to "compute" social class in the United States, weighing factors such as income, the nature of one's employment, and level of education. Taken too literally, these indices are not very meaningful; more broadly speaking, they illustrate the reality that social status is a complex variable that is determined, not always with consensus among observers, by several different variables.

SEGMENTATION, TARGETING, AND POSITIONING

Segmentation, targeting, and positioning together comprise a three stage process. We first (1) determine which kinds of customers exist, then (2) select which ones we are best off trying to serve and, finally, (3) implement our segmentation by optimizing our products/services for that segment and communicating that we have made the choice to distinguish ourselves that way.

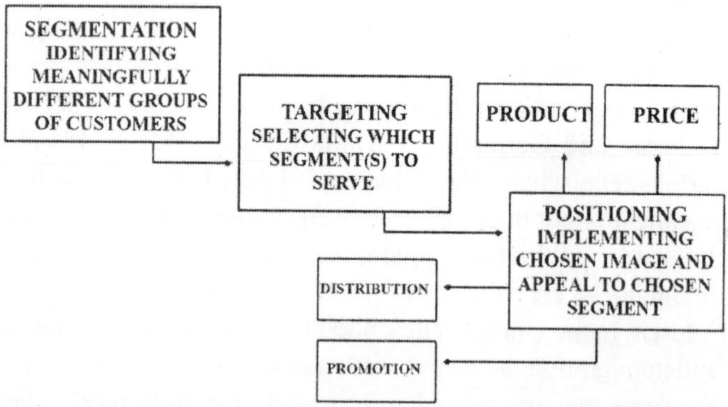

Segmentation involves finding out what kinds of consumers with different needs exist. In the auto market, for example, some consumers demand speed and performance, while others are much more concerned about roominess and safety. In general, it holds true that "You can't be all things to all people," and experience has demonstrated that firms that specialize in meeting the needs of one group of consumers over another tend to be more profitable.

Generically, there are three approaches to marketing. In the undifferentiated strategy, all consumers are treated as the same, with firms not making any specific efforts to satisfy particular groups. This may work when the product is a standard one where one competitor really can't offer much that another one can't. Usually, this is the case only for commodities. In the concentrated strategy, one firm chooses to focus on one of several segments that exist while leaving other segments to competitors. For example, Southwest Airlines focuses on price sensitive consumers who will forego meals and assigned seating for low prices. In contrast, most airlines follow the differentiated strategy: They offer high priced tickets to those who are inflexible in that they cannot tell in advance when they need to fly and find it impractical to stay over a Saturday. These travellers-usually business travellers-pay high fares but can only fill the planes up partially. The same airlines then sell some of the remaining seats to more price sensitive customers who can buy two weeks in advance and stay over.

Note that segmentation calls for some tough choices. There may be a large number of variables that can be used to differentiate consumers of a given product category; yet, in practice, it becomes impossibly cumbersome to work with more than a few at a time. Thus, we need to determine which variables will be most useful in distinguishing different groups of consumers. We might thus decide, for example, that the variables that are most relevant in separating different kinds of soft drink consumers are (1) preference for taste vs. low calories, (2) preference for Cola vs. non-cola taste, (3) price sensitivity-willingness to pay for brand names; and (4) heavy vs. light consumers. We now put these variables together to arrive at various combinations.

Several different kinds of variables can be used for segmentation.

- Demographic variables essentially refer to personal statistics such as income, gender, education, location (rural vs. urban, East vs. West), ethnicity, and family size. Campbell's soup, for instance, has found that Western U.S. consumers on the average prefer spicier soups-thus, you get a different product in the same cans at the East and West coasts. Facing flat sales of guns in the traditional male dominated market, a manufacturer came out with the Lady Remmington, a more compact, handier gun more attractive to women. Taking this a step farther, it is also possible to segment on lifestyle and values."
- Some consumers want to be seen as similar to others, while a different segment wants to stand apart from the crowd.
- Another basis for segmentation is behaviour. Some consumers are "brand loyal"-i.e., they tend to stick with their preferred brands even when a competing one is on sale. Some consumers are "heavy" users while others are "light" users. For example, research conducted by the wine industry shows that some 80% of the product is consumed by 20% of the consumers-presumably a rather intoxicated group.
- One can also segment on benefits sought, essentially bypassing demographic explanatory variables. Some consumers, for example, like scented soap (a segment likely to be attracted to brands such as Irish Spring), while others prefer the "clean" feeling of unscented soap (the "Ivory" segment). Some consumers use toothpaste primarily to promote oral health, while another segment is more interested in breath freshening.

In the next step, we decide to target one or more segments. Our choice should generally depend on several factors. First, how well are existing segments served by other manufacturers? It will be more difficult to appeal to a segment that is already well served than to one whose needs are not currently being served well. Secondly, how large is the segment, and how can we expect it to grow? (Note that a downside to a large, rapidly growing segment is that it tends to attract competition). Thirdly, do we have strengths as a company that will help us appeal particularly to one group of consumers?

Firms may already have an established reputation. While McDonald's has a great reputation for fast, consistent quality, family friendly food, it would be difficult to convince consumers that McDonald's now offers gourmet food. Thus, McD's would probably be better off targeting families in search of consistent quality food in nice, clean restaurants.

Positioning involves implementing our targeting. For example, Apple Computer has chosen to position itself as a maker of user-friendly computers. Thus, Apple has done a lot through its advertising to promote itself, through its unintimidating icons, as a computer for "non-geeks." The Visual C software programming language, in contrast, is aimed a "techies."

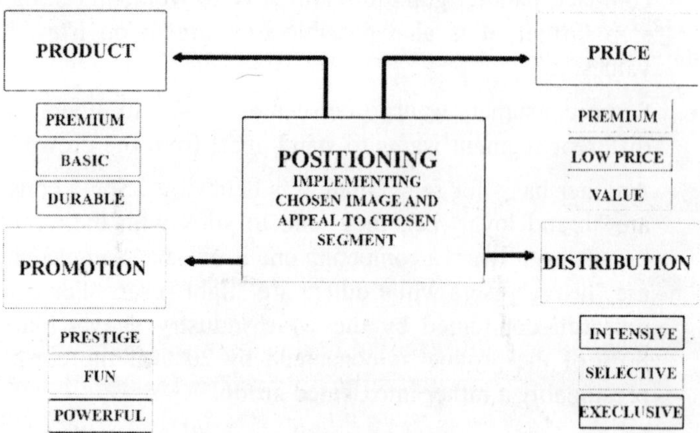

Michael Treacy and Fred Wiersema suggested in their 1993 book The Discipline of Market Leaders that most successful firms fall into one of three categories:

- Operationally excellent firms, which maintain a strong competitive advantage by maintaining exceptional efficiency, thus enabling the firm to provide reliable service to the customer at a significantly lower cost than those of less well organized and well run competitors. The emphasis here is mostly on low cost, subject to reliable performance, and less value is put on customizing the offering for the specific customer. Wal-Mart is an example of this discipline. Elaborate logistical designs allow goods to be moved at the lowest cost, with extensive systems predicting when specific quantities of supplies will be needed.

- Customer intimate firms, which excel in serving the specific needs of the individual customer well. There is less emphasis on efficiency, which is sacrificed for providing more precisely what is wanted by the customer. Reliability is also stressed. Nordstrom's and IBM are examples of this discipline.
- Technologically excellent firms, which produce the most advanced products currently available with the latest technology, constantly maintaining leadership in innovation. These firms, because they work with costly technology that need constant refinement, cannot be as efficient as the operationally excellent firms and often cannot adapt their products as well to the needs of the individual customer. Intel is an example of this discipline.

Treacy and Wiersema suggest that in addition to excelling on one of the three value dimensions, firms must meet acceptable levels on the other two. Wal-Mart, for example, does maintain some level of customer service. Nordstrom's and Intel both must meet some standards of cost effectiveness. The emphasis, beyond meeting the minimum required level in the two other dimensions, is on the dimension of strength.

Repositioning involves an attempt to change consumer perceptions of a brand, usually because the existing position that the brand holds has become less attractive. Sears, for example, attempted to reposition itself from a place that offered great sales but unattractive prices the rest of the time to a store that consistently offered "everyday low prices." Repositioning in practice is very difficult to accomplish. A great deal of money is often needed for advertising and other promotional efforts, and in many cases, the repositioning fails.

To effectively attempt repositioning, it is important to understand how one's brand and those of competitors are perceived. One approach to identifying consumer product perceptions is multidimensional scaling. Here, we identify how products are perceived on two or more "dimensions," allowing us to plot brands against each other. It may then be possible to attempt to "move" one's brand in a more desirable direction by selectively promoting certain points. There are two main approaches to multi-dimensional scaling. In the a priori approach, market researchers identify dimensions of interest and then ask consumers about their perceptions on each dimension for each brand.

This is useful when (1) the market researcher knows which dimensions are of interest and (2) the customer's perception on each dimension is relatively clear (as opposed to being "made up" on the spot to be able to give the researcher a desired answer). In the similarity rating approach, respondents are not asked about their perceptions of brands on any specific dimensions.

Instead, subjects are asked to rate the extent of similarity of different pairs of products (e.g., How similar, on a scale of 1-7, is Snicker's to Kitkat, and how similar is Toblerone to Three Musketeers?) Using a computer algorithms, the computer then identifies positions of each brand on a map of a given number of dimensions.

The computer does not reveal what each dimension means-that must be left to human interpretation based on what the variations in each dimension appears to reveal. This second method is more useful when no specific product dimensions have been identified as being of particular interest or when it is not clear what the variables of difference are for the product category.

INFORMATION SEARCH AND DECISION MAKING

Problem Recognition. One model of consumer decision making involves several steps. The first one is problem recognition-you realize that something is not as it should be. Perhaps, for example, your car is getting more difficult to start and is not accelerating well.

The second step is information search-what are some alternative ways of solving the problem? You might buy a new car, buy a used car, take your car in for repair, ride the bus, ride a taxi, or ride a skateboard to work. The third step involves evaluation of alternatives. A skateboard is inexpensive, but may be ill-suited for long distances and for rainy days.

Finally, we have the purchase stage, and sometimes a post-purchase stage (e.g., you return a product to the store because you did not find it satisfactory). In reality, people may go back and forth between the stages. For example, a person may resume alternative identification during while evaluating already known alternatives.

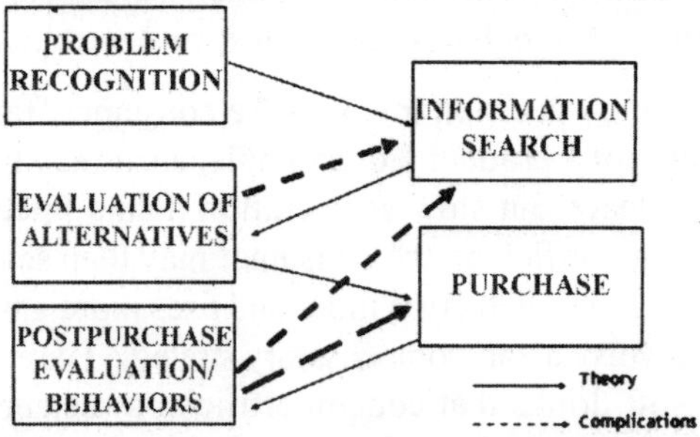

Consumer involvement will tend to vary dramatically depending on the type of product. In general, consumer involvement will be higher for products that are very expensive (e.g., a home, a car) or are highly significant in the consumer's life in some other way (e.g., a word processing program or acne medication).

It is important to consider the consumer's motivation for buying products. To achieve this goal, we can use the Means-End chain, wherein we consider a logical progression of consequences of product use that eventually lead to desired end benefit. Thus, for example, a consumer may see that a car has a large engine, leading to fast acceleration, leading to a feeling of performance, leading to a feeling of power, which ultimately improves the consumer's self-esteem. A handgun may aim bullets with precision, which enables the user to kill an intruder, which means that the intruder will not be able to harm the consumer's family, which achieves the desired end-state of security. In advertising, it is important to portray the desired end-states. Focusing on the large motor will do less good than portraying a successful person driving the car.

Information search and decision making. Consumers engage in both internal and external information search.

Internal search involves the consumer identifying alternatives from his or her memory. For certain low involvement products, it is very important that marketing programs achieve "top of mind" awareness. For example, few people will search the Yellow Pages for fast food restaurants; thus, the consumer must be able to retrieve one's restaurant from memory before it will be considered. For high involvement products, consumers are more likely to use an external search. Before buying a car, for example, the consumer may ask friends' opinions, read reviews in Consumer Reports, consult several web sites, and visit several dealerships. Thus, firms that make products that are selected predominantly through external search must invest in having information available to the consumer in need-e.g., through brochures, web sites, or news coverage.

A compensatory decision involves the consumer "trading off" good and bad attributes of a product. For example, a car may have a low price and good gas mileage but slow acceleration. If the price is sufficiently inexpensive and gas efficient, the consumer may then select it over a car with better acceleration that costs more and uses more gas. Occasionally, a decision will involve a non-compensatory strategy. For example, a parent may reject all soft drinks that contain artificial sweeteners. Here, other good features such as taste and low calories cannot overcome this one "non-negotiable" attribute.

The amount of effort a consumer puts into searching depends on a number of factors such as the market (how many competitors are there, and how great are differences between brands expected to be?), product characteristics (how important is this product? How complex is the product? How obvious are indications of quality?), consumer characteristics (how interested is a consumer, generally, in analyzing product characteristics and making the best possible deal?), and situational characteristics (as previously discussed).

Two interesting issues in decisions are:

- Variety seeking (where consumers seek to try new brands not because these brands are expected to be "better" in any way, but rather because the consumer wants a "change of pace," and
- "Impulse" purchases-unplanned buys. This represents a somewhat "fuzzy" group. For example, a shopper may plan to buy vegetables but only decide in the store to actually buy broccoli and corn. Alternatively, a person may buy an item which is currently on sale, or one that he or she remembers that is needed only once inside the store.

A number of factors involve consumer choices. In some cases, consumers will be more motivated. For example, one may be more careful choosing a gift for an in-law than when buying the same thing for one self. Some consumers are also more motivated to comparison shop for the best prices, while others are more convenience oriented. Personality impacts decisions. Some like variety more than others, and some are more receptive to stimulation and excitement in trying new stores. Perception influences decisions. Some people, for example, can taste the difference between generic and name brand foods while many cannot.

Selective perception occurs when a person is paying attention only to information of interest. For example, when looking for a new car, the consumer may pay more attention to car ads than when this is not in the horizon. Some consumers are put off by perceived risk.

Thus, many marketers offer a money back guarantee. Consumers will tend to change their behaviour through learning-e.g., they will avoid restaurants they have found to be crowded and will settle on brands that best meet their tastes. Consumers differ in the values they hold (e.g., some people are more committed to recycling than others who will not want to go through the hassle). We will consider the issue of lifestyle under segmentation.

FAMILIES AND FAMILY DECISION MAKING

The Family Life Cycle. Individuals and families tend to go through a "life cycle:" The simple life cycle goes from.

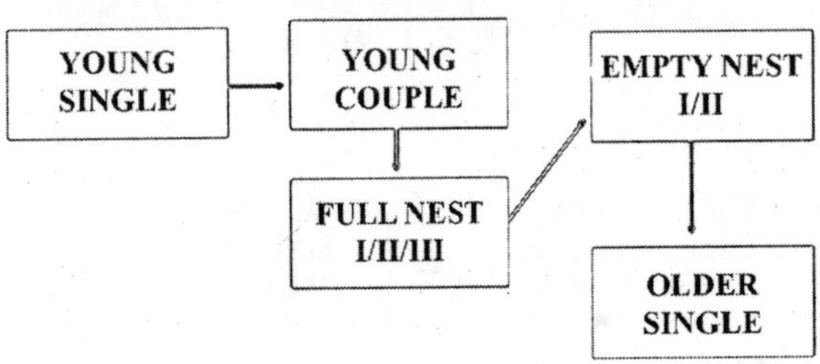

For purposes of this discussion, a "couple" may either be married or merely involve living together. The breakup of a non-marital relationship involving cohabitation is similarly considered equivalent to a divorce.

In real life, this situation is, of course, a bit more complicated. For example, many couples undergo divorce. Then we have one of the scenarios:

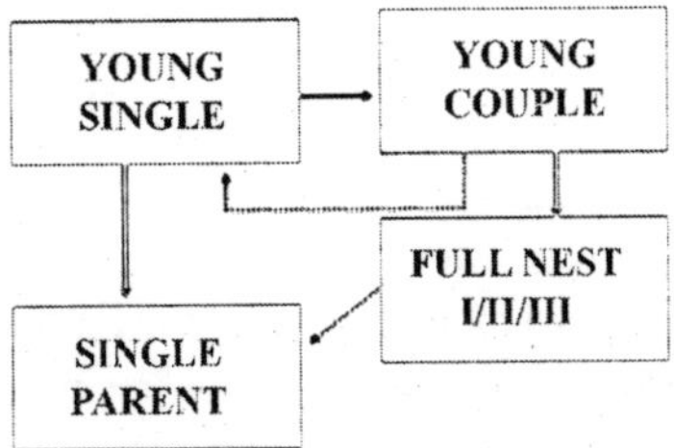

Single parenthood can result either from divorce or from the death of one parent. Divorce usually entails a significant change in the relative wealth of spouses. In some cases, the non-custodial parent (usually the father) will not pay the required child support, and even if he or she does, that still may not leave the custodial parent and children as well off as they were during the marriage. On the other hand, in some cases, some non-custodial parents will be called on to pay a large part of their income in child support. This is particularly a problem when the non-custodial parent remarries and has additional children in the second (or subsequent marriages). In any event, divorce often results in a large demand for:

- Low cost furniture and household items
- Time-saving goods and services

Divorced parents frequently remarry, or become involved in other non-marital relationships; thus, we may see

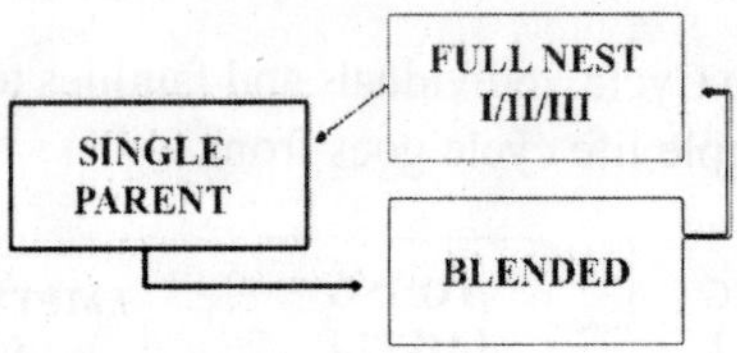

Another variation involves

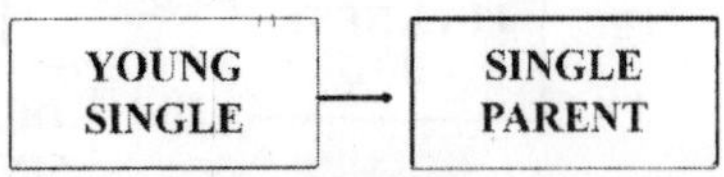

Here, the single parent who assumes responsibility for one or more children may not form a relationship with the other parent of the child.

Integrating all the possibilities discussed, we get the following depiction of the Family Life Cycle:

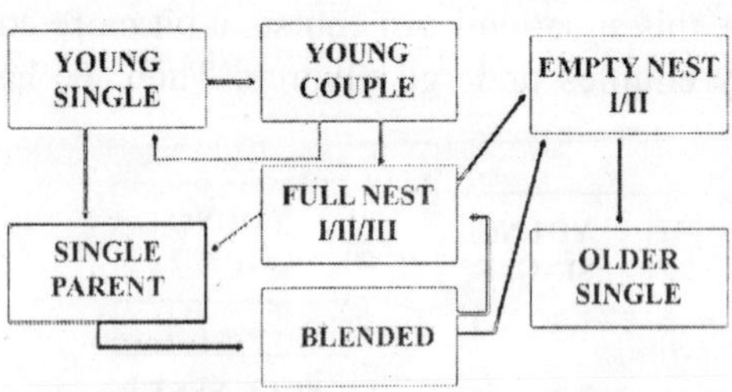

Generally, there are two main themes in the Family Life Cycle, subject to significant exceptions:

- As a person gets older, he or she tends to advance in his or her career and tends to get greater income (exceptions: maternity leave, divorce, retirement).

- Unfortunately, obligations also tend to increase with time (at least until one's mortgage has been paid off). Children and paying for one's house are two of the greatest expenses.

Note that although a single person may have a lower income than a married couple, the single may be able to buy more discretionary items.

Family Decision Making. Individual members of families often serve different roles in decisions that ultimately draw on shared family resources. Some individuals are information gatherers/holders, who seek out information about products of relevance. These individuals often have a great deal of power because they may selectively pass on information that favours their chosen alternatives. Influencers do not ultimately have the power decide between alternatives, but they may make their wishes known by asking for specific products or causing embarrassing situations if their demands are not met. The decision maker(s) have the power to determine issues such as:

- Whether to buy;
- Which product to buy (pick-up or passenger car?);
- Which brand to buy;
- Where to buy it; and
- When to buy.

Note, however, that the role of the decision maker is separate from that of the purchaser. From the point of view of the marketer, this introduces some problems since the purchaser can be targeted by point-of-purchase (POP) marketing efforts that cannot bc aimed at the decision maker. Also note that the distinction between the purchaser and decision maker may be somewhat blurred:

- The decision maker may specify what kind of product to buy, but not which brand;
- The purchaser may have to make a substitution if the desired brand is not in stock;
- The purchaser may disregard instructions (by error or deliberately).

It should be noted that family decisions are often subject to a great deal of conflict. The reality is that few families are wealthy enough to avoid a strong tension between demands on the family's resources. Conflicting pressures are especially likely in families with children and/or when only one spouse works outside the home. Note that many decisions inherently come down to values, and that there is frequently no "objective" way to arbitrate differences. One spouse may believe that it is important to save for the children's future; the other may value spending now (on private schools and computer equipment) to help prepare the children for the future. Who is right? There is no clear answer here. The situation becomes even more complex when more parties-such as children or other relatives-are involved.

Some family members may resort to various strategies to get their way. One is bargaining-one member will give up something in return for someone else. For example, the wife says that her husband can take an expensive course in gourmet cooking if she can buy a new pickup truck. Alternatively, a child may promise to walk it every day if he or she can have a hippopotamus. Another strategy is reasoning-trying to get the other person(s) to accept one's view through logical argumentation.

Note that even when this is done with a sincere intent, its potential is limited by legitimate differences in values illustrated above. Also note that individuals may simply try to "wear down" the other party by endless talking in the guise of reasoning. Various manipulative strategies may also be used.

One is impression management, where one tries to make one's side look good (e.g., argue that a new TV will help the children see educational TV when it is really mostly wanted to see sports programming, or argue that all "decent families make a contribution to the church"). Authority involves asserting one's "right" to make a decision (as the "man of the house," the mother of the children, or the one who makes the most money). Emotion involves making an emotional display to get one's way (e.g., a man cries if his wife will not let him buy a new rap album).

GROUP INFLUENCES

Humans are inherently social animals, and individuals greatly influence each other.

A useful framework of analysis of group influence on the individual is the so called reference group-the term comes about because an individual uses a relevant group as a standard of reference against which oneself is compared. Reference groups come in several different forms.

- The aspirational reference group refers to those others against whom one would like to compare oneself. For example, many firms use athletes as spokespeople, and these represent what many people would ideally like to be.

- Associative reference groups include people who more realistically represent the individuals' current equals or near-equals-e.g., coworkers, neighbours, or members of churches, clubs, and organizations. Paco Underhill, a former anthropologist turned retail consultant and author of the book Why We Buy has performed research suggesting that among many teenagers, the process of clothes buying is a two stage process.

  In the first stage, the teenagers go on a "reconnaissance" mission with their friends to find out what is available and what is "cool." This is often a lengthy process. In the later phase, parents-who will need to pay for the purchases-are brought. This stage is typically much briefer.

- Finally, the dissociative reference group includes people that the individual would not like to be like. For example, the store literally named The Gap came about because many younger people wanted to actively dissociate from parents and other older and "uncool" people. The Quality Paperback Book Club specifically suggests in its advertising that its members are "a breed apart" from conventional readers of popular books.

Reference groups come with various degrees of influence. Primary reference groups come with a great deal of influence-e.g., members of a fraternity/sorority. Secondary reference groups tend to have somewhat less influence-e.g., members of a boating club that one encounters only during week-ends are likely to have their influence limited to consumption during that time period.

Another typology divides reference groups into the informational kind (influence is based almost entirely on members' knowledge), normative (members influence what is perceived to be "right," "proper," "responsible," or "cool"), or identification. The difference between the latter two categories involves the individual's motivation for compliance.

In case of the normative reference group, the individual tends to comply largely for utilitarian reasons-dressing according to company standards is likely to help your career, but there is no real motivation to dress that way outside the job. In contrast, people comply with identification groups' standards for the sake of belonging-for example, a member of a religious group may wear a symbol even outside the house of worship because the religion is a part of the person's identity.

PERCEPTION

Background. Our perception is an approximation of reality. Our brain attempts to make sense out of the stimuli to which we are exposed. This works well, for example, when we "see" a friend three hundred feet away at his or her correct height; however, our perception is sometimes "off"-for example, certain shapes of ice cream containers look like they contain more than rectangular ones with the same volume.

Factors in perception. Several sequential factors influence our perception. Exposure involves the extent to which we encounter a stimulus. For example, we are exposed to numerous commercial messages while driving on the freeway: bill boards, radio advertisements, bumper-stickers on cars, and signs and banners placed at shopping malls that we pass. Most of this exposure is random-we don't plan to seek it out. However, if we are shopping for a car, we may deliberately seek out advertisements and "tune in" when dealer advertisements come on the radio.

Exposure is not enough to significantly impact the individual-at least not based on a single trial (certain advertisements, or commercial exposures such as the "Swoosh" logo, are based on extensive repetition rather than much conscious attention). In order for stimuli to be consciously processed, attention is needed. Attention is actually a matter of degree-our attention may be quite high when we read directions for getting an income tax refund, but low when commercials come on during a television program. Note, however, that even when attention is low, it may be instantly escalated-for example, if an advertisement for a product in which we are interested comes on.

Interpretation involves making sense out of the stimulus. For example, when we see a red can, we may categorize it as a Coke.

Weber's Law suggests that consumers' ability to detect changes in stimulus intensity appear to be strongly related to the intensity of that stimulus to begin with. That is, if you hold an object weighing one pound in your hand, you are likely to notice it when that weight is doubled to two pounds. However, if you are holding twenty pounds, you are unlikely to detect the addition of one pound-a change that you easily detected when the initial weight was one pound. You may be able to eliminate one ounce from a ten ounce container, but you cannot as easily get away with reducing a three ounce container to two (instead, you must accomplish that gradually-e.g., 3.0 --> 2.7 --> 2.5 --> 2.3 --> 2.15 -> 2.00).

Several factors influence the extent to which stimuli will be noticed. One obvious issue is relevance. Consumers, when they have a choice, are also more likely to attend to pleasant stimuli (but when the consumer can't escape, very unpleasant stimuli are also likely to get attention-thus, many very irritating advertisements are remarkably effective). One of the most important factors, however, is repetition. Consumers often do not give much attention to a stimuli-particularly a low priority one such as an advertisement-at any one time, but if it is seen over and over again, the cumulative impact will be greater.

Surprising stimuli are likely to get more attention-survival instinct requires us to give more attention to something unknown that may require action. A greater contrast (difference between the stimulus and its surroundings) as well as greater prominence (e.g., greater size, centre placement) also tend to increase likelihood of processing.

Subliminal stimuli. Back in the 1960s, it was reported that on selected evenings, movie goers in a theatre had been exposed to isolated frames with the words "Drink Coca Cola" and "Eat Popcorn" imbedded into the movie. These frames went by so fast that people did not consciously notice them, but it was reported that on nights with frames present, Coke and popcorn sales were significantly higher than on days they were left off. This led Congress to ban the use of subliminal advertising. First of all, there is a question as to whether this experiment ever took place or whether this information was simply made up. Secondly, no one has been able to replicate these findings. There is research to show that people will start to giggle with embarrassment when they are briefly exposed to "dirty" words in an experimental machine. Here, again, the exposure is so brief that the subjects are not aware of the actual words they saw, but it is evident that something has been recognized by the embarrassment displayed.

LEARNING AND MEMORY

Background. Learning involves "a change in the content or organization of long term memory and/or behaviour." The first part of the definition focuses on what we know (and can thus put to use) while the second focuses on concrete behaviour. For example, many people will avoid foods that they consumed shortly before becoming ill. Learning is not all knowledge based. For example, we may experience the sales people in one store being nicer to us than those in the other. We thus may develop a preference for the one store over the other; however, if pressed, we may not be able to give a conscious explanation as to the reason for our preference.

Much early work on learning was actually done on rats and other animals (and much of this research was unjustifiably cruel, but that is another matter).

Classical conditioning. Pavlov's early work on dogs was known as classical conditioning. Pavlov discovered that when dogs were fed meat powder they salivated. Pavlov then discovered that if a bell were rung before the dogs were fed, the dogs would begin salivating in anticipation of being fed (this was efficient, since they could then begin digesting the meat powder immediately). Pavlov then found that after the meat had been "paired" with the meat powder enough times, Pavlov could ring the bell without feeding the dogs and they would still salivate.

In the jargon of classical conditioning, the meat powder was an unconditioned stimulus (US) and the salivation was, when preceded by the meat powder, an unconditioned response (UR). That is, it is a biologically "hard-wired" response to salivate when you are fed. By pairing the bell with the unconditioned stimulus, the bell became a conditioned stimulus (CS) and salivation in response to the bell (with no meat powder) became a conditioned response (CR).

Many modern day advertisers use classical conditioning in some way. Consider this sequence:

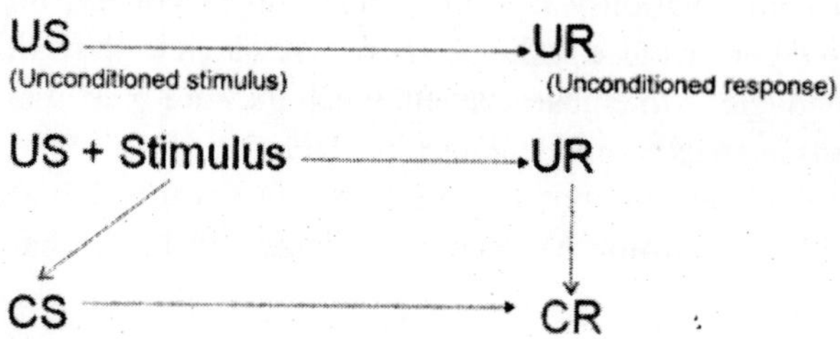

E.g.:

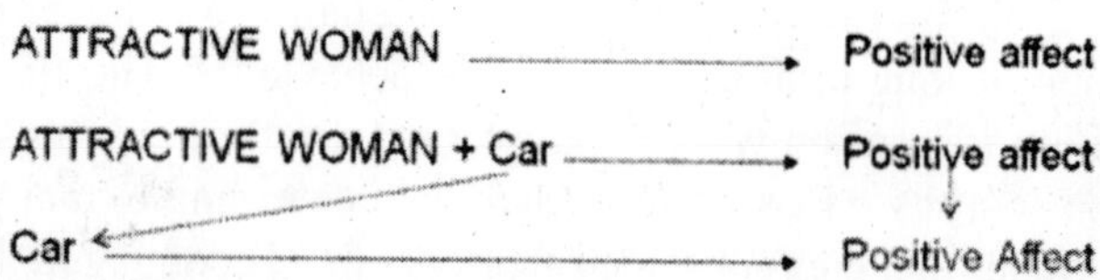

Operant conditioning. Instrumental, or operant, conditioning, involves a different series of events, and this what we usually think of as learning. The general pattern is:

There are three major forms of operant learning. In positive reinforcement, an individual does something and is rewarded. He or she is then more likely to repeat the behaviour. For example, you eat a candy bar (behaviour), it tastes good (consequence), and you are thus more likely to eat a similar candy bar in the future (behavioural change).

Punishment is the opposite. You eat what looks like a piece of candy (behaviour), only to discover that it is a piece of soap with a foul taste (consequences), and subsequently you are less likely to eat anything that looks remotely like that thing ever again (changed behaviour).

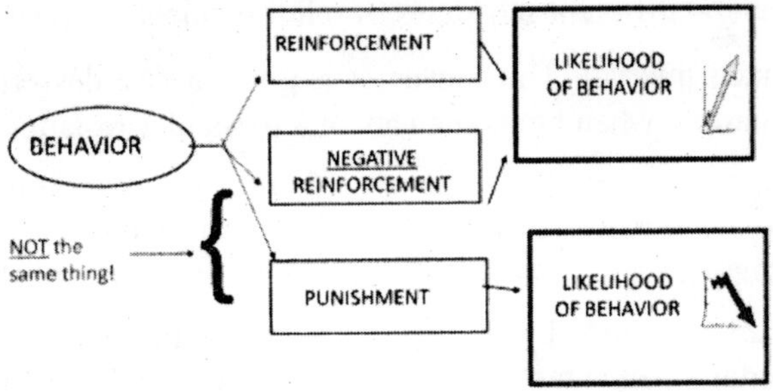

It should be noted that negative reinforcement is very different from punishment. An example of negative reinforcement is an obnoxious sales person who calls you up on the phone, pressuring you into buying something you don't want to do (aversive stimulus). You eventually agree to buy it (changed behaviour), and the sales person leaves you alone (the aversive stimulus is terminated as a result of consequences of your behaviour).

In general, marketers usually have relatively little power to use punishment or negative reinforcement. However, parking meters are often used to discourage consumers from taking up valuable parking space, and manufacturers may void warranties if the consumers take their product to non-authorized repair facilities.

Several factors influence the effectiveness of operant learning. In general, the closer in time the consequences are to the behaviour, the more effective the learning. That is, electric utilities would be more likely to influence consumers to use less electricity at peak hours if the consumers actually had to pay when they used electricity (e.g., through a coin-slot) rather than at the end of the month. Learning is also more likely to occur when the individual can understand a relationship between behaviour and consequences (but learning may occur even if this relationship is not understood consciously).

Another issue is schedules of reinforcement and extinction. Extinction occurs when behaviour stops having consequences and the behaviour then eventually stops occurring. For example, if a passenger learns that yelling at check-in personnel no longer gets her upgraded to first class, she will probably stop that behaviour. Sometimes, an individual is rewarded every time a behaviour is performed (e.g., a consumer gets a soft drink every time coins are put into a vending machine). However, it is not necessary to reward a behaviour every time for learning to occur. Even if a behaviour is only rewarded some of the time, the behaviour may be learned. Several different schedules of reinforcement are possible:

- Fixed interval: The consumer is given a free dessert on every Tuesday when he or she eats in a particular restaurant.
- Fixed ratio: Behaviour is rewarded (or punished) on every nth occasion that it is performed. (E.g., every tenth time a frequent shopper card is presented, a free product is provided).
- Variable ratio: Every time an action is performed, there is a certain percentage chance that a reward will be given. For example, every time the consumer enters the store, he or she is given a lottery ticket. With each ticket, there is a 20% chance of getting a free hamburger. The consumer may get a free hamburger twice in a row, or he or she may go ten times without getting a hamburger even once.

Variable ratio reinforcement is least vulnerable to extinction.

Sometimes, shaping may be necessary to teach the consumer the desired behaviour. That is, it may be impossible to teach the consumer to directly perform the desired behaviour. For example, a consumer may first get a good product for free (the product itself, if good, is a reward), then buy it with a large cents off coupon, and finally buy it at full price. Thus, we reinforce approximations of the desired behaviour. Rather than introducing Coca Cola directly in Indonesia, fruit flavored soft drinks were first introduced, since these were more similar to beverages already consumed.

Vicarious learning. The consumer does not always need to go through the learning process himself or herself-sometimes it is possible to learn from observing the consequences of others. For example, stores may make a big deal out of prosecuting shop lifters not so much because they want to stop that behaviour in the those caught, but rather to deter the behaviour in others. Similarly, viewers may empathize with characters in advertisements who experience (usually positive) results from using a product. The Head 'n' Shoulders advertisement, where a poor man is rejected by women until he treats his dandruff with an effective cure, is a good example of vicarious learning.

Memory ranges in duration on a continuum from extremely short to very long term. Sensory memory includes storage of stimuli that one might not actually notice (e.g., the colour of an advertisement some distance away). For slightly longer duration, when you see an ad on TV for a mail order product you might like to buy, you only keep the phone number in memory until you have dialled it. This is known as short term memory. In order for something to enter into long term memory, which is more permanent, you must usually "rehearse" it several times. For example, when you move and get a new phone number, you will probably repeat it to yourself many times. Alternatively, you get to learn your driver's license or social security numbers with time, not because you deliberately memorize them, but instead because you encounter them numerous times as you look them up.

Several techniques can be used to enhance the memorability of information. "Chunking" involves rearranging information so that fewer parts need to be remembered. For example, consider the phone number (011) 24441000. The eight digits can be more economically remembered as an 800 number (1 piece), four repeated 3 times (2 pieces), and 1000 (1-2 pieces). "Rehearsal" involves the consumer repeating the information over and over so that it can be remembered; this is often done so that a phone number can be remembered while the "memoree" moves to the phone to dial it. "Recirculation" involves repeated exposure to the same information; the information is not learned deliberately, but is gradually absorbed through repetition. Thus, it is to the advantage to a marketer to have an advertisement repeated extensively-especially the brand name. "Elaboration" involves the consumer thinking about the object-e.g., the product in an advertisement-and thinking about as many related issues as possible. For example, when seeing an ad for Dole bananas, the person may think of the colour yellow, going to the zoo seeing a monkey eating a banana, and her grandmother's banana-but bread. The Dole brand name may then be activated when any of those stimuli are encountered.

Memories are not always easily retrievable. This could be because the information was given lower priority than something else-e.g., we have done a lot of things since last buying a replacement furnace filter and cannot remember where this was bought last. Other times, the information can be retrieved but is not readily "available"-e.g., we will be able to remember the location of a restaurant we tried last time we were in Paris, but it may take some thinking before the information emerges.

"Spreading activation" involves the idea of one memory "triggering" another one. For example, one might think of Coke every time one remembers a favourite (and very wise) professor who frequently brought one to class. Coke might also be tied a particular supermarket that always stacked a lot of these beverages by the entrance, and to baseball where this beverage was consumed after the game. It is useful for firms to have their product be activated by as many other stimuli as possible.

There are numerous reasons why retrieval can fail or, in less fancy terms, how we come to forget. One is decay. Here, information that is not accessed frequently essentially "rusts" away. For example, we may not remember the phone number of a friend to whom we have not spoken for several months and may forget what brand of bullets an aunt prefers if we have not gone ammunition shopping with her lately. Other times, the problem may rest in interference. Proactive interference involves something we have learned interfering with what we will late later. Thus, if we remember that everyone in our family always used Tide, we may have more difficulty later remembering what other brands are available. You may be unable to remember what a new, and less important, friend's last name is if that person shares a first name with an old friend. For example, if your best friend for many years has been Jennifer Smith, you may have difficulty remembering that your new friend Jennifer's last name is Silverman. In retroactive interference, the problem is the reverse-learning something new blocks out something old. For example, if you once used WordPerfect than then switched to Microsoft Word, you may have trouble remembering how to use WordPerfect at a friend's house-more so than if you had merely not used any word processing program for some time.

Memorability can be enhanced under certain conditions. One is more likely to remember favourable-or likable stimuli (all other things being equal). Salience-or the extent to which something is highly emphasized or very clearly evident-facilitates memory. Thus, a product which is very visible in an ad, and handled and given attention by the actors, will more likely be remembered. Prototypicality involves the extent to which a stimulus is a "perfect" example of a category. Therefore, people will more likely remember Coke or Kleenex than competing brands. Congruence involves the "fit" with a situation. Since memory is often reconstructed based on what seems plausible, something featured in an appropriate setting-e.g., charcoal on a porch next to a grill rather than in a garage or kitchen-is more likely to be remembered (unless the incongruence triggers an elaboration-life is complicated!) Redundancies involve showing the stimulus several times. Thus, if a given product is shown several places in a house-and if the brand name is repeated-it is more likely to be remembered.

Priming involves tying a stimulus with something so that if "that something" is encountered, the stimulus is more likely to be retrieved. Thus, for example, when one thinks of anniversaries, the Hallmark brand name is more likely to be activated. (This is a special case of spreading activation discussed earlier).

A special issue in memory are so called "scripts," or procedures we remember for doing things. Scripts involve a series of steps for doing various things (e.g., how to send a package). In general, it is useful for firms to have their brand names incorporated into scripts (e.g., to have the consumer reflexively ask the pharmacist for Bayer rather than an unspecified brand of aspirin).

Positioning involves implementing our targeting. For example, Apple Computer has chosen to position itself as a maker of user-friendly computers. Thus, Apple has done a lot through its advertising to promote itself, through its unintimidating icons, as a computer for "non-geeks." The Visual C software programming language, in contrast, is aimed a "techies."

Repositioning involves an attempt to change consumer perceptions of a brand, usually because the existing position that the brand holds has become less attractive. Sears, for example, attempted to reposition itself from a place that offered great sales but unattractive prices the rest of the time to a store that consistently offered "everyday low prices." Repositioning in practice is very difficult to accomplish. A great deal of money is often needed for advertising and other promotional efforts, and in many cases, the repositioning fails.

DIFFUSION OF INNOVATION

Products tend to go through a life cycle. Initially, a product is introduced. Since the product is not well known and is usually expensive (e.g., as microwave ovens were in the late 1970s), sales are usually limited. Eventually, however, many products reach a growth phase-sales increase dramatically. More firms enter with their models of the product. Frequently, unfortunately, the product will reach a maturity stage where little growth will be seen.

For example, in the United States, almost every household has at least one colour TV set. Some products may also reach a decline stage, usually because the product category is being replaced by something better. For example, typewriters experienced declining sales as more consumers switched to computers or other word processing equipment. The product life cycle is tied to the phenomenon of diffusion of innovation. When a new product comes out, it is likely to first be adopted by consumers who are more innovative than others-they are willing to pay a premium price for the new product and take a risk on unproven technology. It is important to be on the good side of innovators since many other later adopters will tend to rely for advice on the innovators who are thought to be more knowledgeable about new products for advice.

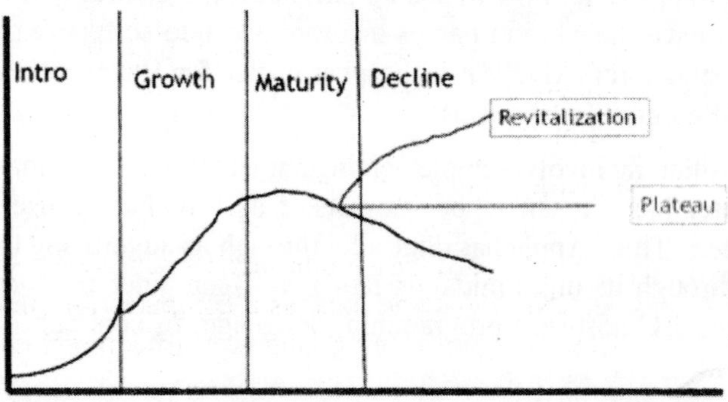

At later phases of the PLC, the firm may need to modify its market strategy. For example, facing a saturated market for baking soda in its traditional use, Arm ü Hammer launched a major campaign to get consumers to use the product to deodorize refrigerators. Deodorizing powders to be used before vacuuming were also created.

It is sometimes useful to think of products as being either new or existing.

Many firms today rely increasingly on new products for a large part of their sales. New products can be new in several ways. They can be new to the market-no one else ever made a product like this before. For example, Chrysler invented the minivan. Products can also be new to the firm-another firm invented the product, but the firm is now making its own version. For example, IBM did not invent the personal computer, but entered after other firms showed the market to have a high potential. Products can be new to the segment-e.g., cellular phones and pagers were first aimed at physicians and other price-insensitive segments. Later, firms decided to target the more price-sensitive mass market. A product can be new for legal purposes. Because consumers tend to be attracted to "new and improved" products, the Federal Trade Commission (FTC) only allows firms to put that label on reformulated products for six months after a significant change has been made.

The diffusion of innovation refers to the tendency of new products, practices, or ideas to spread among people. Usually, when new products or ideas come about, they are only adopted by a small group of people initially; later, many innovations spread to other people.

The bell shaped curve frequently illustrates the rate of adoption of a new product. Cumulative adoptions are reflected by the S-shaped curve. The saturation point is the maximum proportion of consumers likely to adopt a product.

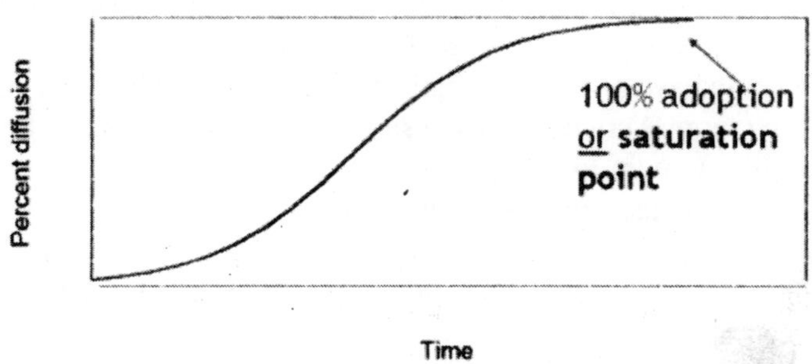

In the case of refrigerators in the U.S., the saturation level is nearly one hundred percent of households; it well below that for video games that, even when spread out to a large part of the population, will be of interest to far from everyone.

Several specific product categories have case histories that illustrate important issues in adoption. Until some time in the 1800s, few physicians bothered to scrub prior to surgery, even though new scientific theories predicted that small microbes not visible to the naked eye could cause infection. Younger and more progressive physicians began scrubbing early on, but they lacked the stature to make their older colleagues follow.

ATM cards spread relatively quickly. Since the cards were used in public, others who did not yet hold the cards could see how convenient they were. Although some people were concerned about security, the convenience factors seemed to be a decisive factor in the "tug-of-war" for and against adoption.

The case of credit cards was a bit more complicated and involved a "chicken-and-egg" paradox. Accepting credit cards was not a particularly attractive option for retailers until they were carried by a large enough number of consumers. Consumers, in contrast, were not particularly interested in cards that were not accepted by a large number of retailers. Thus, it was necessary to "jump start" the process, signing up large corporate accounts, under favourable terms, early in the cycle, after which the cards became worthwhile for retailers to accept.

Rap music initially spread quickly among urban youths in large part because of the low costs of recording. Later, rap music became popular among a very different segment, suburban youths, because of its apparently authentic depiction of an exotic urban lifestyle.

Hybrid corn was adopted only slowly among many farmers. Although hybrid corn provided yields of about 20% more than traditional corn, many farmers had difficulty believing that this smaller seed could provide a superior harvest. They were usually reluctant to try it because a failed harvest could have serious economic consequences, including a possible loss of the farm. Agricultural extension agents then sought out the most progressive farmers to try hybrid corn, also aiming for farmers who were most respected and most likely to be imitated by others. Few farmers switched to hybrid corn outright from year to year. Instead, many started out with a fraction of their land, and gradually switched to 100% hybrid corn when this innovation had proven itself useful.

Several forces often work against innovation. One is risk, which can be either social or financial. For example, early buyers of the CD player risked that few CDs would be recorded before the CD player went the way of the 8 track player. Another risk is being perceived by others as being weird for trying a "fringe" product or idea. For example, Barbara Mandrell sings the song "I Was Country When Country Wasn't Cool." Other sources of resistance include the initial effort needed to learn to use new products (e.g., it takes time to learn to meditate or to learn how to use a computer) and concerns about compatibility with the existing culture or technology. For example, birth control is incompatible with strong religious influences in countries heavily influenced by Islam or Catholicism, and a computer database is incompatible with a large, established card file.

Innovations come in different degrees. A continuous innovation includes slight improvements over time. Very little usually changes from year to year in automobiles, and even automobiles of the 1990s are driven much the same way that automobiles of the 1950 were driven. A dynamically continuous innovation involves some change in technology, although the product is used much the same way that its predecessors were used-e.g., jet vs. propeller aircraft. A discontinuous innovation involves a product that fundamentally changes the way that things are done-e.g., the fax and photocopiers. In general, discontinuous innovations are more difficult to market since greater changes are required in the way things are done, but the rewards are also often significant.

Several factors influence the speed with which an innovation spreads. One issue is relative advantage (i.e., the ratio of risk or cost to benefits). Some products, such as cellular phones, fax machines, and ATM cards, have a strong relative advantage. Other products, such as automobile satellite navigation systems, entail some advantages, but the cost ratio is high. Lower priced products often spread more quickly, and the extent to which the product is trialable (farmers did not have to plant all their land with hybrid corn at once, while one usually has to buy a cellular phone to try it out) influence the speed of diffusion. Finally, the extent of switching difficulties influences speed-many offices were slow to adopt computers because users had to learn how to use them.

Some cultures tend to adopt new products more quickly than others, based on several factors:

- Modernity: The extent to which the culture is receptive to new things. In some countries, such as Britain and Saudi Arabia, tradition is greatly valued-thus, new products often don't fare too well. The United States, in contrast, tends to value progress.
- Homophily: The more similar to each other that members of a culture are, the more likely an innovation is to spread-people are more likely to imitate similar than different models. The two most rapidly adopting countries in the World are the U.S. and Japan. While the U.S. interestingly scores very low, Japan scores high.
- Physical distance: The greater the distance between people, the less likely innovation is to spread.
- Opinion leadership: The more opinion leaders are valued and respected, the more likely an innovation is to spread. The style of opinion leaders moderates this influence, however. In less

innovative countries, opinion leaders tend to be more conservative, i.e., to reflect the local norms of resistance.

It should be noted that innovation is not always an unqualifiedly good thing. Some innovations, such as infant formula adopted in developing countries, may do more harm than good. Individuals may also become dependent on the innovations. For example, travel agents who get used to booking online may be unable to process manual reservations.

Sometimes innovations are disadopted. For example, many individuals disadopt cellular phones if they find out that they don't end up using them much.

ATTITUDES

Introduction. Consumer attitudes are a composite of a consumer's (1) beliefs about, (2) feelings about, (3) and behavioural intentions toward some object--within the context of marketing, usually a brand or retail store. These components are viewed together since they are highly interdependent and together represent forces that influence how the consumer will react to the object.

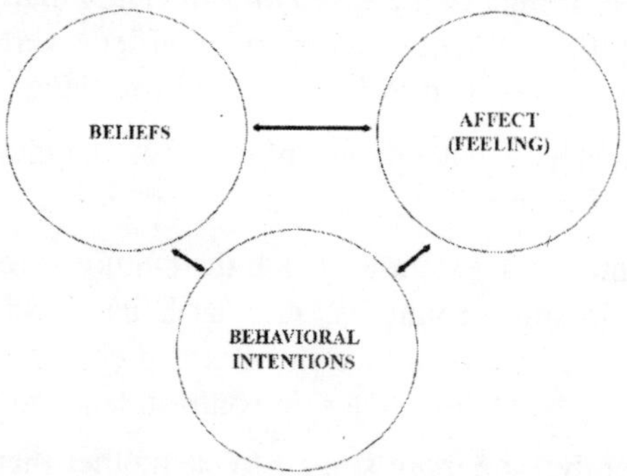

Beliefs. The first component is beliefs. A consumer may hold both positive beliefs toward an object (e.g., coffee tastes good) as well as negative beliefs (e.g., coffee is easily spilled and stains papers). In addition, some beliefs may be neutral (coffee is black), and some may be differ in valance depending on the person or the situation (e.g., coffee is hot and stimulates--good on a cold morning, but not good on a hot summer evening when one wants to sleep). Note also that the beliefs that consumers hold need not be accurate (e.g., that pork contains little fat), and some beliefs may, upon closer examination, be contradictory (e.g., that a historical figure was a good person but also owned slaves).

Since a consumer holds many beliefs, it may often be difficult to get down to a "bottom line" overall belief about whether an object such as McDonald's is overall good or bad. The Multiattribute (also sometimes known as the Fishbein) Model attempts to summarize overall attitudes into one score using the equation:

$$A_b = \sum_{i=1}^{n} W_i X_{ib}$$

That is, for each belief, we take the weight or importance (Wi) of that belief and multiply it with its evaluation (Xib). For example, a consumer believes that the taste of a beverage is moderately important, or a 4 on a scale from 1 to 7. He or she believes that coffee tastes very good, or a 6 on a scale from 1 to 7. Thus, the product here is 4(6)=24. On the other hand, he or she believes that the potential of a drink to stain is extremely important (7), and coffee fares moderately badly, at a score -4, on this attribute (since this is a negative belief, we now take negative numbers from -1 to -7, with -7 being worst). Thus, we now have 7(-4)=-28. Had these two beliefs been the only beliefs the consumer held, his or her total, or aggregated, attitude would have been 24+(-28)=-4. In practice, of course, consumers tend to have many more beliefs that must each be added to obtain an accurate measurement.

Affect. Consumers also hold certain feelings toward brands or other objects. Sometimes these feelings are based on the beliefs (e.g., a person feels nauseated when thinking about a hamburger because of the tremendous amount of fat it contains), but there may also be feelings which are relatively independent of beliefs. For example, an extreme environmentalist may believe that cutting down trees is morally wrong, but may have positive affect toward Christmas trees because he or she unconsciously associates these trees with the experience that he or she had at Christmas as a child.

Behavioural Intention. The behavioural intention is what the consumer plans to do with respect to the object (e.g., buy or not buy the brand). As with affect, this is sometimes a logical consequence of beliefs (or affect), but may sometimes reflect other circumstances--e.g., although a consumer does not really like a restaurant, he or she will go there because it is a hangout for his or her friends.

Attitude-Behaviour Consistency. Consumers often do not behave consistently with their attitudes for several reasons:

- Ability. He or she may be unable to do so. Although junior high school student likes pick-up trucks and would like to buy one, she may lack a driver's license.

- Competing demands for resources. Although the above student would like to buy a pickup truck on her sixteenth birthday, she would rather have a computer, and has money for only one of the two.
- Social influence. A student thinks that smoking is really cool, but since his friends think it's disgusting, he does not smoke.
- Measurement problems. Measuring attitudes is difficult. In many situations, consumers do not consciously set out to enumerate how positively or negatively they feel about mopeds, and when a market researcher asks them about their beliefs about mopeds, how important these beliefs are, and their evaluation of the performance of mopeds with respect to these beliefs, consumers often do not give very reliable answers. Thus, the consumers may act consistently with their true attitudes, which were never uncovered because an erroneous measurement was made.

Attitude Change Strategies. Changing attitudes is generally very difficult, particularly when consumers suspect that the marketer has a self-serving agenda in bringing about this change (e.g., to get the consumer to buy more or to switch brands).

Changing affect. One approach is to try to change affect, which may or may not involve getting consumers to change their beliefs. One strategy uses the approach of classical conditioning try to "pair" the product with a liked stimulus. For example, we "pair" a car with a beautiful woman. Alternatively, we can try to get people to like the advertisement and hope that this liking will "spill over" into the purchase of a product. For example, the Pillsbury Doughboy does not really emphasize the conveyance of much information to the consumer; instead, it attempts to create a warm, fuzzy image. Although Energizer Bunny ads try to get people to believe that their batteries last longer, the main emphasis is on the likeable bunny. Finally, products which are better known, through the mere exposure effect, tend to be better liked--that is, the more a product is advertised and seen in stores, the more it will generally be liked, even if consumers to do not develop any specific beliefs about the product.

Changing behaviour. People like to believe that their behaviour is rational; thus, once they use our products, chances are that they will continue unless someone is able to get them to switch. One way to get people to switch to our brand is to use temporary price discounts and coupons; however, when consumers buy a product on deal, they may justify the purchase based on that deal (i.e., the low price) and may then switch to other brands on deal later. A better way to get people to switch to our brand is to at least temporarily obtain better shelf space so that the product is more convenient. Consumers are less likely to use this availability as a rationale for their purchase and may continue to buy the product even when the product is less conveniently located. (Notice, by the way, that this represents a case of shaping).

Changing beliefs. Although attempting to change beliefs is the obvious way to attempt attitude change, particularly when consumers hold unfavourable or inaccurate ones, this is often difficult to achieve because consumers tend to resist. Several approaches to belief change exist:

1. Change currently held beliefs. It is generally very difficult to attempt to change beliefs that people hold, particularly those that are strongly held, even if they are inaccurate. For example, the petroleum industry advertised for a long time that its profits were lower than were commonly believed, and provided extensive factual evidence in its advertising to support this reality. Consumers were suspicious and rejected this information, however.
2. Change the importance of beliefs. Although the sugar manufacturers would undoubtedly like to decrease the importance of healthy teeth, it is usually not feasible to make beliefs less important--consumers are likely to reason, why, then, would you bother bringing them up in the first place? However, it may be possible to strengthen beliefs that favour us--e.g., a vitamin supplement manufacturer may advertise that it is extremely important for women to replace iron lost through menstruation. Most consumers already agree with this, but the belief can be made stronger.
3. Add beliefs. Consumers are less likely to resist the addition of beliefs so long as they do not conflict with existing beliefs. Thus, the beef industry has added beliefs that beef (1) is convenient and (2) can be used to make a number of creative dishes. Vitamin manufacturers attempt to add the belief that stress causes vitamin depletion, which sounds quite plausible to most people.
4. Change ideal. It usually difficult, and very risky, to attempt to change ideals, and only few firms succeed. For example, Hard Candy may have attempted to change the ideal away from traditional beauty toward more unique self expression.

One-sided vs. two-sided appeals. Attitude research has shown that consumers often tend to react more favourably to advertisements which either (1) admit something negative about the sponsoring brand (e.g., the Volvo is a clumsy car, but very safe) or (2) admits something positive about a competing brand (e.g., a competing supermarket has slightly lower prices, but offers less service and selection). Two-sided appeals must, contain overriding arguments why the sponsoring brand is ultimately superior--that is, in the above examples, the "but" part must be emphasized.

The Elaboration Likelihood Model (ELM) and Celebrity Endorsements. The ELM suggests that consumers will scrutinize claims more in important situations than in unimportant ones. For example, we found that in the study of people trying to get ahead of others in a line to use photo copiers, the compliance rate was about fifty percent when people just asked to get ahead. However, when the justification "... because I have to make copies" was added, compliance increased to 80%. Since the reason offered really did not add substantive information, we conclude that it was not extensively analyzed--in the jargon of the theory, "elaboration" was low.

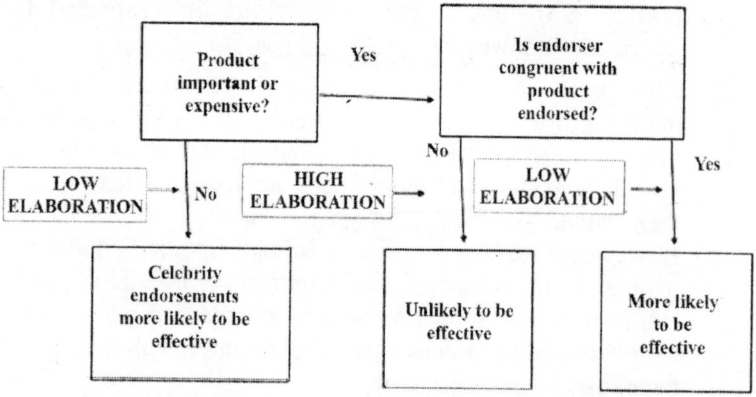

The ELM suggests that for "unimportant" products, elaboration will be low, and thus Bill Cosby is able to endorse Coke and Jell-O without having any special credentials to do so. However, for products which are either expensive or important for some other reason (e.g., a pain reliever given to a child that could be harmed by using dangerous substances), elaboration is likely to be more extensive, and the endorser is expected to be "congruent," or compatible, with the product. For example, a basket ball player is likely to be effective in endorsing athletic shoes, but not in endorsing automobiles. On the other hand, a nationally syndicated auto columnist would be successful in endorsing cars, but not athletic shoes. All of them, however, could endorse fast food restaurants effectively.

Appeal Approaches. Several approaches to appeal may be used. The use of affect to induce empathy with advertising characters may increase attraction to a product, but may backfire if consumers believe that people's feelings are being exploited. Fear appeals appear to work only if (1) an optimal level of fear is evoked--not so much that people tune it out, but enough to scare people into action and (2) a way to avoid the feared stimulus is explicitly indicated--e.g., gingivitis and tooth loss can be avoided by using this mouth wash. Humour appears to be effective in gaining attention, but does not appear to increase persuasion in practice. In addition, a more favourable attitude toward the advertisement may be created by humorous advertising, which may in turn result in increased sales. Comparative advertising, which is illegal in many countries, often increases sales for the sponsoring brand, but may backfire in certain cultures.

E-COMMERCE

Online marketing can serve several purposes:

- Actual sales of products-e.g., Amazon.com.
- Promotion/advertising: Customers can be quite effectively targeted in many situations because of the context that they, themselves, have sought out. For example, when a consumer searches for a specific term in a search engine, a "banner" or link to a firm selling products in that area can be displayed. Print and television advertisements can also feature the firm's web address, thus inexpensively drawing in those who would like additional information.
- Customer service: The site may contain information for those who no longer have their manuals handy and, for electronic products, provide updated drivers and software patches.
- Market research: Data can be collected relatively inexpensively on the Net. However, the response rates are likely to be very unrepresentative and recent research shows that it is very difficult to get consumers to read instructions. This is one of the reasons why the quality of data collected online is often suspect.

ECONOMICS OF ELECTRONIC COMMERCE

SELLING ONLINE IS USUALLY MORE EXPENSIVE

Some people have suggested that the Internet may be a less expensive way to distribute products than traditional "brick-and-mortar" stores.

However, in most cases, selling online will probably be more costly than selling in traditional stores due to the high costs of processing orders and direct shipping to the customer. Some products may, however, be economically marketed online. Some factors that are relevant in assessing the potential for e-commerce to be an effective way to sell a specific products are:

- "Value-to-bulk" ratio. Products that have a lot of value squeezed into a small volume (e.g., high end jewellery and certain electronic products) are often more cost-effective to ship to end-customers than are bulkier products with less value (e.g., low end furniture).
- Absolute margins. Some products may have a rather high percentage margin-e.g., a scarf bought at wholesale at $10 and marked up 100% to be sold at $20. However, the absolute margin is only $20-$10=$10. In contrast, a laptop computer may be bought at $1,000 and be marked up by only 15%, or $150, for a total price of $1,150. Here, however, the absolute margin will be larger--$150. This allows the merchant to spend money on processing, packaging, and shipping the order. Ten dollars, in contrast, can only cover a small amount of employee time and very limited packaging and shipping. Some online merchants do charge for shipping, but doing so will ultimately make the online merchant less competitive.
- Extent of customization needed. Some products need to be customized-e.g., checks have to be personalized and airline tickets have to be issued for a specific departure site, destination time, and travel time. Here, online processing may be useful because the customer can do much of the work.
- Willingness of customers to pay for convenience. Some consumers may be willing to pay for the convenience of having products delivered to their door. For example, delivering high bulk, generally low value groceries is generally not efficient. However, for some customers, it may be worthwhile to pay to avoid an inconvenient trip to the grocery store.
- Geographic dispersal of customers. Electronic commerce, when value-to-bulk ratios and absolute margins are not favourable, is often not viable when customers are located conveniently close to a retail outlet. However, for some products-e.g., bee keeping equipment-customers are widely geographically

dispersed and thus, a centralized distribution centre may be more economically viable. Specialty books-e.g., for collectors of vintage automobiles-may not be worthwhile for bookstores to stock, and these may thus be economically sold online.

- Vulnerability of inventory to loss of value. Some products-especially high tech products-have a very high effective carrying costs. It has been estimated that because of the rapid technological progress made in the computer field, computer parts may lose as much as 1.5% of their value per week. If shipping directly to the customer can reduce the channel time by five weeks, this potentially "rescues" as much as 7.5% of the product value. In such a situation, then, trying to reach the customer directly may make sense, even if the direct costs of distribution are higher, because of the inventory value issue.

There are a number of economic realities of online competition:

- As discussed, costs of handling online orders is often higher than that of distributing through traditional stores.
- Even if online selling is more cost effective in some situations, a firm selling online will, in the long run, be competing with other online merchants-not just against traditional "brick-and-mortar" stores. By the forces of supply and demand, online prices will then be driven down so that the profit from selling online will be no greater than that from traditional retailing. Any reduced costs would then be expected to go to customers.
- Competition will be greater for products that have large markets than for those where markets are smaller and more specialized. Amazon.com, for example, has found it necessary to discount best selling books deeply. Higher prices-closer to the list price-can be charged for specialty books, but for a large part of the market, competition will be intense.
- A new online merchant will face competition from established traditional merchants. These will often have the cash reserves to stay in business for a long time even with temporary competition. The online merchant, if it has no cash reserves other than stockholders' investment, may run out of cash before it can become profitable.

ISSUES IN WEB SITE DESIGN

Web site design: The web designer must make various issues into consideration:

- Speed vs. aesthetics: As we saw, some of the fancier sites have serious problems functioning practically. Consumers may be impressed by a fancy site, or may lack confidence in a firm that offers a simple one. Yet, fancier sites with extensive graphics take time to download-particularly for users dialling in with a modem as opposed to being "hard" wired-and may result in site crashes.
- Keeping users on the site: A large number of "baskets" are abandoned online as consumers fail to complete the "check-out" process for the products they have selected. One problem here is that many consumers are drawn away from a site and then are unlikely to come back. A large number of links may be desirable to consumers, but they tend to draw people away. Taking banner advertisers on your site from other sites may be profitable, but it may result in customers lost.
- Information collection: An increasing number of consumers resist collection of information about them, and a number of consumers have set up their browsers to disallow "cookies," files that contain information about their computers and shopping habits.

Cyber-consumer behaviour: In principle, it is fairly easy to search and compare online, and it was feared that this might wipe out all margins online. More recent research suggests that consumers in fact do not tend to search very intently and that large price differences between sites persist. We saw above the problem of keeping consumers from prematurely departing from one's site.

Site content: The content of a site should generally be based on the purposes of operating a site. For most sites, however, having a clear purpose be evident is essential. The site should generally provide some evidence for this position. For example, if the site claims a large selection, the vast choices offered should be evident. Sites that claim convenience should make this evident. A main purpose of the Internet is to make information readily available, and the site should be designed so that finding the needed information among all the content of the site is as easy as possible. Since it is easy for consumers to move to other sites, the site should be made interesting. To provide the information and options desired by customers, two-way interaction capabilities are essential.

WEB SITE TRAFFIC GENERATION

The web is now so large that getting traffic to any one site can be difficult. One method is search engine optimization, a topic that will be covered below. Other methods include "viral" campaigns wherein current users are used to spread the word about a site, firm, or service. For example, Hotmail attaches a message to every e-mail sent from its service alerting the recipient that a free e-mail account can be had there. Google offers a free e-mail account with a full gigabyte of storage. This is available only by invitation from others who have such e-mail accounts. Amazon.com at one point invited people, when they had completed a purchase, to automatically e-mail friends whose e-mail addresses they provided with a message about what they had just bought. If the friend bought any of the same items, both the original customer and the friend would get a discount.

Another method of gaining traffic is through online advertising. Sites like Yahoo! are mainly sponsored by advertisers, as are many sites for newspapers and magazines. Individuals who see an ad on these sites can usually click to go to the sponsor's web site. Occasionally, a firm may advertise their sites in traditional media. Geico, Dell Computer, and Progressive Insurance do this. Overstock.com has also advertised a lot on traditional TV programs. Conventional advertising may also contain a web site address as part of a larger advertising message.

Viral marketing is more suitable for some products than for others. To get others involved in spreading the word, the product usually must be interesting and unique. It must also be simple enough so that it can be explained briefly. It is most useful when switching or trial costs are low. It is more difficult, for example, getting people to sign up for a satellite system or cellular phone service where equipment has to be bought up front and/or a long term contract is required makes viral marketing more difficult. Viral marketing does raise some problems about control of the campaign. For example, if a service is aimed at higher income countries and residents there spread the word to consumers in lower income countries, people attracted may be unprofitable. For Google's one gigabyte e-mail account, for example, there are large costs that may be covered by advertising revenues from ads aimed at people who can afford to buy products and services. Advertisers, however, may not be willing to pay for targets who cannot afford their products. It is also difficult to control "word of mouth" (or "word of keyboard"). Measuring the effectiveness of a campaign may be difficult. When a viral campaign relies on e-mail, messages received may be considered spam by some recipients, leading to potential brand damage and loss of goodwill.

Online promotions: One way to generate traffic is promotions. Many sites often offer new customers discounts or free gifts. This can be expensive, but sometimes, the gifts can be ones that have a low marginal cost. For example, once the firms pays for the development of a game, the cost of letting new users download it is modest. The U.S. army uses this approach in making a game available. To be allowed to use some of the "cooler" features, the user has to go through various stages of "basic training."

SEARCH ENGINE OPTIMIZATION

Many Internet users find desired information and sites through search engines such as Google. Research shows that a large proportion of the traffic goes to the first three sites listed, and few people go so sites that appear beyond the first "page" or screen. On Google, the default screen size is ten sites, so being in the top ten is essential.

Because of the importance of search engines, getting a good ranking or coming up early on the list for important keywords is vitally important. Many consultants offer, for large fees, to help improve a site's ranking.

There are several types of sites that are similar to search engines. Directories involve sites that index information based on human analysis. Yahoo! started out that way, but now most of the information is accessed through search engine features. Some sites contain link collections as part of their sites-e.g., business magazines may have links to business information sites.

Several issues in search engines and directories are important. Some search engines, such as Google, base rankings strictly on merit (although sites are allowed to get preferred paid listings on the right side of the screen). Other search engines allow sites to "bid" to get listed first. Some sites may end up paying as much as a dollar for each surfer who clicks through. If a potential customer is valuable enough, it may be worth paying for enhanced listings. Often, however, it is better to be listed as number two or three since only more serious searchers are likely to go beyond the first site. The first listed site may attract a number of people who click through without much serious inspection of the site.

Some search engines are more specific than others. The goal of Google, Yahoo! and MSN is to contain as many sites as possible. Others may specialize in sites of a specific type to reduce the amount of irrelevant information that may come up.

Search engines often have different types of strategies. Google is very much technology oriented while Yahoo! appears to be more market oriented. Another major goal of Google is speed. Some sites may contain more content of one type than another. For example, AltaVista appears to have more images, as opposed to text pages, indexed.

Search engine rankings. The order in which different sites are listed for a given term is determined by a secret algorithm developed by the search engine. An algorithm is a collection of rules put together to identify the most relevant sites. The specific algorithms are highly guarded trade secrets, but most tend to heavily weigh the number of links from other sites to a site and the keywords involved. More credit is given for a link from a highly rated site. On any given page, the weight given from a link will depend on the total number of links on that page. Having one of one hundred links will count less than being the only one. One source reports that the weight appears to be proportional so that one out of one hundred links would carry one percent of the weight of being the sole link, but that may change and/or vary among search engines.

For Google, some of the main ranking factors appear to be:

- Number and quality of links to the site, as discussed above.
- Relevant keywords. Note that the ranking algorithm tests for "spam." Reckless repeating keywords may actually count against the rating of the site.
- The "click-through" share of the site. Since late 2006 or early 2007, Google reportedly fine-tunes rankings by observing the percentage of the time that a particular site is chosen for a given set of search terms. Sites that are selected more frequently may improve in rank and those less frequently selected-despite their merits presumed from the other factors-may move down.

Types of search engines: Some engines, such as Google, are general purpose search engines. Some are specialized. Some are hybrids, containing some directory structure in addition to search engine capabilities. Some "reward" sites attract people by allowing them to enter a lottery when doing a search. Some sites are aggregator sites-they do not have their own databases but instead combine the results from simultaneous searches on other search engines.

Text optimization: It is important to repeat important words as much as possible subject to credibility. Search engines today are increasingly sophisticated in identifying "spamming" through frivolous repetition of the same words or early use of words that are not relevant to the main content of the site. Words that appear early in the text and on the index page will tend to be weighted more heavily. For some search engines, it may be useful to include common misspellings of a word so that the site will come up when that spelling is used. For aesthetic reasons, many firms may object to having much text on the front page, but text may be put below the graphic elements. Some web site owners have attempted to include hidden text so that a search engine would find the desired words while the visitor would see something else. Some web designers, for example, would hide text behind a graphic, make the text in a very small font, and/or make the font colour the same, or nearly the same, as the background. Other web site designers have made a "legitimate" site, only to have a command to move the visitor to another site when they go to the searched site. Search engines today are increasingly able to detect this type of abuse, and sites may be penalized as a result.

Early search engines relied heavily on "meta tags" where the web site creator specified what he or she believed to be appropriate keywords, content descriptions, and titles. Because these tags are subject to a lot of abuse, these no longer appear to be significant.

Link optimization. Many web sites engage in "link exchanges"-that is, complementary sites will agree to feature links to each other. It may be useful for a webmaster to ask firms whose content does not compete for a link.

The bottom line on Google. Today, the most significant factor in search engine rankings appears to be the "value" of the links that reach a site. Links from "low value" sites (those that are not rated highly, and especially those considered to the "spam") count for very little. Links from highly rated sites on the relevant keywords count for literally thousands-sometimes tens and hundreds of thousands-times as much as less important site. In the past, the presence of important key terms on a site was the main driver of rankings, subject to some rudimentary safeguards against obvious "spamming" sites which used the words as a way to gain rankings without providing relevant information. Now, the effect of keywords is secondary except for searches that involve a very unique key term. Within the last year, it appears that Google has incorporated the frequency of "click-through" for a site when it is listed in search ("organic") results. That is, if a relatively high proportion of searchers go to the site, its ranking is likely to decrease. However, if relatively few searchers actually end up going to a highly ranked site when it shows up in search listings, that site is likely to lose rank. Search engines cannot usually measure the amount of traffic that goes to a site. Traditionally, then, the traffic of a site was not directly incorporated into the ranking system. Today, however, Google is reported to weigh the percentage that a site is chosen for click-through when the site comes up in a search. That is, if a site is initially highly ranked, if a small proportion of searchers actually choose to go to that site, this site is likely to have its rank reduced.

Google now offers a set of "Analytics" tools, including a set of web traffic statistics. Webmasters can sign up voluntarily to participate in this by placing certain "meta tag" code in their web pages. (This code is invisible to people viewing the respective web page in its regular display mode). Therefore, for such sites, Google does, in principle, have access to traffic information from all sources, including other search engines or links from other sites. It is not clear whether Google actually uses this information, however.

ORGANIZATIONAL BUYERS

A large portion of the market for goods and services is attributable to organizational, as opposed to individual, buyers. In general, organizational buyers, who make buying decisions for their companies for a living, tend to be somewhat more sophisticated than ordinary consumers. However, these organizational buyers are also often more risk averse. There is a risk in going with a new, possibly better (lower price or higher quality) supplier whose product is unproven and may turn out to be problematic. Often the fear of running this risk is greater than the potential rewards for getting a better deal. In the old days, it used to be said that "You can't get fired for buying IBM." This attitude is beginning to soften a bit today as firms face increasing pressures to cut costs.

Organizational buyers come in several forms. Resellers involve either wholesalers or retailers that buy from one organization and resell to some other entity. For example, large grocery chains sometimes buy products directly from the manufacturer and resell them to end-consumers. Wholesalers may sell to retailers who in turn sell to consumers. Producers also buy products from sub-manufacturers to create a finished product. For example, rather than manufacturing the parts themselves, computer manufacturers often buy hard drives, motherboards, cases, monitors, keyboards, and other components from manufacturers and put them together to create a finished product. Governments buy a great deal of things. For example, the military needs an incredible amount of supplies to feed and equip troops. Finally, large institutions buy products in huge quantities. For example, UCR probably buys thousands of reams of paper every month.

Organizational buying usually involves more people than individual buying. Often, many people are involved in making decisions as to (a) whether to buy, (b) what to buy, (c) at what quantity, and (d) from whom. An engineer may make a specification as to what is needed, which may be approved by a manager, with the final purchase being made by a purchase specialist who spends all his or her time finding the best deal on the goods that the organization needs. Often, such long purchase processes can cause long delays. In the government, rules are often especially stringent-e.g., vendors of fruit cake have to meet fourteen pages of specifications put out by the General Services Administration. In many cases, government buyers are also heavily bound to go with the lowest price. Even if it is obvious that a higher priced vendor will offer a superior product, it may be difficult to accept that bid.

Note: Avocent designs, manufactures, licenses, and sells software and hardware products, which provides connectivity and centralized management of information technology (IT) infrastructure. The company primarily operates in the US. It is headquartered in Alabama, United States and employs 1,099 people. For detailed information related to this chapter reader can visit www.avocent.com

16

Consumer Buying Behaviour

Researchers in marketing have studied most areas of consumer behaviour including the impact of everything from music to lighting on how people behave and how they consume products. This is not surprising considering the fact that we live in a consumption-driven culture. We will focus on the basic constructs accepted today in the study of buying behaviour.

CONSUMER DECISION-MAKING

Most studies of the decision-making process in marketing have used an adaptation of the scientific method. This decision-making process is as follows:

- Problem recognition - the consumer recognizes a problem. For example, her car has had major mechanical problems for the last two months.
- Information search - internal and external. The consumer thinks about options she may have to remedy her situation (internal search). And then she seeks external sources of information such as friends, newspapers, TV, and the internet.
- Alternative identification and evaluation - she has some ideas about what alternatives she has and how to approach them. She now must compare and contrast the options she has.
- Choice and purchase - based on this process of consideration the consumer now purchases the most attractive option she has identified.
- Post purchase evaluatlon - the consumer experiences her choice and determines if she is happy with it.

- Feedback learning for future consumption behaviour - the consumer remembers how she feels about her purchase and makes note of it for future reference (internal search).

As a student, learning this approach is worthwhile for you so that you will have a general framework to understand your purchasing behaviour and the purchasing behaviour of others for purposes of marketing research.

Of course, there are exceptions to the rather rigid, mechanistic process above. First, we often don't go through all of the steps. This fact sometimes has to do with 'involvement'. Involvement can be defined as the personal importance and social significance of the purchase. The importance can be a function of how much the product or service costs and whether there are any social risks involved. Involvement is often classified as 'high' or 'low'. We would add 'medium' to the categories, because many products we buy fit into that area. For example, we rarely buy new cars, laser surgery for vision correction, and new houses (all three of these would be high involvement) and while we frequently buy low involvement products (coffee, soft drinks, chewing gum) we also buy many more durable products that can be considered medium involvement. For example, if a college student buys a new CD player for his car or a new sports-coat, both of these would probably be considered medium involvement because they are in the medium price range as far as his budget is concerned and there is some level of risk surrounding the purchase.

There is also another important consideration called situational effects. Situational effects are all of the circumstances surrounding our purchases that may strongly impact our decision-making process. For example, a female college student is preparing to go out with her friends for the evening. She and her 'buds' have decided to go to a club where there will be music, dancing, and, most importantly, young men. The student decides to go to Dillard's and buy a new blouse and a pair of new 'dressy' slacks in preparation for the night out. She also buys some makeup and fragrance. Just last night in the midst of studying for an exam when the same student went out with her friends for pizza at a local pizza parlour, she wore jeans and a ragged sweatshirt. Why was there such a difference in her dress and preparation? The social nature of the two evenings was very different, thus situational effects strongly impacted this person's buying behaviour. We have all had a battery 'go out' in our car and most of us don't think of shopping for a battery until our present battery goes dead. Again, the situation strongly impacts what are willing and able to do as far as buying behaviour. Usually, we just try to find a battery wherever we can and as soon as we can to solve our problem.

We, as consumers, feel no responsibility 'to follow the rules' thus we may engage in unorthodox buying behaviour that defies classification. For example, go to Walmart and observe customers there. You will see all types of people buying all kinds of things: some of those purchases will be planned and some will be unplanned, although, of course, you won't be able to tell which is which. Often, a 'shopping trip' is directed not to a specific, planned purchase but just to 'see what available' - so while the cognitive perspective on shopping is useful, there is also a lot of buying behaviour that defies understanding. For example, think a situation in which you engaged in an 'impulse purchase.' An impulse purchase is an unplanned purchase in which we just decide to buy the product with very little prior consideration.

GROUP/SOCIAL VARIABLES IMPACTING BUYING BEHAVIOUR

While there are many different impacts on consumer buying behaviour that have to do with groups, we consider the following three as the most important overall.

REFERENCE GROUPS

First, reference groups are collections of other people who strongly affect what we buy and how we go about buying it. What do you think is the most influential reference group for most people? If you guessed "family" you are absolutely right. The family is not only the most important reference group for children, a person's family background can impact his or her buying behaviour throughout life in many ways. Sometimes adults buy 'what our family bought' and sometimes they 'won't touch what my family liked'. This has been shown to be true in durable goods such as cars and appliances, as well as, nondurable goods like laundry detergent and shampoo. The family is a membership reference group whereas other reference groups may be nonmembership reference groups. This brings another factor into consideration. If you consider the reference groups available to you, some will be groups you would like to be a member of but are not and other groups you would not like to be a member of: perhaps an example would be the "winning lottery ticket losers club."

Groups you would like to be a member of but are not, are called Aspirant Reference Groups, groups to which you don't really expect membership, but still want to be somehow related to are called Associative Reference Groups and groups in which you would not seek membership are termed Disassociative Reference Groups.

Many adopt the appearance of their aspirant or associative groups by engaging in consumption behaviour to express their personal sentiment. For example, one may buy a Colorado Rockies Hat and wear in public because s/he is a fan of that particular baseball team. This person would belong to an associative reference group but not be a member of an aspirant reference group because in our example the fan does not really expect to be able to join the Rockies team in any official capacity.

ETHNICITY - CULTURE/SUB CULTURE

The ethnic landscape of the U.S. has changed constantly over the last few thousand years and that process continues. Native Americans continually shifted geographic habitat due to weather and other human adversaries. As our country developed in the eighteenth, nineteenth, and twentieth centuries, different ethnic groups joined the growing population. Today the ethnic composition of the India is still changing.

Incumbent in these changes in ethnicity are changes in Culture for the India. Historically dominated by the thoughts and mores of a Western European tradition, the India is changing rapidly to accommodate many new ideas and ways of doing things. We define "culture" as the totality of artefacts and behaviours handed down from one generation to the next. A subculture can be any segment of society that hands down its own beliefs across an extended period of time. Thus, different subcultures intermingle their ideas and art forms in a ethnically diverse society.

INDIVIDUAL/PSYCHOLOGICAL VARIABLES IMPACTING BUYING BEHAVIOUR

LEARNING

We, as human beings are constantly learning about our environment and a portion of this learning is related to what we consume and when and how we consume it. Therefore, learning is an important concept in consumer buying behaviour. Learning can be defined as "changes in attitudes or behaviour based on experience." We learn constantly about products and services available and adjust our consumption patterns to what we learn. However, we sometimes obtain knowledge that does impact our consumption patterns for some time. Marketers cannot assess such learning easily. Although as a marketing person you can't assess it, you must remain aware and track changes occurring in the environment. For example, today most people do not perceive significant risks in consuming hamburger meat, however, that may be changing quietly across our U.S. population in response the "Mad Cow" and "foot and mouth disease" outbreaks in the United. Many people are aware of this threat presently, and it would not take much to drive them away from consuming beef and hamburger meat in all forms. If you were a marketing manager for a food company, you would be well advised to continually gather information on and be aware of this trend as consumers become more aware of this threat to health.

ATTITUDE

There are probably more studies of attitude in the marketing literature than any other individual variable affecting consumer buying behaviour. An attitude can be defined 'predisposition to respond to stimuli.' In plain English, an attitude is simply how we feel about something. If you are apathetic about a certain product or issue, you don't really have an attitude related to it. "Neutral attitude" is an oxymoron, it is internally contradictory. Attitude formation can follow several different patterns. However, we can use a simple approach to understand how people form an attitude towards a product or service. Attitudes are usually comprised of three parts: cognitive, evaluative, and behavioural. That is, a consumer normally goes through three stages when forming an attitude. The stages may differ in the order they occur. For example, for a high involvement product, most consumers will probably first think about a product (cognitive stage), develop a feeling towards that product (evaluative stage) and then, if s/he likes the product, purchase it (behavioural stage). We will expand our discussion of attitude formation in the chapter on marketing communications.

The most common attitude model applied in business is the 'belief/ importance weight model' also called the 'multiattribute attitude model (MAM).' The MAM orientation to measuring attitudes is a simple but effective way to understand how people feel about products and services.

PERCEPTION

Perception can be defined as 'the way we experience life.' That is, perception is how we attach meaning to all of the inputs that we are exposed to in daily living. These inputs can be new words, a new song, or an advertisement about a product. Marketers have been interested in perception because they are constantly trying to communicate product and service ideas to their target markets and they need to understand how that information will be received and understood. Humans normally go through several stages in the process of perceiving meaning. These stages include exposure, attention, attached meaning, and retention. You may see a TV ad for Coca Cola. For example, first, you were present by the TV to be exposed to the ad. Second, it may have gained your attention because you liked the music in the ad. Third, you attached meaning to the ad, recognizing the product and the musical theme, and finally, you find yourself humming the musical theme "Life tastes good" later in the day.

Much has been written about 'subliminal perception' over the years. Several popular writers have made considerable money on books they published warning consumers that "You are being manipulated and you don't even know it." While, this is really an exciting conspiracy theory that persists in media study, you as a college student, and soon to be graduate, should be in possession of the facts.

Subliminal perception means literally 'below the level of consciousness' thus if you can identify symbols or words in an ad, you are not dealing with subliminal perception. Research indicates that while subliminal perception exists, if exposed to subliminal stimuli, you may see a red bottle of Coca-Cola and decide you are seeing Santa Claus. That is, subliminal perception is not efficient at all.

Perception remains an important construct in marketing because the study of perception can give information to marketing communications professionals about when and how people receive and make sense of information.

RISK

Risk, in the consumer buying behaviour area, can be defined as the potential negative consequence of a certain action including buying or using a certain product or service. In marketing, we usually use the term 'perceived risk' because the person or persons we are trying to understand determine the amount of risk. That is, we can advertise that there is no risk associated with taking aspirin for a headache, but some of the populace will perceive a health risk (physical risk) because they have heard that aspirin is dangerous. There are several types of risk that have been identified in research. We will cover four kinds of risk:

a. Physiological risk - associated with threats to one's health

b. Financial risk - risk associated with the loss of economic wealth or financial security

c. Psychological risk - threats associated with some psychological construct, for example, a threat to one's self-esteem

d. Social risk - a threat to one's social standing or social comfort

Surely, you are familiar with each type of risk as a consumer. You can see that marketers want to understand not only how they can use risk to make their products more appealing for purchase (for example, home security systems). Also, one can see how companies live in fear of hoaxes that will cause consumers to avoid the company's products (check out these websites to see some present hoaxes in our society.

ORGANIZATIONAL BUYING BEHAVIOUR

ORGANIZATIONAL DECISION-MAKING

Organizations often make decisions in a very similar fashion to consumers. In fact, there has been substantial disagreement about whether the differences in consumer decision-making and organizational decision-making are adequate to justify separate models of decision-making for the two. We agree that the differences are small, and don't necessarily justify separate treatment. However, we do want to point out a couple of important differences that exist in a fairly universal way. First, organizational purchase decisions are frequently made by a group of individuals. One might argue that families are similar and we would agree. However, the group decision-making approach is consistent across most organizations whereas families may be less oriented to this form of decision-making at least for many decisions. Second, the decision-making process for organizations is certainly more formalized. Most families don't consider any structured approach to their decision-making as a group and many organizations find it necessary to codify many details about how purchase decisions shall be made. Government agencies are legend for incredibly complex buying approaches.

Thus, marketers must strive to understand how organizations in their chosen markets reach the buying decision. In considering the organizational purchase process we would recommend that the student remember two differences between consumer decision-making and organizational decision-making related to purchasing. First, we would suggest adding a stage to the consumer decision-making process covered earlier in this chapter. Organizations often solicit bids from an approved bidder list or publish specifications related to the product they are seeking to obtain. Second, there has been considerable research on the 'roles' assumed by people who impact the buying decision. These people, taken as a group, are called the buying centre.

A list of the roles usually existing in the buying centre might include:

- Initiator - this person first recognizes the need for the product or service and may or may not have a say in the purchase decision.
- User - this person will be responsible for operating the product that is bought or consuming the service that is purchased. Again, this person may or may not have a say in what is purchased.
- Influencer - this person's role may be only tangential to product use, but s/he will still have an impact on the purchase decision.
- Buyer - this person is responsible for obtaining the product, though s/he may or may not have any impact on what is purchased.
- Decider - this person is responsible for the final determination of what will be purchased.

You should become familiar with these roles and be able to understand how they would be expressed in a group-buying scenario. You should also be able to explain why a marketer would be interested in who plays what role.

GROUP/SOCIAL VARIABLES THAT IMPACT ORGANIZATIONAL BUYING BEHAVIOUR

While there are group variables that affect organizational buying behaviour, the amount of research in this area is relatively small. Certainly, organizational relationships and organizational culture, for example, may have a strong impact on what is ultimately purchased.

INDIVIDUAL/PSYCHOLOGICAL VARIABLES THAT IMPACT ORGANIZATIONAL BUYING BEHAVIOUR

While there has been a limited amount of research regarding these variables, the average business-to-business marketer doesn't really have easy access to much knowledge in this area. There are some studies on perceived risk that indicate risk is an important personal consideration for industrial buyers as supported by the saying "No one have ever been fired for buying from IBM."

Other individual/psychological variables including learning, perception, attitudes, and organizational culture also are important considerations in organizational buying as well as consumer decision-making. There is still a lot to be learned in this area.

CUSTOMER RELATIONSHIP MANAGEMENT (CRM)

This area of organizational marketing is one of the most vibrant, intriguing areas in today's marketing landscape. While many marketers have realized for years that the key to long-term success is at least in part customer knowledge and customer care. However, this initiative is often lost in promotion without creation of a service delivery system to ensure that customers are treated as 'number one.'

While this catch phrase has gained added space in trade magazines and academic journals, some companies will see this as another opportunity to be 'sales driven' and use the concept as a way to promote their 'customer care' programs. Sadly, such programs often are not really directed at customer satisfaction and relationship building but only represent something else to advertise that may increase sales. Many organizations that aggressively advertise such programs haven't really done the research and made the commitment necessary to make the programs successful in the long term.

However, many businesses in organizational markets have realized the importance of relationship building and have made this a priority in their business planning activities.

Note: VF Corporation (VFC) offers branded lifestyle apparel and related products in various product categories including jeanswear, outerwear, packs, footwear, sportswear and occupational apparel. The company operates in the US, Europe, Asia, Canada and Latin America. It is headquartered in Greensboro, North Carolina, and employs 46,600 people. For a case study visit company's site www.vfc.com

17

Consumer Psychology

The study of consumers helps firms and organizations improve their marketing strategies by understanding issues such as how

- The psychology of how consumers think, feel, reason, and select between different alternatives (e.g., brands, products);
- The psychology of how the consumer is influenced by his or her environment (e.g., culture, family, signs, media);
- The behavior of consumers while shopping or making other marketing decisions;
- Limitations in consumer knowledge or information processing abilities influence decisions and marketing outcome;
- How consumer motivation and decision strategies differ between products that differ in their level of importance or interest that they entail for the consumer; and
- How marketers can adapt and improve their marketing campaigns and marketing strategies to more effectively reach the consumer.

One "official" definition of consumer behavior is "The study of individuals, groups, or organizations and the processes they use to select, secure, use, and dispose of products, services, experiences, or ideas to satisfy needs and the impacts that these processes have on the consumer and society." Although it is not necessary to memorize this definition, it brings up some useful points:

- Behavior occurs either for the individual, or in the context of a group (e.g., friends influence what kinds of clothes a person wears) or an organization (people on the job make decisions as to which products the firm should use).

- Consumer behavior involves the use and disposal of products as well as the study of how they are purchased. Product use is often of great interest to the marketer, because this may influence how a product is best positioned or how we can encourage increased consumption. Since many environmental problems result from product disposal (e.g., motor oil being sent into sewage systems to save the recycling fee, or garbage piling up at landfills) this is also an area of interest.
- Consumer behavior involves services and ideas as well as tangible products.
- The impact of consumer behavior on society is also of relevance. For example, aggressive marketing of high fat foods, or aggressive marketing of easy credit, may have serious repercussions for the national health and economy.

There are four main applications of consumer behavior:

- The most obvious is for marketing strategy—i.e., for making better marketing campaigns. For example, by understanding that consumers are more receptive to food advertising when they are hungry, we learn to schedule snack advertisements late in the afternoon. By understanding that new products are usually initially adopted by a few consumers and only spread later, and then only gradually, to the rest of the population, we learn that (1) companies that introduce new products must be well financed so that they can stay afloat until their products become a commercial success and (2) it is important to please initial customers, since they will in turn influence many subsequent customers' brand choices.
- A second application is public policy. In the 1980s, Accutane, a near miracle cure for acne, was introduced. Unfortunately, Accutane resulted in severe birth defects if taken by pregnant women. Although physicians were instructed to warn their female patients of this, a number still became pregnant while taking the drug. To get consumers' attention, the Federal Drug Administration (FDA) took the step of requiring that very graphic pictures of deformed babies be shown on the medicine containers.
- Social marketing involves getting ideas across to consumers rather than selling something. Marty Fishbein, a marketing professor, went on sabbatical to work for the Centers for

Disease Control trying to reduce the incidence of transmission of diseases through illegal drug use. The best solution, obviously, would be if we could get illegal drug users to stop. This, however, was deemed to be infeasible. It was also determined that the practice of sharing needles was too ingrained in the drug culture to be stopped. As a result, using knowledge of consumer attitudes, Dr. Fishbein created a campaign that encouraged the cleaning of needles in bleach before sharing them, a goal that was believed to be more realistic.

- As a final benefit, studying consumer behavior should make us better consumers. Common sense suggests, for example, that if you buy a 64 liquid ounce bottle of laundry detergent, you should pay less per ounce than if you bought two 32 ounce bottles. In practice, however, you often pay a size premium by buying the larger quantity. In other words, in this case, knowing this fact will sensitize you to the need to check the unit cost labels to determine if you are really getting a bargain.

There are several units in the market that can be analyzed. Our main thrust in this course is the consumer. However, we will also need to analyze our own firm's strengths and weaknesses and those of competing firms. Suppose, for example, that we make a product aimed at older consumers, a growing segment. A competing firm that targets babies, a shrinking market, is likely to consider repositioning toward our market. To assess a competing firm's potential threat, we need to examine its assets (e.g., technology, patents, market knowledge, awareness of its brands) against pressures it faces from the market. Finally, we need to assess conditions (the marketing environment). For example, although we may have developed a product that offers great appeal for consumers, a recession may cut demand dramatically.

CONSUMER RESEARCH METHODS

Market research is often needed to ensure that we produce what customers really want and not what we think they want.

PRIMARY AND SECONDARY RESEARCH METHODS

There are two main approaches to marketing. Secondary research involves using information that others have already put together. For example, if you are thinking about starting a business making clothes for tall people, you don't need to question people about how tall they are to find out how many tall people exist—that information has already been published by the U.S. Government. Primary research, in contrast, is research that you design and conduct yourself. For example, you may need to find out whether consumers would prefer that your soft drinks be sweater or tarter.

Research will often help us reduce risks associated with a new product, but it cannot take the risk away entirely. It is also important to ascertain whether the research has been complete. For example, Coca Cola did a great deal of research prior to releasing the New Coke, and consumers seemed to prefer the taste. However, consumers were not prepared to have this drink replace traditional Coke.

Several tools are available to the market researcher—e.g., mail questionnaires, phone surveys, observation, and focus groups. Surveys are useful for getting a great deal of specific information. Surveys can contain open-ended questions (e.g., "In which city and state were you born? ____________") or closed-ended, where the respondent is asked to select answers from a brief list (e.g., "__Male ___ Female." Open ended questions have the advantage that the respondent is not limited to the options listed, and that the respondent is not being influenced by seeing a list of responses. However, open-ended questions are often skipped by respondents, and coding them can be quite a challenge. In general, for surveys to yield meaningful responses, sample sizes of over 100 are usually required because precision is essential. For example, if a market share of twenty percent would result in a loss while thirty percent would be profitable, a confidence interval of 20-35% is too wide to be useful.

Surveys come in several different forms. Mail surveys are relatively inexpensive, but response rates are typically quite low—typically from 5-20%. Phone-surveys get somewhat higher response rates, but not many questions can be asked because many answer options have to be repeated and few people are willing to stay on the phone for more than five minutes. Mall intercepts are a convenient way to reach consumers, but respondents may be reluctant to discuss anything sensitive face-to-face with an interviewer.

Surveys, as any kind of research, are vulnerable to bias. The wording of a question can influence the outcome a great deal. For example, more people answered no to the question "Should speeches against democracy be allowed?" than answered yes to "Should speeches against democracy be forbidden?" For face-to-face interviews, interviewer bias is a danger, too. Interviewer bias occurs when the interviewer influences the way the respondent answers. For example, unconsciously an interviewer that works for the firm manufacturing the product in question may smile a little when something good is being said about the product and frown a little when something negative is being said. The respondent may catch on and say something more positive than his or her real opinion. Finally, a response bias may occur—if only part of the sample responds to a survey, the respondents' answers may not be representative of the population.

Focus groups are useful when the marketer wants to launch a new product or modify an existing one. A focus group usually involves having some 8-12 people come together in a room to discuss their consumption preferences and experiences. The group is usually led by a moderator, who will start out talking broadly about topics related broadly to the product without mentioning the product itself. For example, a focus group aimed at sugar-free cookies might first address consumers' snacking preferences, only gradually moving toward the specific product of sugar-free cookies. By not mentioning the product up front, we avoid biasing the participants into thinking only in terms of the specific product brought out. Thus, instead of having consumers think primarily in terms of what might be good or bad about the product, we can ask them to discuss more broadly the ultimate benefits they really seek. For example, instead of having consumers merely discuss what they think about some sugar-free cookies that we are considering releasing to the market, we can have consumers speak about their motivations for using snacks and what general kinds of benefits they seek. Such a discussion might reveal a concern about healthfulness and a desire for wholesome foods. Probing on the meaning of wholesomeness, consumers might indicate a desire to avoid artificial ingredients. This would be an important concern in the marketing of sugar-free cookies, but might not have come up if consumers were asked to comment directly on the product where the use of artificial ingredients is, by virtue of the nature of the product, necessary.

Focus groups are well suited for some purposes, but poorly suited for others. In general, focus groups are very good for getting breadth—i.e., finding out what kinds of issues are important for consumers in a given product category. Here, it is helpful that focus groups are completely "open-ended:" The consumer mentions his or her preferences and opinions, and the focus group moderator can ask the consumer to elaborate. In a questionnaire, if one did not think to ask about something, chances are that few consumers would take the time to write out an elaborate answer. Focus groups also have some drawbacks, for example:

- They represent small sample sizes. Because of the cost of running focus groups, only a few groups can be run. Suppose you run four focus groups with ten members each. This will result in an n of 4(10)=40, which is too small to generalize from. Therefore, focus groups cannot give us a good idea of:
- What proportion of the population is likely to buy the product.
- What price consumers are willing to pay.
- The groups are inherently social. This means that:
- Consumers will often say things that may make them look good (i.e., they watch public television rather than soap operas or cook fresh meals for their families daily) even if that is not true.
- Consumers may be reluctant to speak about embarrassing issues (e.g., weight control, birth control).

Personal interviews involve in-depth questioning of an individual about his or her interest in or experiences with a product. The benefit here is that we can get really into depth (when the respondent says something interesting, we can ask him or her to elaborate), but this method of research is costly and can be extremely vulnerable to interviewer bias.

To get a person to elaborate, it may help to try a common tool of psychologists and psychiatrists—simply repeating what the person said. He or she will often become uncomfortable with the silence that follows and will then tend to elaborate. This approach has the benefit that it minimizes the interference with the respondent's own ideas and thoughts. He or she is not influenced by a new question but will, instead, go more in depth on what he or she was saying.

Personal interviews are highly susceptible to inadvertent "signaling" to the respondent. Although an interviewer is looking to get at the truth, he or she may have a significant interest in a positive consumer response. Unconsciously, then, he or she may inadvertently smile a little when something positive is said and frown a little when something negative is said. Consciously, this will often not be noticeable, and the respondent often will not consciously be aware that he or she is being "reinforced" and "punished" for saying positive or negative things, but at an unconscious level, the cumulative effect of several facial expressions are likely to be felt. Although this type of conditioning will not get a completely negative respondent to say all positive things, it may "swing" the balance a bit so that respondents are more likely to say positive thoughts and withhold, or limit the duration of, negative thoughts.

Projective techniques are used when a consumer may feel embarrassed to admit to certain opinions, feelings, or preferences. For example, many older executives may not be comfortable admitting to being intimidated by computers. It has been found that in such cases, people will tend to respond more openly about "someone else." Thus, we may ask them to explain reasons why a friend has not yet bought a computer, or to tell a story about a person in a picture who is or is not using a product. The main problem with this method is that it is difficult to analyze responses.

Projective techniques are inherently inefficient to use. The elaborate context that has to be put into place takes time and energy away from the main question. There may also be real differences between the respondent and the third party. Saying or thinking about something that "hits too close to home" may also influence the respondent, who may or may not be able to see through the ruse.

Observation of consumers is often a powerful tool. Looking at how consumers select products may yield insights into how they make decisions and what they look for. For example, some American manufacturers were concerned about low sales of their products in Japan. Observing Japanese consumers, it was found that many of these Japanese consumers scrutinized packages looking for a name of a major manufacturer—the product specific-brands that are common in the U.S. (e.g., Tide) were not impressive to the Japanese, who wanted a name of a major firm like Mitsubishi or Proctor & Gamble. Observation may help us determine how much time consumers spend comparing prices, or whether nutritional labels are being consulted.

A question arises as to whether this type of "spying" inappropriately invades the privacy of consumers. Although there may be cause for some concern in that the particular individuals have not consented to be part of this research, it should be noted that there is no particular interest in what the individual customer being watched does. The question is what consumers—either as an entire group or as segments—do. Consumers benefit, for example, from stores that are designed effectively to promote efficient shopping. If it is found that women are more uncomfortable than men about others standing too close, the areas of the store heavily trafficked by women can be designed accordingly. What is being reported here, then, are averages and tendencies in response. The intent is not to find "juicy" observations specific to one customer.

The video clip with Paco Underhill that we saw in class demonstrated the application of observation research to the retail setting. By understanding the phenomena such as the tendency toward a right turn, the location of merchandise can be observed. It is also possible to identify problem areas where customers may be overly vulnerable to the "but brush," or overly close encounter with others. This method can be used to identify problems that the customer experiences, such as difficulty finding a product, a mirror, a changing room, or a store employee for help.

Online research methods. The Internet now reaches the great majority of households in the U.S., and thus, online research provides new opportunity and has increased in use.

One potential benefit of online surveys is the use of "conditional branching." In conventional paper and pencil surveys, one question might ask if the respondent has shopped for a new car during the last eight months. If the respondent answers "no," he or she will be asked to skip ahead several questions—e.g., going straight to question 17 instead of proceeding to number 9. If the respondent answered "yes," he or she would be instructed to go to the next question which, along with the next several ones, would address issues related to this shopping experience. Conditional branching allows the computer to skip directly to the appropriate question. If a respondent is asked which brands he or she considered, it is also possible to customize brand comparison questions to those listed. Suppose, for example, that the respondent considered Ford, Toyota, and Hyundai, it would be possible to ask the subject questions about his or her view of the relative quality of each respective pair—in this case, Ford vs. Toyota, Ford vs. Hyundai, and Toyota vs. Hyundai.

There are certain drawbacks to online surveys. Some consumers may be more comfortable with online activities than others—and not all households will have access. Today, however, this type of response bias is probably not significantly greater than that associated with other types of research methods. A more serious problem is that it has consistently been found in online research that it is very difficult—if not impossible—to get respondents to carefully read instructions and other information online—there is a tendency to move quickly. This makes it difficult to perform research that depends on the respondent's reading of a situation or product description.

Online search data and page visit logs provides valuable ground for analysis. It is possible to see how frequently various terms are used by those who use a firm's web site search feature or to see the route taken by most consumers to get to the page with the information they ultimately want. If consumers use a certain term frequently that is not used by the firm in its product descriptions, the need to include this term in online content can be seen in search logs. If consumers take a long, "torturous" route to information frequently accessed, it may be appropriate to redesign the menu structure and/or insert hyperlinks in "intermediate" pages that are found in many users' routes.

Many consumers are members of supermarket "clubs." In return for signing p for a card and presenting this when making purchases, consumers are often eligible for considerable discounts on selected products.

Researchers use a more elaborate version of this type of program in some communities. Here, a number of consumers receive small payments and/or other incentives to sign up to be part of a research panel. They then receive a card that they are asked to present any time they go shopping. Nearly all retailers in the area usually cooperate. It is now possible to track what the consumer bought in all stores and to have a historical record.

The consumer's shopping record is usually combined with demographic information (e.g., income, educational level of adults in the household, occupations of adults, ages of children, and whether the family owns and rents) and the family's television watching habits. What brand in a given product category was bought during the last, or a series of past, purchase occasions;

- Whether, and if so, how many times a consumer has seen an ad for the brand in question or a competing one;
- Whether the target brand (and/or a competing one) is on sale during the store visit;
- Whether any brand had preferential display space;
- The impact of income and/or family size on purchase patterns; and
- Whether a coupon was used for the purchase and, if so, its value.

A "split cable" technology allows the researchers to randomly select half the panel members in a given community to receive one advertising treatment and the other half another. The selection is truly random since each household, as opposed to neighborhood, is selected to get one treatment or the other. Thus, observed differences should, allowing for sampling error, the be result of advertising exposure since there are no other systematic differences between groups.

Interestingly, it has been found that consumers tend to be more influenced by commercials that they "zap" through while channel surfing even if they only see part of the commercial. This most likely results from the reality that one must pay greater attention while channel surfing than when watching a commercial in order to determine which program is worth watching.

Scanner data is, at the present time, only available for certain grocery item product categories—e.g., food items, beverages, cleaning items, laundry detergent, paper towels, and toilet paper. It is not available for most non-grocery product items. Scanner data analysis is most useful for frequently purchased items (e.g., drinks, food items, snacks, and toilet paper) since a series of purchases in the same product category yield more information with greater precision than would a record of one purchase at one point in time. Even if scanner data were available for electronic products such as printers, computers, and MP3 players, for example, these products would be purchased quite infrequently. A single purchase, then, would not be as effective in effectively distinguishing the effects of different factors—e.g., advertising, shelf space, pricing of the product and competitors, and availability of a coupon—since we have at most one purchase instance during a long period of time during which several of these factors would apply at the same time. In the case of items that are purchased frequently, the consumer has the opportunity to buy a product, buy a competing product, or buy nothing at all depending on the status of the brand of interest and competing brands. In the case of the purchase of an MP3 player, in contrast, there may be promotions associated with several brands going on at the same time, and each may advertise. It may also be that the purchase was motivated by the breakdown of an existing product or dissatisfaction or a desire to add more capabilities.

Physiological measures are occasionally used to examine consumer response. For example, advertisers may want to measure a consumer's level of arousal during various parts of an advertisement. This can be used to assess possible discomfort on the negative side and level of attention on the positive side.

By attaching a tiny camera to plain eye glasses worn by the subject while watching an advertisement, it is possible to determine where on screen or other ad display the subject focuses at any one time. If the focus remains fixed throughout an ad sequence where the interesting and active part area changes, we can track whether the respondent is following the sequence intended.

If he or she is not, he or she is likely either not to be paying as much attention as desired or to be confused by an overly complex sequence. In situations where the subject's eyes do move, we can assess whether this movement is going in the intended direction.

Mind-reading would clearly not be ethical and is, at the present time, not possible in any event. However, it is possible to measure brain waves by attaching electrodes. These readings will not reveal what the subject actually thinks, but it is possible to distinguish between beta waves—indicating active thought and analysis—and alpha waves, indicating lower levels of attention.

An important feature of physiological measures is that we can often track performance over time. A subject may, for example, be demonstrating good characteristics—such as appropriate level of arousal and eye movement—during some of the ad sequence and not during other parts. This, then, gives some guidance as to which parts of the ad are effective and which ones need to be reworked.

In a variation of direct physiological measures, a subject may be asked, at various points during an advertisement, to indicate his or her level of interest, liking, comfort, and approval by moving a lever or some instrument (much like one would adjust the volume on a radio or MP3 player). Republican strategist used this technique during the impeachment and trial of Bill Clinton in the late 1990s. By watching approval during various phases of a speech by the former President, it was found that viewers tended to respond negatively when he referred to "speaking truthfully" but favorably when the President referred to the issues in controversy as part of his "private life."

The Republican researchers were able to separate average results from Democrats, Independents, and Republicans, effectively looking at different segments to make sure that differences between each did not cancel out effects of the different segments. (For example, if at one point Democrats reacted positively and Republicans responded negatively with the same intensity, the average result of apparent indifference would have been very misleading).

Research sequence: In general, if more than one type of research is to be used, the more flexible and less precise method—such as focus groups and/or individual interviews—should generally be used before the less flexible but more precise methods (e.g., surveys and scanner data) are used. Focus groups and interviews are flexible and allow the researcher to follow up on interesting issues raised by participants who can be probed. However, because the sample sizes are small and because participants in a focus group are influenced by each other, few data points are collected. If we run five focus groups with eight people each, for example, we would have a total of forty responses. Even if we assume that these are independent, a sample size of forty would give very imprecise results. We might conclude, for example, that somewhere between 5% and 40% of the target market would be interested in the product we have to offer. This is usually no more precise than what we already reasonably new. Questionnaires, in contrast, are highly inflexible. It is not possible to ask follow-up questions. Therefore, we can use our insights from focus groups and interviews to develop questionnaires that contain specific questions that can be asked to a larger number of people. There will still be some sampling error, but with a sample size of 1,000+ responses, we may be able to narrow the 95% confidence interval for the percentage of the target market that is seriously interested in our product to, say, 17-21%, a range that is much more meaningful.

Cautions: Some cautions should be heeded in marketing research. First, in general, research should only be commissioned when it is worth the cost. Thus, research should normally be useful in making specific decisions (what size should the product be? Should the product be launched? Should we charge $1.75 or $2.25?)

Secondly, marketing research can be, and often is, abused. Managers frequently have their own "agendas" (e.g., they either would like a product to be launched or would prefer that it not be launched so that the firm will have more resources left over to tackle their favorite products). Often, a way to get your way is to demonstrate through "objective" research that your opinions make economic sense. One example of misleading research, which was reported nationwide in the media, involved the case of "The Pentagon Declares War on Rush Limbaugh." The Pentagon, within a year of the election of Democrat Bill Clinton, reported that only 4.2% of soldiers listening to the Armed Forces Network wanted to hear Rush Limbaugh. However, although this finding was reported without question in the media, it was later found that the conclusion was based on the question "What single thing can we do to improve programming?" If you did not write in something like "Carry Rush Limbaugh," you were counted as not wanting to hear him.

CULTURE AND SUBCULTURE

Culture is part of the external influences that impact the consumer. That is, culture represents influences that are imposed on the consumer by other individuals.

The definition of culture offered in one textbook is "That complex whole which includes knowledge, belief, art, morals, custom, and any other capabilities and habits acquired by man person as a member of society." From this definition, we make the following observations:

- Culture, as a "complex whole," is a system of interdependent components.
- Knowledge and beliefs are important parts. In the U.S., we know and believe that a person who is skilled and works hard will get ahead. In other countries, it may be believed that differences in outcome result more from luck. "Chunking," the name for China in Chinese, literally means "The Middle Kingdom." The belief among ancient Chinese that they were in the center of the universe greatly influenced their thinking.
- Other issues are relevant. Art, for example, may be reflected in the rather arbitrary practice of wearing ties in some countries and wearing turbans in others. Morality may be exhibited in the view in the United States that one should not be naked in public. In Japan, on the other hand, groups of men and women may take steam baths together without perceived as improper. On the other extreme, women in some Arab countries are not even allowed to reveal their faces. Notice, by the way, that what at least some countries view as moral may in fact be highly immoral by the standards of another country. For example, the law that once banned interracial marriages in South Africa was named the "Immorality Act," even though in most civilized countries this law, and any degree of explicit racial prejudice, would itself be considered highly immoral.

Culture has several important characteristics:

1. Culture is comprehensive. This means that all parts must fit together in some logical fashion. For example, bowing and a strong desire to avoid the loss of face are unified in their manifestation of the importance of respect.
2. Culture is learned rather than being something we are born with. We will consider the mechanics of learning later in the course.

3. Culture is manifested within boundaries of acceptable behavior. For example, in American society, one cannot show up to class naked, but wearing anything from a suit and tie to shorts and a T-shirt would usually be acceptable. Failure to behave within the prescribed norms may lead to sanctions, ranging from being hauled off by the police for indecent exposure to being laughed at by others for wearing a suit at the beach.
4. Conscious awareness of cultural standards is limited. One American spy was intercepted by the Germans during World War II simply because of the way he held his knife and fork while eating.
5. Cultures fall somewhere on a continuum between static and dynamic depending on how quickly they accept change. For example, American culture has changed a great deal since the 1950s, while the culture of Saudi Arabia has changed much less.

DEALING WITH CULTURE

Culture is a problematic issue for many marketers since it is inherently nebulous and often difficult to understand. One may violate the cultural norms of another country without being informed of this, and people from different cultures may feel uncomfortable in each other's presence without knowing exactly why (for example, two speakers may unconsciously continue to attempt to adjust to reach an incompatible preferred interpersonal distance).

WARNING ABOUT STEREOTYPING

When observing a culture, one must be careful not to over-generalize about traits that one sees. Research in social psychology has suggested a strong tendency for people to perceive an "outgroup" as more homogenous than an "ingroup," even when they knew what members had been assigned to each group purely by chance. When there is often a "grain of truth" to some of the perceived differences, the temptation to over-generalize is often strong. Note that there are often significant individual differences within cultures.

CULTURAL LESSONS

We considered several cultural lessons in class; the important thing here is the big picture. For example, within the Muslim tradition, the dog is considered a "dirty" animal, so portraying it as "man's best friend" in an advertisement is counter-productive. Packaging, seen as a reflection of the quality of the "real" product, is considerably more important in Asia than in the U.S., where there is a tendency to focus on the contents which "really count." Many cultures observe significantly greater levels of formality than that typical in the U.S., and Japanese negotiator tend to observe long silent pauses as a speaker's point is considered.

CULTURAL CHARACTERISTICS AS A CONTINUUM

There is a tendency to stereotype cultures as being one way or another (e.g., individualistic rather than collectivistic). Note, however, countries fall on a continuum of cultural traits. Hofstede's research demonstrates a wide range between the most individualistic and collectivistic countries, for example—some fall in the middle.

HOFSTEDE'S DIMENSIONS

Gert Hofstede, a Dutch researcher, was able to interview a large number of IBM executives in various countries, and found that cultural differences tended to center around four key dimensions:

- Individualism vs. collectivism: To what extent do people believe in individual responsibility and reward rather than having these measures aimed at the larger group? Contrary to the stereotype, Japan actually ranks in the middle of this dimension, while Indonesia and West Africa rank toward the collectivistic side. The U.S., Britain, and the Netherlands rate toward individualism.
- Power distance: To what extent is there a strong separation of individuals based on rank? Power distance tends to be particularly high in Arab countries and some Latin American ones, while it is more modest in Northern Europe and the U.S.
- Masculinity vs. femininity involves a somewhat more nebulous concept. "Masculine" values involve competition and "conquering" nature by means such as large construction projects, while "feminine" values involve harmony and environmental protection. Japan is one of the more masculine countries, while the Netherlands rank relatively low. The U.S. is close to the middle, slightly toward the masculine side. (The fact that these values are thought of as "masculine" or "feminine" does not mean that they are consistently held by members of each respective gender—there are very large "within-group" differences. There is, however, often a large correlation of these cultural values with the status of women.)

- Uncertainty avoidance involves the extent to which a "structured" situation with clear rules is preferred to a more ambiguous one; in general, countries with lower uncertainty avoidance tend to be more tolerant of risk. Japan ranks very high. Few countries are very low in any absolute sense, but relatively speaking, Britain and Hong Kong are lower, and the U.S. is in the lower range of the distribution.

Although Hofstede's original work did not address this, a fifth dimension of long term vs. short term orientation has been proposed. In the U.S., managers like to see quick results, while Japanese managers are known for take a long term view, often accepting long periods before profitability is obtained.

HIGH VS. LOW CONTEXT CULTURES

In some cultures, "what you see is what you get"—the speaker is expected to make his or her points clear and limit ambiguity. This is the case in the U.S.—if you have something on your mind, you are expected to say it directly, subject to some reasonable standards of diplomacy. In Japan, in contrast, facial expressions and what is not said may be an important clue to understanding a speaker's meaning. Thus, it may be very difficult for Japanese speakers to understand another's written communication. The nature of languages may exacerbate this phenomenon—while the German language is very precise, Chinese lacks many grammatical features, and the meaning of words may be somewhat less precise. English ranks somewhere in the middle of this continuum.

ETHNOCENTRISM AND THE SELF-REFERENCE CRITERION

The self-reference criterion refers to the tendency of individuals, often unconsciously, to use the standards of one's own culture to evaluate others. For example, Americans may perceive more traditional societies to be "backward" and "unmotivated" because they fail to adopt new technologies or social customs, seeking instead to preserve traditional values. In the 1960s, a supposedly well read American psychology professor referred to India's culture of "sick" because, despite severe food shortages, the Hindu religion did not allow the eating of cows. The psychologist expressed disgust that the cows were allowed to roam free in villages, although it turns out that they provided valuable functions by offering milk and fertilizing fields. Ethnocentrism is the tendency to view one's culture to be superior to others. The important thing here is to consider how these biases may come in the way in dealing with members of other cultures.

It should be noted that there is a tendency of outsiders to a culture to overstate the similarity of members of that culture to each other. In the United States, we are well aware that there is a great deal of heterogeneity within our culture; however, we often underestimate the diversity within other cultures. For example, in Latin America, there are great differences between people who live in coastal and mountainous areas; there are also great differences between social classes.

LANGUAGE ISSUES

Language is an important element of culture. It should be realized that regional differences may be subtle. For example, one word may mean one thing in one Latin American country, but something off-color in another. It should also be kept in mind that much information is carried in non-verbal communication. In some cultures, we nod to signify "yes" and shake our heads to signify "no;" in other cultures, the practice is reversed. Within the context of language:

- There are often large variations in regional dialects of a given language. The differences between U.S., Australian, and British English are actually modest compared to differences between dialects of Spanish and German.
- Idioms involve "figures of speech" that may not be used, literally translated, in other languages. For example, baseball is a predominantly North and South American sport, so the notion of "in the ball park" makes sense here, but the term does not carry the same meaning in cultures where the sport is less popular.
- Neologisms involve terms that have come into language relatively recently as technology or society involved. With the proliferation of computer technology, for example, the idea of an "add-on" became widely known. It may take longer for such terms to "diffuse" into other regions of the world. In parts of the World where English is heavily studied in schools, the emphasis is often on grammar and traditional language rather than on current terminology, so neologisms have a wide potential not to be understood.
- Slang exists within most languages. Again, regional variations are common and not all people in a region where slang is used

will necessarily understand this. There are often significant generation gaps in the use of slang.

In English and Northern European languages, there is an emphasis on organization and conciseness. Here, a point is made by building up to it through background. An introduction will often foreshadow what is to be said. In Romance languages such as Spanish, French, and Portuguese, this style is often considered "boring" and "inelegant." Detours are expected and are considered a sign of class, not of poor organization. In Asian languages, there is often a great deal of circularity. Because of concerns about potential loss of face, opinions may not be expressed directly. Instead, speakers may hint at ideas or indicate what others have said, waiting for feedback from the other speaker before committing to a point of view.

Because of differences in values, assumptions, and language structure, it is not possible to meaningfully translate "word-for-word" from one language to another. A translator must keep "unspoken understandings" and assumptions in mind in translating. The intended meaning of a word may also differ from its literal translation. For example, the Japanese word hai is literally translated as "yes." To Americans, that would imply "Yes, I agree." To the Japanese speaker, however, the word may mean "Yes, I hear what you are saying" (without any agreement expressed) or even "Yes, I hear you are saying something even though I am not sure exactly what you are saying."

Differences in cultural values result in different preferred methods of speech. In American English, where the individual is assumed to be more in control of his or her destiny than is the case in many other cultures, there is a preference for the "active" tense (e.g., "I wrote the marketing plan") as opposed to the passive (e.g., "The marketing plan was written by me.")

Because of the potential for misunderstandings in translations, it is dangerous to rely on a translation from one language to another made by one person. In the "decentering" method, multiple translators are used.

The text is first translated by one translator—say, from German to Mandarin Chinese. A second translator, who does not know what the original German text said, will then translate back to German from Mandarin Chinese translation. The text is then compared. If the meaning is not similar, a third translator, keeping in mind this feedback, will then translate from German to Mandarin. The process is continued until the translated meaning appears to be satisfactory.

Different perspectives exist in different cultures on several issues; e.g.:

- Monochronic cultures tend to value precise scheduling and doing one thing at a time; in polychronic cultures, in contrast, promptness is valued less, and multiple tasks may be performed simultaneously. (See text for more detail).
- Space is perceived differently. Americans will feel crowded where people from more densely populated countries will be comfortable.
- Symbols differ in meaning. For example, while white symbols purity in the U.S., it is a symbol of death in China. Colors that are considered masculine and feminine also differ by culture.
- Americans have a lot of quite shallow friends toward whom little obligation is felt; people in European and some Asian cultures have fewer, but more significant friends. For example, one Ph.D. student from India, with limited income, felt obligated to try buy an airline ticket for a friend to go back to India when a relative had died.
- In the U.S. and much of Europe, agreements are typically rather precise and contractual in nature; in Asia, there is a greater tendency to settle issues as they come up. As a result, building a relationship of trust is more important in Asia, since you must be able to count on your partner being reasonable.
- In terms of etiquette, some cultures have more rigid procedures than others. In some countries, for example, there are explicit standards as to how a gift should be presented. In some cultures, gifts should be presented in private to avoid embarrassing the recipient; in others, the gift should be made publicly to ensure that no perception of secret bribery could be made.

DEMOGRAPHICS

Demographics are clearly tied to subculture and segmentation. Here, however, we shift our focus from analyzing specific subcultures to trying to understand the implications for an entire population of its makeup.

Several issues are useful in the structure of a population. For example, in some rapidly growing countries, a large percentage of the population is concentrated among younger generations. In countries such as Korea,

China, and Taiwan, this has helped stimulate economic growth, while in certain poorer countries, it puts pressures on society to accommodate an increasing number of people on a fixed amount of land. Other countries such as Japan and Germany, in contrast, experience problems with a "graying" society, where fewer non-retired people are around to support an increasing number of aging seniors. Because Germany actually hovers around negative population growth, the German government has issued large financial incentives, in the forms of subsidies, for women who have children. In the United States, population growth occurs both through births and immigration. Since the number of births is not growing, problems occur for firms that are dependent on population growth (e.g., Gerber, a manufacturer of baby food).

Social class is a somewhat nebulous subject that involves stratifying people into groups with various amounts of prestige, power, and privilege. In part because of the pioneering influence in American history, status differentiations here are quite vague. We cannot, for example, associate social class with income, because a traditionally low status job as a plumber may today come with as much income as a traditionally more prestigious job as a school teacher. In certain other cultures, however, stratification is more clear-cut. Although the caste system in India is now illegal, it still maintains a tremendous influence on that society. While some mobility exists today, social class awareness is also somewhat greater in Britain, where social status is in part reinforced by the class connotations of the accent with which one speaks.

Textbooks speak of several indices that have been used to "compute" social class in the United States, weighing factors such as income, the nature of one's employment, and level of education. Taken too literally, these indices are not very meaningful; more broadly speaking, they illustrate the reality that social status is a complex variable that is determined, not always with consensus among observers, by several different variables.

SEGMENTATION, TARGETING, AND POSITIONING

Segmentation, targeting, and positioning together comprise a three stage process. We first (1) determine which kinds of customers exist, then (2) select which ones we are best off trying to serve and, finally, (3) implement our segmentation by optimizing our products/services for that segment and communicating that we have made the choice to distinguish ourselves that way.

Segmentation involves finding out what kinds of consumers with different needs exist. In the auto market, for example, some consumers demand speed and performance, while others are much more concerned about roominess and safety. In general, it holds true that "You can't be all things to all people," and experience has demonstrated that firms that specialize in meeting the needs of one group of consumers over another tend to be more profitable.

Generically, there are three approaches to marketing. In the undifferentiated strategy, all consumers are treated as the same, with firms not making any specific efforts to satisfy particular groups. This may work when the product is a standard one where one competitor really can't offer much that another one can't. Usually, this is the case only for commodities. In the concentrated strategy, one firm chooses to focus on one of several segments that exist while leaving other segments to competitors. For example, Southwest Airlines focuses on price sensitive consumers who will forego meals and assigned seating for low prices. In contrast, most airlines follow the differentiated strategy: They offer high priced tickets to those who are inflexible in that they cannot tell in advance when they need to fly and find it impractical to stay over a Saturday. These travelers—usually business travelers—pay high fares but can only fill the planes up partially. The same airlines then sell some of the remaining seats to more price sensitive customers who can buy two weeks in advance and stay over.

Note that segmentation calls for some tough choices. There may be a large number of variables that can be used to differentiate consumers of a given product category; yet, in practice, it becomes impossibly cumbersome to work with more than a few at a time. Thus, we need to determine which variables will be most useful in distinguishing different groups of consumers. We might thus decide, for example, that the variables that are most relevant in separating different kinds of soft drink consumers are (1) preference for taste vs. low calories, (2) preference for Cola vs. non-cola taste, (3) price sensitivity—willingness to pay for brand names; and (4) heavy vs. light consumers. We now put these variables together to arrive at various combinations.

Several different kinds of variables can be used for segmentation.

- Demographic variables essentially refer to personal statistics such as income, gender, education, location (rural vs. urban, East vs. West), ethnicity, and family size. Campbell's soup, for instance, has found that Western U.S. consumers on the average prefer spicier soups—thus, you get a different product in the same cans at the East and West coasts. Facing flat sales of guns in the traditional male dominated market, a manufacturer came out with the Lady Remmington, a more compact, handier gun more attractive to women. Taking this a step farther, it is also possible to segment on lifestyle and values."

- Some consumers want to be seen as similar to others, while a different segment wants to stand apart from the crowd.
- Another basis for segmentation is behavior. Some consumers are "brand loyal"—i.e., they tend to stick with their preferred brands even when a competing one is on sale. Some consumers are "heavy" users while others are "light" users. For example, research conducted by the wine industry shows that some 80% of the product is consumed by 20% of the consumers—presumably a rather intoxicated group.
- One can also segment on benefits sought, essentially bypassing demographic explanatory variables. Some consumers, for example, like scented soap (a segment likely to be attracted to brands such as Irish Spring), while others prefer the "clean" feeling of unscented soap (the "Ivory" segment). Some consumers use toothpaste primarily to promote oral health, while another segment is more interested in breath freshening.

In the next step, we decide to target one or more segments. Our choice should generally depend on several factors. First, how well are existing segments served by other manufacturers? It will be more difficult to appeal to a segment that is already well served than to one whose needs are not currently being served well. Secondly, how large is the segment, and how can we expect it to grow? (Note that a downside to a large, rapidly growing segment is that it tends to attract competition). Thirdly, do we have strengths as a company that will help us appeal particularly to one group of consumers? Firms may already have an established reputation. While McDonald's has a great reputation for fast, consistent quality, family friendly food, it would be difficult to convince consumers that McDonald's now offers gourmet food. Thus, McD's would probably be better off targeting families in search of consistent quality food in nice, clean restaurants.

Positioning involves implementing our targeting. For example, Apple Computer has chosen to position itself as a maker of user-friendly computers. Thus, Apple has done a lot through its advertising to promote itself, through its unintimidating icons, as a computer for "non-geeks."

The Visual C software programming language, in contrast, is aimed a "techies."

Michael Treacy and Fred Wiersema suggested in their 1993 book The Discipline of Market Leaders that most successful firms fall into one of three categories:

- Operationally excellent firms, which maintain a strong competitive advantage by maintaining exceptional efficiency, thus enabling the firm to provide reliable service to the customer at a significantly lower cost than those of less well organized and well run competitors. The emphasis here is mostly on low cost, subject to reliable performance, and less value is put on customizing the offering for the specific customer. Wal-Mart is an example of this discipline. Elaborate logistical designs allow goods to be moved at the lowest cost, with extensive systems predicting when specific quantities of supplies will be needed.
- Customer intimate firms, which excel in serving the specific needs of the individual customer well. There is less emphasis on efficiency, which is sacrificed for providing more precisely what is wanted by the customer. Reliability is also stressed. Nordstrom's and IBM are examples of this discipline.
- Technologically excellent firms, which produce the most advanced products currently available with the latest technology, constantly maintaining leadership in innovation. These firms, because they work with costly technology that need constant refinement, cannot be as efficient as the operationally excellent firms and often cannot adapt their products as well to the needs of the individual customer. Intel is an example of this discipline.

Treacy and Wiersema suggest that in addition to excelling on one of the three value dimensions, firms must meet acceptable levels on the other two. Wal-Mart, for example, does maintain some level of customer service. Nordstrom's and Intel both must meet some standards of cost effectiveness. The emphasis, beyond meeting the minimum required level in the two other dimensions, is on the dimension of strength.

Repositioning involves an attempt to change consumer perceptions of a brand, usually because the existing position that the brand holds has become less attractive. Sears, for example, attempted to reposition itself from a place that offered great sales but unattractive prices the rest of the time to a store that consistently offered "everyday low prices." Repositioning in practice is very difficult to accomplish. A great deal of money is often needed for advertising and other promotional efforts, and in many cases, the repositioning fails.

To effectively attempt repositioning, it is important to understand how one's brand and those of competitors are perceived. One approach to identifying consumer product perceptions is multidimensional scaling. Here, we identify how products are perceived on two or more "dimensions," allowing us to plot brands against each other. It may then be possible to attempt to "move" one's brand in a more desirable direction by selectively promoting certain points. There are two main approaches to multi-dimensional scaling. In the a priori approach, market researchers identify dimensions of interest and then ask consumers about their perceptions on each dimension for each brand. This is useful when (1) the market researcher knows which dimensions are of interest and (2) the customer's perception on each dimension is relatively clear (as opposed to being "made up" on the spot to be able to give the researcher a desired answer). In the similarity rating approach, respondents are not asked about their perceptions of brands on any specific dimensions. Instead, subjects are asked to rate the extent of similarity of different pairs of products (e.g., How similar, on a scale of 1-7, is Snicker's to Kitkat, and how similar is Toblerone to Three Musketeers?) Using a computer algorithms, the computer then identifies positions of each brand on a map of a given number of dimensions. The computer does not reveal what each dimension means—that must be left to human interpretation based on what the variations in each dimension appears to reveal. This second method is more useful when no specific product dimensions have been identified as being of particular interest or when it is not clear what the variables of difference are for the product category.

INFORMATION SEARCH AND DECISION MAKING

One model of consumer decision making involves several steps. The first one is problem recognition—you realize that something is not as it should be. Perhaps, for example, your car is getting more difficult to start and is not accelerating well. The second step is information search—what are some alternative ways of solving the problem? You might buy a new car, buy a used car, take your car in for repair, ride the bus, ride a taxi, or ride a skateboard to work. The third step involves evaluation of alternatives. A skateboard is inexpensive, but may be ill-suited for long distances and for rainy days. Finally, we have the purchase stage, and sometimes a post-purchase stage (e.g., you return a product to the store because you did not find it satisfactory). In reality, people may go back and forth between the stages.

Consumer involvement will tend to vary dramatically depending on the type of product. In general, consumer involvement will be higher for products that are very expensive (e.g., a home, a car) or are highly significant in the consumer's life in some other way (e.g., a word processing program or acne medication).

It is important to consider the consumer's motivation for buying products. To achieve this goal, we can use the Means-End chain, wherein we consider a logical progression of consequences of product use that eventually lead to desired end benefit. Thus, for example, a consumer may see that a car has a large engine, leading to fast acceleration, leading to a feeling of performance, leading to a feeling of power, which ultimately improves the consumer's self-esteem. A handgun may aim bullets with precision, which enables the user to kill an intruder, which means that the intruder will not be able to harm the consumer's family, which achieves the desired end-state of security. In advertising, it is important to portray the desired end-states. Focusing on the large motor will do less good than portraying a successful person driving the car.

Consumers engage in both internal and external information search. Internal search involves the consumer identifying alternatives from his or her memory. For certain low involvement products, it is very important that marketing programs achieve "top of mind" awareness. For example, few people will search the Yellow Pages for fast food restaurants; thus, the consumer must be able to retrieve one's restaurant from memory before it will be considered. For high involvement products, consumers are more likely to use an external search. Before buying a car, for example, the consumer may ask friends' opinions, read reviews in Consumer Reports, consult several web sites, and visit several dealerships. Thus, firms that make products that are selected predominantly through external search must invest in having information available to the consumer in need—e.g., through brochures, web sites, or news coverage.

A compensatory decision involves the consumer "trading off" good and bad attributes of a product. For example, a car may have a low price and good gas mileage but slow acceleration. If the price is sufficiently inexpensive and gas efficient, the consumer may then select it over a car with better acceleration that costs more and uses more gas. Occasionally, a decision will involve a non-compensatory strategy. For example, a parent may reject all soft drinks that contain artificial sweeteners. Here, other good features such as taste and low calories cannot overcome this one "non-negotiable" attribute.

The amount of effort a consumer puts into searching depends on a number of factors such as the market (how many competitors are there, and how great are differences between brands expected to be?), product characteristics (how important is this product? How complex is the product? How obvious are indications of quality?), consumer characteristics (how interested is a consumer, generally, in analyzing product characteristics and making the best possible deal?), and situational characteristics (as previously discussed).

Two interesting issues in decisions are:

- Variety seeking (where consumers seek to try new brands not because these brands are expected to be "better" in any way, but rather because the consumer wants a "change of pace," and
- "Impulse" purchases—unplanned buys. This represents a somewhat "fuzzy" group. For example, a shopper may plan to buy vegetables but only decide in the store to actually buy broccoli and corn. Alternatively, a person may buy an item which is currently on sale, or one that he or she remembers that is needed only once inside the store.

A number of factors involve consumer choices. In some cases, consumers will be more motivated. For example, one may be more careful choosing a gift for an in-law than when buying the same thing for one self. Some consumers are also more motivated to comparison shop for the best prices, while others are more convenience oriented. Personality impacts decisions. Some like variety more than others, and some are more receptive to stimulation and excitement in trying new stores. Perception influences decisions. Some people, for example, can taste the difference between generic and name brand foods while many cannot. Selective perception occurs when a person is paying attention only to information of interest. For example, when looking for a new car, the consumer may pay more attention to car ads than when this is not in the horizon. Some consumers are put off by perceived risk. Thus, many marketers offer a money back guarantee. Consumers will tend to change their behavior through learning—e.g., they will avoid restaurants they have found to be crowded and will settle on brands that best meet their tastes. Consumers differ in the values they hold (e.g., some people are more committed to recycling than others who will not want to go through the hassle). We will consider the issue of lifestyle under segmentation.

FAMILIES AND FAMILY DECISION MAKING

The Family Life Cycle. Individuals and families tend to go through a "life cycle:" For purposes of this discussion, a "couple" may either be married or merely involve living together. The breakup of a non-marital relationship involving cohabitation is similarly considered equivalent to a divorce.

In real life, this situation is, of course, a bit more complicated. For example, many couples undergo divorce. Then we have one of the scenarios:

Single parenthood can result either from divorce or from the death of one parent. Divorce usually entails a significant change in the relative wealth of spouses. In some cases, the non-custodial parent (usually the father) will not pay the required child support, and even if he or she does, that still may not leave the custodial parent and children as well off as they were during the marriage. On the other hand, in some cases, some non-custodial parents will be called on to pay a large part of their income in child support. This is particularly a problem when the non-custodial parent remarries and has additional children in the second (or subsequent marriages). In any event, divorce often results in a large demand for:

- Low cost furniture and household items
- Time-saving goods and services

Divorced parents frequently remarry, or become involved in other non-marital relationships; thus, we may see

Another variation involves the single parent who assumes responsibility for one or more children may not form a relationship with the other parent of the child.

Integrating all the possibilities discussed, we get the following depiction of the Family Life Cycle:

Generally, there are two main themes in the Family Life Cycle, subject to significant exceptions:

- As a person gets older, he or she tends to advance in his or her career and tends to get greater income (exceptions: maternity leave, divorce, retirement).

- Unfortunately, obligations also tend to increase with time (at least until one's mortgage has been paid off). Children and paying for one's house are two of the greatest expenses.

Note that although a single person may have a lower income than a married couple, the single may be able to buy more discretionary items.

FAMILY DECISION MAKING

Individual members of families often serve different roles in decisions that ultimately draw on shared family resources. Some individuals are information gatherers/holders, who seek out information about products of relevance. These individuals often have a great deal of power because they may selectively pass on information that favors their chosen alternatives. Influencers do not ultimately have the power decide between alternatives, but they may make their wishes known by asking for specific products or causing embarrassing situations if their demands are not met. The decision maker(s) have the power to determine issues such as:

- Whether to buy;
- Which product to buy (pick-up or passenger car?);
- Which brand to buy;
- Where to buy it; and
- When to buy.

Note, however, that the role of the decision maker is separate from that of the purchaser. From the point of view of the marketer, this introduces some problems since the purchaser can be targeted by point-of-purchase (POP) marketing efforts that cannot be aimed at the decision maker. Also note that the distinction between the purchaser and decision maker may be somewhat blurred:

- The decision maker may specify what kind of product to buy, but not which brand;
- The purchaser may have to make a substitution if the desired brand is not in stock;
- The purchaser may disregard instructions (by error or deliberately).

It should be noted that family decisions are often subject to a great deal of conflict. The reality is that few families are wealthy enough to avoid a strong tension between demands on the family's resources. Conflicting pressures are especially likely in families with children and/or when only one spouse works outside the home. Note that many decisions inherently come down to values, and that there is frequently no "objective" way to arbitrate differences. One spouse may believe that it is important to save for the children's future; the other may value spending now (on private schools and computer equipment) to help prepare the children for the future. Who is right? There is no clear answer here. The situation becomes even more complex when more parties—such as children or other relatives—are involved.

Some family members may resort to various strategies to get their way. One is bargaining—one member will give up something in return for someone else. For example, the wife says that her husband can take an expensive course in gourmet cooking if she can buy a new pickup truck. Alternatively, a child may promise to walk it every day if he or she can have a hippopotamus. Another strategy is reasoning—trying to get the other person(s) to accept one's view through logical argumentation. Note that even when this is done with a sincere intent, its potential is limited by legitimate differences in values illustrated above.

Also note that individuals may simply try to "wear down" the other party by endless talking in the guise of reasoning (this is a case of negative reinforcement as we will see subsequently). Various manipulative strategies may also be used. One is impression management, where one tries to make one's side look good (e.g., argue that a new TV will help the children see educational TV when it is really mostly wanted to see sports programming, or argue that all "decent families make a contribution to the church"). Authority involves asserting one's "right" to make a decision (as the "man of the house," the mother of the children, or the one who makes the most money). Emotion involves making an emotional display to get one's way (e.g., a man cries if his wife will not let him buy a new rap album).

GROUP INFLUENCES

Humans are inherently social animals, and individuals greatly influence each other.

A useful framework of analysis of group influence on the individual is the so called reference group—the term comes about because an individual uses a relevant group as a standard of reference against which oneself is compared. Reference groups come in several different forms.

- The aspirational reference group refers to those others against whom one would like to compare oneself. For example, many firms use athletes as spokespeople, and these represent what many people would ideally like to be.

- Associative reference groups include people who more realistically represent the individuals' current equals or near-equals—e.g., coworkers, neighbors, or members of churches, clubs, and organizations. Paco Underhill, a former anthropologist turned retail consultant and author of the book Why We Buy has performed research suggesting that among many teenagers, the process of clothes buying is a two stage process. In the first stage, the teenagers go on a "reconnaissance" mission with their friends to find out what is available and what is "cool." This is often a lengthy process. In the later phase, parents—who will need to pay for the purchases—are brought. This stage is typically much briefer.
- Finally, the dissociative reference group includes people that the individual would not like to be like. For example, the store literally named The Gap came about because many younger people wanted to actively dissociate from parents and other older and "uncool" people. The Quality Paperback Book Club specifically suggests in its advertising that its members are "a breed apart" from conventional readers of popular books.

Reference groups come with various degrees of influence. Primary reference groups come with a great deal of influence—e.g., members of a fraternity/sorority. Secondary reference groups tend to have somewhat less influence—e.g., members of a boating club that one encounters only during week-ends are likely to have their influence limited to consumption during that time period.

Another typology divides reference groups into the informational kind (influence is based almost entirely on members' knowledge), normative (members influence what is perceived to be "right," "proper," "responsible," or "cool"), or identification. The difference between the latter two categories involves the individual's motivation for compliance. In case of the normative reference group, the individual tends to comply largely for utilitarian reasons—dressing according to company standards is likely to help your career, but there is no real motivation to dress that way outside the job. In contrast, people comply with identification groups' standards for the sake of belonging—for example, a member of a religious group may wear a symbol even outside the house of worship because the religion is a part of the person's identity.

PERCEPTION

Background. Our perception is an approximation of reality. Our brain attempts to make sense out of the stimuli to which we are exposed. This works well, for example, when we "see" a friend three hundred feet away at his or her correct height; however, our perception is sometimes "off"—for example, certain shapes of ice cream containers look like they contain more than rectangular ones with the same volume.

FACTORS IN PERCEPTION

Several sequential factors influence our perception. Exposure involves the extent to which we encounter a stimulus. For example, we are exposed to numerous commercial messages while driving on the freeway: bill boards, radio advertisements, bumper-stickers on cars, and signs and banners placed at shopping malls that we pass. Most of this exposure is random—we don't plan to seek it out. However, if we are shopping for a car, we may deliberately seek out advertisements and "tune in" when dealer advertisements come on the radio.

Exposure is not enough to significantly impact the individual—at least not based on a single trial (certain advertisements, or commercial exposures such as the "Swoosh" logo, are based on extensive repetition rather than much conscious attention). In order for stimuli to be consciously processed, attention is needed. Attention is actually a matter of degree—our attention may be quite high when we read directions for getting an income tax refund, but low when commercials come on during a television program. Note, however, that even when attention is low, it may be instantly escalated—for example, if an advertisement for a product in which we are interested comes on.

Interpretation involves making sense out of the stimulus. For example, when we see a red can, we may categorize it as a CokeÒ.

Weber's Law suggests that consumers' ability to detect changes in stimulus intensity appear to be strongly related to the intensity of that stimulus to begin with. That is, if you hold an object weighing one pound in your hand, you are likely to notice it when that weight is doubled to two pounds. However, if you are holding twenty pounds, you are unlikely to detect the addition of one pound—a change that you easily detected when the initial weight was one pound. You may be able to eliminate one ounce from a ten ounce container, but you cannot as easily get away with reducing a three ounce container to two (instead, you must accomplish that gradually—e.g., 3.0 —> 2.7 —> 2.5 —> 2.3 —> 2.15 -> 2.00).

Several factors influence the extent to which stimuli will be noticed. One obvious issue is relevance. Consumers, when they have a choice, are also more likely to attend to pleasant stimuli (but when the consumer can't escape, very unpleasant stimuli are also likely to get attention—thus, many very irritating advertisements are remarkably effective). One of the most important factors, however, is repetition. Consumers often do not give much attention to a stimuli—particularly a low priority one such as an advertisement—at any one time, but if it is seen over and over again, the cumulative impact will be greater.

Surprising stimuli are likely to get more attention—survival instinct requires us to give more attention to something unknown that may require action. A greater contrast (difference between the stimulus and its surroundings) as well as greater prominence (e.g., greater size, center placement) also tend to increase likelihood of processing.

Subliminal stimuli. Back in the 1960s, it was reported that on selected evenings, movie goers in a theater had been exposed to isolated frames with the words "Drink Coca Cola" and "Eat Popcorn" imbedded into the movie. These frames went by so fast that people did not consciously notice them, but it was reported that on nights with frames present, Coke and popcorn sales were significantly higher than on days they were left off. This led Congress to ban the use of subliminal advertising. First of all, there is a question as to whether this experiment ever took place or whether this information was simply made up. Secondly, no one has been able to replicate these findings. There is research to show that people will start to giggle with embarrassment when they are briefly exposed to "dirty" words in an experimental machine. Here, again, the exposure is so brief that the subjects are not aware of the actual words they saw, but it is evident that something has been recognized by the embarrassment displayed.

LEARNING AND MEMORY

Background. Learning involves "a change in the content or organization of long term memory and/or behavior." The first part of the definition focuses on what we know (and can thus put to use) while the second focuses on concrete behavior. For example, many people will avoid foods that they consumed shortly before becoming ill. Learning is not all knowledge based. For example, we may experience the sales people in one store being nicer to us than those in the other. We thus may develop a preference for the one store over the other; however, if pressed, we may not be able to give a conscious explanation as to the reason for our preference.

Much early work on learning was actually done on rats and other animals (and much of this research was unjustifiably cruel, but that is another matter).

Classical conditioning. Pavlov's early work on dogs was known as classical conditioning. Pavlov discovered that when dogs were fed meat powder they salivated. Pavlov then discovered that if a bell were rung before the dogs were fed, the dogs would begin salivating in anticipation of being fed (this was efficient, since they could then begin digesting the meat powder immediately). Pavlov then found that after the meat had been "paired" with the meat powder enough times, Pavlov could ring the bell without feeding the dogs and they would still salivate.

In the jargon of classical conditioning, the meat powder was an unconditioned stimulus (US) and the salivation was, when preceded by the meat powder, an unconditioned response (UR). That is, it is a biologically "hard-wired" response to salivate when you are fed. By pairing the bell with the unconditioned stimulus, the bell became a conditioned stimulus (CS) and salivation in response to the bell (with no meat powder) became a conditioned response (CR).

Operant conditioning. Instrumental, or operant, conditioning, involves a different series of events, and this what we usually think of as learning.

There are three major forms of operant learning. In positive reinforcement, an individual does something and is rewarded. He or she is then more likely to repeat the behavior. For example, you eat a candy bar (behavior), it tastes good (consequence), and you are thus more likely to eat a similar candy bar in the future (behavioral change). Punishment is the opposite. You eat what looks like a piece of candy (behavior), only to discover that it is a piece of soap with a foul taste (consequences), and subsequently you are less likely to eat anything that looks remotely like that thing ever again (changed behavior).

It should be noted that negative reinforcement is very different from punishment. An example of negative reinforcement is an obnoxious sales person who calls you up on the phone, pressuring you into buying something you don't want to do (aversive stimulus). You eventually agree to buy it (changed behavior), and the sales person leaves you alone (the aversive stimulus is terminated as a result of consequences of your behavior).

In general, marketers usually have relatively little power to use punishment or negative reinforcement. However, parking meters are often used to discourage consumers from taking up valuable parking space, and manufacturers may void warranties if the consumers take their product to non-authorized repair facilities.

Several factors influence the effectiveness of operant learning. In general, the closer in time the consequences are to the behavior, the more effective the learning. That is, electric utilities would be more likely to influence consumers to use less electricity at peak hours if the consumers actually had to pay when they used electricity (e.g., through a coin-slot) rather than at the end of the month. Learning is also more likely to occur when the individual can understand a relationship between behavior and consequences (but learning may occur even if this relationship is not understood consciously).

Another issue is schedules of reinforcement and extinction. Extinction occurs when behavior stops having consequences and the behavior then eventually stops occurring. For example, if a passenger learns that yelling at check-in personnel no longer gets her upgraded to first class, she will probably stop that behavior. Sometimes, an individual is rewarded every time a behavior is performed (e.g., a consumer gets a soft drink every time coins are put into a vending machine). However, it is not necessary to reward a behavior every time for learning to occur. Even if a behavior is only rewarded some of the time, the behavior may be learned. Several different schedules of reinforcement are possible:

- Fixed interval: The consumer is given a free dessert on every Tuesday when he or she eats in a particular restaurant.
- Fixed ratio: Behavior is rewarded (or punished) on every nth occasion that it is performed. (E.g., every tenth time a frequent shopper card is presented, a free product is provided).
- Variable ratio: Every time an action is performed, there is a certain percentage chance that a reward will be given. For example, every time the consumer enters the store, he or she is given a lottery ticket. With each ticket, there is a 20% chance of getting a free hamburger. The consumer may get a free hamburger twice in a row, or he or she may go ten times without getting a hamburger even once.

Variable ratio reinforcement is least vulnerable to extinction.

Sometimes, shaping may be necessary to teach the consumer the desired behavior. That is, it may be impossible to teach the consumer to directly perform the desired behavior. For example, a consumer may first get a good product for free (the product itself, if good, is a reward), then buy it with a large cents off coupon, and finally buy it at full price. Thus, we reinforce approximations of the desired behavior. Rather than introducing Coca Cola directly in Indonesia, fruit flavored soft drinks were first introduced, since these were more similar to beverages already consumed.

VICARIOUS LEARNING

The consumer does not always need to go through the learning process himself or herself—sometimes it is possible to learn from observing the consequences of others. For example, stores may make a big deal out of prosecuting shop lifters not so much because they want to stop that behavior in the those caught, but rather to deter the behavior in others. Similarly, viewers may empathize with characters in advertisements who experience (usually positive) results from using a product. The Head 'n' Shoulders advertisement, where a poor man is rejected by women until he treats his dandruff with an effective cure, is a good example of vicarious learning.

Memory ranges in duration on a continuum from extremely short to very long term. Sensory memory includes storage of stimuli that one might not actually notice (e.g., the color of an advertisement some distance away). For slightly longer duration, when you see an ad on TV for a mail order product you might like to buy, you only keep the phone number in memory until you have dialed it. This is known as short term memory. In order for something to enter into long term memory, which is more permanent, you must usually "rehearse" it several times. For example, when you move and get a new phone number, you will probably repeat it to yourself many times. Alternatively, you get to learn your driver's license or social security numbers with time, not because you deliberately memorize them, but instead because you encounter them numerous times as you look them up.

Several techniques can be used to enhance the memorability of information. "Chunking" involves rearranging information so that fewer parts need to be remembered. For example, consider the phone number (800) 444-1000. The eight digits can be more economically remembered as an 800 number (1 piece), four repeated 3 times (2 pieces), and 1000 (1-2 pieces). "Rehearsal" involves the consumer repeating the information over and over so that it can be remembered; this is often done so that a phone number can be remembered while the "memoree" moves to the phone to dial it. "Recirculation" involves repeated exposure to the same information; the information is not learned deliberately, but is gradually absorbed through repetition. Thus, it is to the advantage to a marketer to have an advertisement repeated extensively—especially the brand name. "Elaboration" involves the consumer thinking about the object—e.g., the product in an advertisement—and thinking about as many related issues as possible. For example, when seeing an ad for Dole bananas, the person may think of the color yellow, going to the zoo seeing a monkey eating a banana, and her grandmother's banana-but bread. The Dole brand name may then be activated when any of those stimuli are encountered.

Memories are not always easily retrievable. This could be because the information was given lower priority than something else—e.g., we have done a lot of things since last buying a replacement furnace filter and cannot remember where this was bought last. Other times, the information can be retrieved but is not readily "available"—e.g., we will be able to remember the location of a restaurant we tried last time we were in Paris, but it may take some thinking before the information emerges.

"Spreading activation" involves the idea of one memory "triggering" another one. For example, one might think of Coke every time one remembers a favorite (and very wise) professor who frequently brought one to class. Coke might also be tied a particular supermarket that always stacked a lot of these beverages by the entrance, and to baseball where this beverage was consumed after the game. It is useful for firms to have their product be activated by as many other stimuli as possible.

There are numerous reasons why retrieval can fail or, in less fancy terms, how we come to forget. One is decay. Here, information that is not accessed frequently essentially "rusts" away. For example, we may not remember the phone number of a friend to whom we have not spoken for several months and may forget what brand of bullets an aunt prefers if we have not gone ammunition shopping with her lately. Other times, the problem may rest in interference. Proactive interference involves something we have learned interfering with what we will late later. Thus, if we remember that everyone in our family always used Tide, we may have more difficulty later remembering what other brands are available. You may be unable to remember what a new, and less important, friend's last name is if that person shares a first name with an old friend. For example, if your best friend for many years has been Jennifer Smith, you may have difficulty remembering that your new friend Jennifer's last name is Silverman. In retroactive interference, the problem is the reverse—learning something new blocks out something old. For example, if you once used WordPerfect than then switched to Microsoft Word, you may have trouble remembering how to use WordPerfect at a friend's house—more so than if you had merely not used any word processing program for some time.

Memorability can be enhanced under certain conditions. One is more likely to remember favorable—or likable stimuli (all other things being equal). Salience—or the extent to which something is highly emphasized or very clearly evident—facilitates memory. Thus, a product which is very visible in an ad, and handled and given attention by the actors, will more likely be remembered. Prototypicality involves the extent to which a stimulus is a "perfect" example of a category.

Therefore, people will more likely remember Coke or Kleenex than competing brands. Congruence involves the "fit" with a situation. Since memory is often reconstructed based on what seems plausible, something featured in an appropriate setting—e.g., charcoal on a porch next to a grill rather than in a garage or kitchen—is more likely to be remembered (unless the incongruence triggers an elaboration—life is complicated!) Redundancies involve showing the stimulus several times. Thus, if a given product is shown several places in a house—and if the brand name is repeated—it is more likely to be remembered.

Priming involves tying a stimulus with something so that if "that something" is encountered, the stimulus is more likely to be retrieved. Thus, for example, when one thinks of anniversaries, the Hallmark brand name is more likely to be activated. (This is a special case of spreading activation discussed earlier).

A special issue in memory are so called "scripts," or procedures we remember for doing things. Scripts involve a series of steps for doing various things (e.g., how to send a package). In general, it is useful for firms to have their brand names incorporated into scripts (e.g., to have the consumer reflexively ask the pharmacist for Bayer rather than an unspecified brand of aspirin).

Positioning involves implementing our targeting. For example, Apple Computer has chosen to position itself as a maker of user-friendly computers. Thus, Apple has done a lot through its advertising to promote itself, through its unintimidating icons, as a computer for "non-geeks." The Visual C software programming language, in contrast, is aimed a "techies."

Repositioning involves an attempt to change consumer perceptions of a brand, usually because the existing position that the brand holds has become less attractive. Sears, for example, attempted to reposition itself from a place that offered great sales but unattractive prices the rest of the time to a store that consistently offered "everyday low prices." Repositioning in practice is very difficult to accomplish. A great deal of money is often needed for advertising and other promotional efforts, and in many cases, the repositioning fails.

DIFFUSION OF INNOVATION

Products tend to go through a life cycle. Initially, a product is introduced. Since the product is not well known and is usually expensive (e.g., as microwave ovens were in the late 1970s), sales are usually limited. Eventually, however, many products reach a growth phase—sales increase dramatically. More firms enter with their models of the product. Frequently, unfortunately, the product will reach a maturity stage where little growth will be seen. For example, in the United States, almost every household has at least one color TV set. Some products may also reach a decline stage, usually because the product category is being replaced by something better. For example, typewriters experienced declining sales as more consumers switched to computers or other word processing equipment. The product life cycle is tied to the phenomenon of diffusion of innovation. When a new product comes out, it is likely to first be adopted by consumers who are more innovative than others—they are willing to pay a premium price for the new product and take a risk on unproven technology. It is important to be on the good side of innovators since many other later adopters will tend to rely for advice on the innovators who are thought to be more knowledgeable about new products for advice.

At later phases of the PLC, the firm may need to modify its market strategy. For example, facing a saturated market for baking soda in its traditional use, Arm ü Hammer launched a major campaign to get consumers to use the product to deodorize refrigerators. Deodorizing powders to be used before vacuuming were also created.

It is sometimes useful to think of products as being either new or existing.

Many firms today rely increasingly on new products for a large part of their sales. New products can be new in several ways. They can be new to the market—noone else ever made a product like this before. For example, Chrysler invented the minivan. Products can also be new to the firm—another firm invented the product, but the firm is now making its own version. For example, IBM did not invent the personal computer, but entered after other firms showed the market to have a high potential. Products can be new to the segment—e.g., cellular phones and pagers were first aimed at physicians and other price-insensitive segments. Later, firms decided to target the more price-sensitive mass market. A product can be new for legal purposes. Because consumers tend to be attracted to "new and improved" products, the Federal Trade Commission (FTC) only allows firms to put that label on reformulated products for six months after a significant change has been made.

The diffusion of innovation refers to the tendency of new products, practices, or ideas to spread among people. Usually, when new products or ideas come about, they are only adopted by a small group of people initially; later, many innovations spread to other people.

The bell shaped curve frequently illustrates the rate of adoption of a new product. Cumulative adoptions are reflected by the S-shaped curve. The saturation point is the maximum proportion of consumers likely to adopt a product.

In the case of refrigerators in the U.S., the saturation level is nearly one hundred percent of households; it well below that for video games that, even when spread out to a large part of the population, will be of interest to far from everyone.

Several specific product categories have case histories that illustrate important issues in adoption. Until some time in the 1800s, few physicians bothered to scrub prior to surgery, even though new scientific theories predicted that small microbes not visible to the naked eye could cause infection. Younger and more progressive physicians began scrubbing early on, but they lacked the stature to make their older colleagues follow.

ATM cards spread relatively quickly. Since the cards were used in public, others who did not yet hold the cards could see how convenient they were. Although some people were concerned about security, the convenience factors seemed to be a decisive factor in the "tug-of-war" for and against adoption.

The case of credit cards was a bit more complicated and involved a "chicken-and-egg" paradox. Accepting credit cards was not a particularly attractive option for retailers until they were carried by a large enough number of consumers. Consumers, in contrast, were not particularly interested in cards that were not accepted by a large number of retailers. Thus, it was necessary to "jump start" the process, signing up large corporate accounts, under favorable terms, early in the cycle, after which the cards became worthwhile for retailers to accept.

Rap music initially spread quickly among urban youths in large part because of the low costs of recording. Later, rap music became popular among a very different segment, suburban youths, because of its apparently authentic depiction of an exotic urban lifestyle.

Hybrid corn was adopted only slowly among many farmers. Although hybrid corn provided yields of about 20% more than traditional corn, many farmers had difficulty believing that this smaller seed could provide a superior harvest. They were usually reluctant to try it because a failed harvest could have serious economic consequences, including a possible loss of the farm. Agricultural extension agents then sought out the most progressive farmers to try hybrid corn, also aiming for farmers who were most respected and most likely to be imitated by others. Few farmers switched to hybrid corn outright from year to year. Instead, many started out with a fraction of their land, and gradually switched to 100% hybrid corn when this innovation had proven itself useful.

Several forces often work against innovation. One is risk, which can be either social or financial. For example, early buyers of the CD player risked that few CDs would be recorded before the CD player went the way of the 8 track player. Another risk is being perceived by others as being weird for trying a "fringe" product or idea. For example, Barbara Mandrell sings the song "I Was Country When Country Wasn't Cool." Other sources of resistance include the initial effort needed to learn to use new products (e.g., it takes time to learn to meditate or to learn how to use a computer) and concerns about compatibility with the existing culture or technology. For example, birth control is incompatible with strong religious influences in countries heavily influenced by Islam or Catholicism, and a computer database is incompatible with a large, established card file.

Innovations come in different degrees. A continuous innovation includes slight improvements over time. Very little usually changes from year to year in automobiles, and even automobiles of the 1990s are driven much the same way that automobiles of the 1950 were driven. A dynamically continuous innovation involves some change in technology, although the product is used much the same way that its predecessors were used—e.g., jet vs. propeller aircraft. A discontinous innovation involves a product that fundamentally changes the way that things are done—e.g., the fax and photocopiers. In general, discontinuous innovations are more difficult to market since greater changes are required in the way things are done, but the rewards are also often significant.

Several factors influence the speed with which an innovation spreads. One issue is relative advantage (i.e., the ratio of risk or cost to benefits). Some products, such as cellular phones, fax machines, and ATM cards, have a strong relative advantage. Other products, such as automobile satellite navigation systems, entail some advantages, but the cost ratio is high. Lower priced products often spread more quickly, and the extent to which the product is trialable (farmers did not have to plant all their land with hybrid corn at once, while one usually has to buy a cellular phone to try it out) influence the speed of diffusion. Finally, the extent of switching difficulties influences speed—many offices were slow to adopt computers because users had to learn how to use them.

Some cultures tend to adopt new products more quickly than others, based on several factors:

- Modernity: The extent to which the culture is receptive to new things. In some countries, such as Britain and Saudi Arabia, tradition is greatly valued—thus, new products often don't fare too well. The United States, in contrast, tends to value progress.
- Homophily: The more similar to each other that members of a culture are, the more likely an innovation is to spread—people are more likely to imitate similar than different models. The two most rapidly adopting countries in the World are the U.S. and Japan. While the U.S. interestingly scores very low, Japan scores high.
- Physical distance: The greater the distance between people, the less likely innovation is to spread.
- Opinion leadership: The more opinion leaders are valued and respected, the more likely an innovation is to spread. The style of opinion leaders moderates this influence, however. In less innovative countries, opinion leaders tend to be more conservative, i.e., to reflect the local norms of resistance.

It should be noted that innovation is not always an unqualifiedly good thing. Some innovations, such as infant formula adopted in developing countries, may do more harm than good. Individuals may also become dependent on the innovations. For example, travel agents who get used to booking online may be unable to process manual reservations.

Sometimes innovations are disadopted. For example, many individuals disadopt cellular phones if they find out that they don't end up using them much.

ATTITUDES

Consumer attitudes are a composite of a consumer's (1) beliefs about, (2) feelings about, (3) and behavioral intentions toward some object—within the context of marketing, usually a brand or retail store. These components are viewed together since they are highly interdependent and together represent forces that influence how the consumer will react to the object.

BELIEFS

The first component is beliefs. A consumer may hold both positive beliefs toward an object (e.g., coffee tastes good) as well as negative beliefs (e.g., coffee is easily spilled and stains papers). In addition, some beliefs may be neutral (coffee is black), and some may be differ in valance depending on the person or the situation (e.g., coffee is hot and stimulates—good on a cold morning, but not good on a hot summer evening when one wants to sleep). Note also that the beliefs that consumers hold need not be accurate (e.g., that pork contains little fat), and some beliefs may, upon closer examination, be contradictory (e.g., that a historical figure was a good person but also owned slaves).

Since a consumer holds many beliefs, it may often be difficult to get down to a "bottom line" overall belief about whether an object such as McDonald's is overall good or bad.

AFFECT

Consumers also hold certain feelings toward brands or other objects. Sometimes these feelings are based on the beliefs (e.g., a person feels nauseated when thinking about a hamburger because of the tremendous amount of fat it contains), but there may also be feelings which are relatively independent of beliefs. For example, an extreme environmentalist may believe that cutting down trees is morally wrong, but may have positive affect toward Christmas trees because he or she unconsciously associates these trees with the experience that he or she had at Christmas as a child.

BEHAVIORAL INTENTION

The behavioral intention is what the consumer plans to do with respect to the object (e.g., buy or not buy the brand). As with affect, this is sometimes a logical consequence of beliefs (or affect), but may sometimes reflect other circumstances—e.g., although a consumer does not really like a restaurant, he or she will go there because it is a hangout for his or her friends.

ATTITUDE-BEHAVIOR CONSISTENCY

Consumers often do not behave consistently with their attitudes for several reasons:

Ability. He or she may be unable to do so. Although junior high school student likes pick-up trucks and would like to buy one, she may lack a driver's license.

Competing demands for resources. Although the above student would like to buy a pickup truck on her sixteenth birthday, she would rather have a computer, and has money for only one of the two.

Social influence. A student thinks that smoking is really cool, but since his friends think it's disgusting, he does not smoke.

Measurement problems. Measuring attitudes is difficult. In many situations, consumers do not consciously set out to enumerate how positively or negatively they feel about mopeds, and when a market researcher asks them about their beliefs about mopeds, how important these beliefs are, and their evaluation of the performance of mopeds with respect to these beliefs, consumers often do not give very reliable answers. Thus, the consumers may act consistently with their true attitudes, which were never uncovered because an erroneous measurement was made.

ATTITUDE CHANGE STRATEGIES

Changing attitudes is generally very difficult, particularly when consumers suspect that the marketer has a self-serving agenda in bringing about this change (e.g., to get the consumer to buy more or to switch brands).

Changing affect. One approach is to try to change affect, which may or may not involve getting consumers to change their beliefs. One strategy uses the approach of classical conditioning try to "pair" the product with a liked stimulus. For example, we "pair" a car with a beautiful woman. Alternatively, we can try to get people to like the advertisement and hope that this liking will "spill over" into the purchase of a product. For example, the Pillsbury Doughboy does not really emphasize the conveyance of much information to the consumer; instead, it attempts to create a warm, fuzzy image. Although Energizer Bunny ads try to get people to believe that their batteries last longer, the main emphasis is on the likeable bunny. Finally, products which are better known, through the mere exposure effect, tend to be better liked—that is, the more a product is advertised and seen in stores, the more it will generally be liked, even if consumers to do not develop any specific beliefs about the product.

Changing behavior. People like to believe that their behavior is rational; thus, once they use our products, chances are that they will continue unless someone is able to get them to switch. One way to get people to switch to our brand is to use temporary price discounts and coupons; however, when consumers buy a product on deal, they may justify the purchase based on that deal (i.e., the low price) and may then switch to other brands on deal later. A better way to get people to switch to our brand is to at least temporarily obtain better shelf space so that the product is more convenient. Consumers are less likely to use this availability as a rationale for their purchase and may continue to buy the product even when the product is less conveniently located. (Notice, by the way, that this represents a case of shaping).

Changing beliefs. Although attempting to change beliefs is the obvious way to attempt attitude change, particularly when consumers hold unfavorable or inaccurate ones, this is often difficult to achieve because consumers tend to resist. Several approaches to belief change exist:

1. Change currently held beliefs. It is generally very difficult to attempt to change beliefs that people hold, particularly those that are strongly held, even if they are inaccurate. For example, the petroleum industry advertised for a long time that its profits were lower than were commonly believed, and provided extensive factual evidence in its advertising to support this reality. Consumers were suspicious and rejected this information, however.

2. Change the importance of beliefs. Although the sugar manufacturers would undoubtedly like to decrease the importance of healthy teeth, it is usually not feasible to make beliefs less important—consumers are likely to reason, why, then, would you bother bringing them up in the first place?

However, it may be possible to strengthen beliefs that favor us—e.g., a vitamin supplement manufacturer may advertise that it is extremely important for women to replace iron lost through menstruation. Most consumers already agree with this, but the belief can be made stronger.

3. Add beliefs. Consumers are less likely to resist the addition of beliefs so long as they do not conflict with existing beliefs. Thus, the beef industry has added beliefs that beef (1) is convenient and (2) can be used to make a number of creative dishes. Vitamin manufacturers attempt to add the belief that stress causes vitamin depletion, which sounds quite plausible to most people.
4. Change ideal. It usually difficult, and very risky, to attempt to change ideals, and only few firms succeed. For example, Hard Candy may have attempted to change the ideal away from traditional beauty toward more unique self expression.

ONE-SIDED VS. TWO-SIDED APPEALS

Attitude research has shown that consumers often tend to react more favorably to advertisements which either (1) admit something negative about the sponsoring brand (e.g., the Volvo is a clumsy car, but very safe) or (2) admits something positive about a competing brand (e.g., a competing supermarket has slightly lower prices, but offers less service and selection). Two-sided appeals must, contain overriding arguments why the sponsoring brand is ultimately superior—that is, in the above examples, the "but" part must be emphasized.

THE ELABORATION LIKELIHOOD MODEL (ELM) AND CELEBRITY ENDORSEMENTS

The ELM suggests that consumers will scrutinize claims more in important situations than in unimportant ones. For example, we found that in the study of people trying to get ahead of others in a line to use photo copiers, the compliance rate was about fifty percent when people just asked to get ahead. However, when the justification "... because I have to make copies" was added, compliance increased to 80%. Since the reason offered really did not add substantive information, we conclude that it was not extensively analyzed—in the jargon of the theory, "elaboration" was low.

The ELM suggests that for "unimportant" products, elaboration will be low, and thus Bill Cosby is able to endorse Coke and Jell-O without having any special credentials to do so. However, for products which are either expensive or important for some other reason (e.g., a pain reliever given to a child that could be harmed by using dangerous substances), elaboration is likely to be more extensive, and the endorser is expected to be "congruent," or compatible, with the product. For example, a basket ball player is likely to be effective in endorsing athletic shoes, but not in endorsing automobiles. On the other hand, a nationally syndicated auto columnist would be successful in endorsing cars, but not athletic shoes. All of them, however, could endorse fast food restaurants effectively.

APPEAL APPROACHES

Several approaches to appeal may be used. The use of affect to induce empathy with advertising characters may increase attraction to a product, but may backfire if consumers believe that people's feelings are being exploited. Fear appeals appear to work only if (1) an optimal level of fear is evoked—not so much that people tune it out, but enough to scare people into action and (2) a way to avoid the feared stimulus is explicitly indicated—e.g., gingivitis and tooth loss can be avoided by using this mouth wash. Humor appears to be effective in gaining attention, but does not appear to increase persuasion in practice. In addition, a more favorable attitude toward the advertisement may be created by humorous advertising, which may in turn result in increased sales. Comparative advertising, which is illegal in many countries, often increases sales for the sponsoring brand, but may backfire in certain cultures.

Online marketing can serve several purposes:

- Actual sales of products—e.g., Amazon.com.
- Promotion/advertising: Customers can be quite effectively targeted in many situations because of the context that they, themselves, have sought out. For example, when a consumer searches for a specific term in a search engine, a "banner" or link to a firm selling products in that area can be displayed. Print and television advertisements can also feature the firm's web address, thus inexpensively drawing in those who would like additional information.
- Customer service: The site may contain information for those who no longer have their manuals handy and, for electronic products, provide updated drivers and software patches.
- Market research: Data can be collected relatively inexpensively on the Net. However, the response rates are likely to be very

unrepresentative and recent research shows that it is very difficult to get consumers to read instructions. This is one of the reasons why the quality of data collected online is often suspect.

ECONOMICS OF ELECTRONIC COMMERCE

Some people have suggested that the Internet may be a less expensive way to distribute products than traditional "brick-and-mortar" stores. However, in most cases, selling online will probably be more costly than selling in traditional stores due to the high costs of processing orders and direct shipping to the customer. Some products may, however, be economically marketed online. Some factors that are relevant in assessing the potential for e-commerce to be an effective way to sell a specific products are:

- "Value-to-bulk" ratio. Products that have a lot of value squeezed into a small volume (e.g., high end jewelry and certain electronic products) are often more cost-effective to ship to end-customers than are bulkier products with less value (e.g., low end furniture).
- Absolute margins. Some products may have a rather high percentage margin—e.g., a scarf bought at wholesale at $10 and marked up 100% to be sold at $20. However, the absolute margin is only $20-$10=$10. In contrast, a laptop computer may be bought at $1,000 and be marked up by only 15%, or $150, for a total price of $1,150. Here, however, the absolute margin will be larger—$150. This allows the merchant to spend money on processing, packaging, and shipping the order. Ten dollars, in contrast, can only cover a small amount of employee time and very limited packaging and shipping. Some online merchants do charge for shipping, but doing so will ultimately make the online merchant less competitive.
- Extent of customization needed. Some products need to be customized—e.g., checks have to be personalized and airline tickets have to be issued for a specific departure site, destination time, and travel time. Here, online processing may be useful because the customer can do much of the work.
- Willingness of customers to pay for convenience. Some consumers may be willing to pay for the convenience of having products delivered to their door. For example, delivering high

bulk, generally low value groceries is generally not efficient. However, for some customers, it may be worthwhile to pay to avoid an inconvenient trip to the grocery store.

- Geographic dispersal of customers. Electronic commerce, when value-to-bulk ratios and absolute margins are not favorable, is often not viable when customers are located conveniently close to a retail outlet. However, for some products—e.g., bee keeping equipment—customers are widely geographically dispersed and thus, a centralized distribution center may be more economically viable. Specialty books—e.g., for collectors of vintage automobiles—may not be worthwhile for bookstores to stock, and these may thus be economically sold online.
- Vulnerability of inventory to loss of value. Some products—especially high tech products—have a very high effective carrying costs. It has been estimated that because of the rapid technological progress made in the computer field, computer parts may lose as much as 1.5% of their value per week. If shipping directly to the customer can reduce the channel time by five weeks, this potentially "rescues" as much as 7.5% of the product value. In such a situation, then, trying to reach the customer directly may make sense, even if the direct costs of distribution are higher, because of the inventory value issue.

There are a number of economic realities of online competition:

- As discussed, costs of handling online orders is often higher than that of distributing through traditional stores.
- Even if online selling is more cost effective in some situations, a firm selling online will, in the long run, be competing with other online merchants—not just against traditional "brick-and-mortar" stores. By the forces of supply and demand, online prices will then be driven down so that the profit from selling online will be no greater than that from traditional retailing. Any reduced costs would then be expected to go to customers.

  Competition will be greater for products that have large markets than for those where markets are smaller and more specialized. Amazon.com, for example, has found it necessary to discount best selling books deeply. Higher prices—closer to the list price—can be charged for specialty books, but for a large part of the market, competition will be intense.

- A new online merchant will face competition from established traditional merchants. These will often have the cash reserves to stay in business for a long time even with temporary competition. The online merchant, if it has no cash reserves other than stockholders' investment, may run out of cash before it can become profitable.

ISSUES IN WEB SITE DESIGN

Web site design: The web designer must make various issues into consideration:

- Speed vs. aesthetics: As we saw, some of the fancier sites have serious problems functioning practically. Consumers may be impressed by a fancy site, or may lack confidence in a firm that offers a simple one. Yet, fancier sites with extensive graphics take time to download—particularly for users dialing in with a modem as opposed to being "hard" wired—and may result in site crashes.
- Keeping users on the site: A large number of "baskets" are abandoned online as consumers fail to complete the "check-out" process for the products they have selected. One problem here is that many consumers are drawn away from a site and then are unlikely to come back. A large number of links may be desirable to consumers, but they tend to draw people away. Taking banner advertisers on your site from other sites may be profitable, but it may result in customers lost.
- Information collection: An increasing number of consumers resist collection of information about them, and a number of consumers have set up their browsers to disallow "cookies," files that contain information about their computers and shopping habits.

Cyber-consumer behavior: In principle, it is fairly easy to search and compare online, and it was feared that this might wipe out all margins online. More recent research suggests that consumers in fact do not tend to search very intently and that large price differences between sites persist. We saw above the problem of keeping consumers from prematurely departing from one's site.

Site content. The content of a site should generally be based on the purposes of operating a site. For most sites, however, having a clear purpose be evident is essential. The site should generally provide some evidence for this position. For example, if the site claims a large selection, the vast choices offered should be evident. Sites that claim convenience should make this evident. A main purpose of the Internet is to make information readily available, and the site should be designed so that finding the needed information among all the content of the site is as easy as possible. Since it is easy for consumers to move to other sites, the site should be made interesting. To provide the information and options desired by customers, two-way interaction capabilities are essential.

WEB SITE TRAFFIC GENERATION

The web is now so large that getting traffic to any one site can be difficult. One method is search engine optimization, a topic that will be covered below. Other methods include "viral" campaigns wherein current users are used to spread the word about a site, firm, or service. For example, Hotmail attaches a message to every e-mail sent from its service alerting the recipient that a free e-mail account can be had there. Google offers a free e-mail account with a full gigabyte of storage. This is available only by invitation from others who have such e-mail accounts. Amazon.com at one point invited people, when they had completed a purchase, to automatically e-mail friends whose e-mail addresses they provided with a message about what they had just bought. If the friend bought any of the same items, both the original customer and the friend would get a discount.

Another method of gaining traffic is through online advertising. Sites like Yahoo! are mainly sponsored by advertisers, as are many sites for newspapers and magazines. Individuals who see an ad on these sites can usually click to go to the sponsor's web site. Occasionally, a firm may advertise their sites in traditional media. Geico, Dell Computer, and Progressive Insurance do this. Overstock.com has also advertised a lot on traditional TV programs. Conventional advertising may also contain a web site address as part of a larger advertising message.

Viral marketing is more suitable for some products than for others. To get others involved in spreading the word, the product usually must be interesting and unique. It must also be simple enough so that it can be explained briefly. It is most useful when switching or trial costs are low. It is more difficult, for example, getting people to sign up for a satellite system or cellular phone service where equipment has to be bought up front and/or a long term contract is required makes viral marketing more difficult. Viral marketing does raise some problems about control of the campaign. For example, if a service is aimed at higher income countries and residents there spread the word to consumers in lower income countries, people attracted may be unprofitable. For Google's one gigabyte e-mail account, for example, there are large costs that may be covered by advertising revenues from ads aimed at people who can afford to buy products and services. Advertisers, however, may not be willing to pay for targets who cannot afford their products. It is also difficult to control "word of mouth" (or "word of keyboard"). Measuring the effectiveness of a campaign may be difficult. When a viral campaign relies on e-mail, messages received may be considered spam by some recipients, leading to potential brand damage and loss of goodwill.

One way to generate traffic is promotions. Many sites often offer new customers discounts or free gifts. This can be expensive, but sometimes, the gifts can be ones that have a low marginal cost. For example, once the firms pays for the development of a game, the cost of letting new users download it is modest. The U.S. army uses this approach in making a game available. To be allowed to use some of the "cooler" features, the user has to go through various stages of "basic training."

SEARCH ENGINE OPTIMIZATION

Many Internet users find desired information and sites through search engines such as Google. Research shows that a large proportion of the traffic goes to the first three sites listed, and few people go so sites that appear beyond the first "page" or screen. On Google, the default screen size is ten sites, so being in the top ten is essential.

Because of the importance of search engines, getting a good ranking or coming up early on the list for important keywords is vitally important. Many consultants offer, for large fees, to help improve a site's ranking.

There are several types of sites that are similar to search engines. Directories involve sites that index information based on human analysis. Several issues in search engines and directories are important. Some search engines, such as Google, base rankings strictly on merit (although sites are allowed to get preferred paid listings on the right side of the screen). Other search engines allow sites to "bid" to get listed first. Some sites may end up paying as much as a dollar for each surfer who clicks through. If a potential customer is valuable enough, it may be worth paying for enhanced listings. Often, however, it is better to be listed as number two or three since only more serious searchers are likely to go beyond the first site. The first listed site may attract a number of people who click through without much serious inspection of the site.

Some search engines are more specific than others. The goal of Google, Yahoo! and MSN is to contain as many sites as possible. Others may specialize in sites of a specific type to reduce the amount of irrelevant information that may come up.

Search engines often have different types of strategies. Google is very much technology oriented while Yahoo! appears to be more market oriented. Another major goal of Google is speed. Some sites may contain more content of one type than another. For example, AltaVista appears to have more images, as opposed to text pages, indexed.

SEARCH ENGINE RANKINGS

The order in which different sites are listed for a given term is determined by a secret algorithm developed by the search engine. An algorithm is a collection of rules put together to identify the most relevant sites. The specific algorithms are highly guarded trade secrets, but most tend to heavily weigh the number of links from other sites to a site and the keywords involved.

More credit is given for a link from a highly rated site—thus, having a link from CNN.com would count much more than one from the site of the Imperial Valley Press. On any given page, the weight given from a link will depend on the total number of links on that page. Having one of one hundred links will count less than being the only one. One source reports that the weight appears to be proportional so that one out of one hundred links would carry one percent of the weight of being the sole link, but that may change and/or vary among search engines.

For Google, some of the main ranking factors appear to be:

- Number and quality of links to the site, as discussed above.
- Relevant keywords. Note that the ranking algorithm tests for "spam." Reckless repeating keywords may actually count against the rating of the site.
- The "click-through" share of the site. Since late 2006 or early 2007, Google reportedly fine-tunes rankings by observing the percentage of the time that a particular site is chosen for a given set of search terms. Sites that are selected more frequently may improve in rank and those less frequently selected—despite their merits presumed from the other factors—may move down.

TYPES OF SEARCH ENGINES

Some engines, such as Google, are general purpose search engines. Some are specialized. Some are hybrids, containing some directory structure in addition to search engine capabilities. Some "reward" sites such as iwon.com attract people by allowing them to enter a lottery when doing a search. Some sites are aggregator sites—they do not have their own databases but instead combine the results from simultaneous searches on other search engines.

TEXT OPTIMIZATION

It is important to repeat important words as much as possible subject to credibility. Search engines today are increasingly sophisticated in identifying "spamming" through frivolous repetition of the same words or early use of words that are not relevant to the main content of the site. Words that appear early in the text and on the index page will tend to be weighted more heavily. For some search engines, it may be useful to include common misspellings of a word so that the site will come up when that spelling is used. Some web site owners have attempted to include hidden text so that a search engine would find the desired words while the visitor would see something else. Some web designers, for example, would hide text behind a graphic, make the text in a very small font, and/or make the font color the same, or nearly the same, as the background. Other web site designers have made a "legitimate" site, only to have a command to move the visitor to another site when they go to the searched site. Search engines today are increasingly able to detect this type of abuse, and sites may be penalized as a result.

Early search engines relied heavily on "meta tags" where the web site creator specified what he or she believed to be appropriate keywords, content descriptions, and titles. Because these tags are subject to a lot of abuse, these no longer appear to be significant.

LINK OPTIMIZATION

Many web sites engage in "link exchanges"—that is, complementary sites will agree to feature links to each other. It may be useful for a webmaster to ask firms whose content does not compete for a link. Sites should register with the Open Directory Project at http://www.dmoz.org since, if a site is classified favorably, this may help rankings.

Today, the most significant factor in search engine rankings appears to be the "value" of the links that reach a site. Links from "low value" sites (those that are not rated highly, and especially those considered to the "spam") count for very little. Links from highly rated sites on the relevant keywords count for literally thousands—sometimes tens and hundreds of thousands—times as much as less important site. In the past, the presence of important key terms on a site was the main driver of rankings, subject to some rudimentary safeguards against obvious "spamming" sites which used the words as a way to gain rankings without providing relevant information. Now, the effect of keywords is secondary except for searches that involve a very unique key term. Within the last year, it appears that Google has incorporated the frequency of "click-through" for a site when it is listed in search ("organic") results. That is, if a relatively high proportion of searchers go to the site, its ranking is likely to decrease. However, if relatively few searchers actually end up going to a highly ranked site when it shows up in search listings, that site is likely to lose rank. Search engines cannot usually measure the amount of traffic that goes to a site. Traditionally, then, the traffic of a site was not directly incorporated into the ranking system. Today, however, Google is reported to weigh the percentage that a site is chosen for click-through when the site comes up in a search. That is, if a site is initially highly ranked, if a small proportion of searchers actually choose to go to that site, this site is likely to have its rank reduced.

Google now offers a set of "Analytics" tools, including a set of web traffic statistics. Webmasters can sign up voluntarily to participate in this by placing certain "meta tag" code in their web pages. (This code is invisible to people viewing the respective web page in its regular display mode). Therefore, for such sites, Google does, in principle, have access to traffic information from all sources, including other search engines or links from other sites. It is not clear whether Google actually uses this information, however.

ORGANIZATIONAL BUYERS

A large portion of the market for goods and services is attributable to organizational, as opposed to individual, buyers. In general, organizational buyers, who make buying decisions for their companies for a living, tend to be somewhat more sophisticated than ordinary consumers. However, these organizational buyers are also often more risk averse. There is a risk in going with a new, possibly better (lower price or higher quality) supplier whose product is unproven and may turn out to be problematic. Often the fear of running this risk is greater than the potential rewards for getting a better deal. In the old days, it used to be said that "You can't get fired for buying IBM." This attitude is beginning to soften a bit today as firms face increasing pressures to cut costs.

Organizational buyers come in several forms. Resellers involve either wholesalers or retailers that buy from one organization and resell to some other entity. For example, large grocery chains sometimes buy products directly from the manufacturer and resell them to end-consumers. Wholesalers may sell to retailers who in turn sell to consumers. Producers also buy products from sub-manufacturers to create a finished product. For example, rather than manufacturing the parts themselves, computer manufacturers often buy hard drives, motherboards, cases, monitors, keyboards, and other components from manufacturers and put them together to create a finished product. Governments buy a great deal of things. For example, the military needs an incredible amount of supplies to feed and equip troops. Finally, large institutions buy products in huge quantities. For example, UCR probably buys thousands of reams of paper every month.

Organizational buying usually involves more people than individual buying. Often, many people are involved in making decisions as to a) whether to buy, (b) what to buy, (c) at what quantity, and (d) from whom. An engineer may make a specification as to what is needed, which may be approved by a manager, with the final purchase being made by a purchase specialist who spends all his or her time finding the best deal on the goods that the organization needs. Often, such long purchase processes can cause long delays. In the government, rules are often especially stringent—e.g., vendors of fruit cake have to meet fourteen pages of specifications put out by the General Services Administration. In many cases, government buyers are also heavily bound to go with the lowest price. Even if it is obvious that a higher priced vendor will offer a superior product, it may be difficult to accept that bid.

Note: MICROS Systems is a designer, manufacturer and marketer of enterprise information solutions for the global hospitality and specialty retail industries. Its offerings include software, hardware, and services comprising enterprise systems integration, consulting and support. The company operates in the US, Europe, Pacific Rim and Latin America. It is headquartered in Columbia, Maryland and employs 4,619 people. For a very good case study regarding this topic, reader can visit company's website www.micros.com

Bibliography

A. A. Luchak, "What Kind of Voice Do Loyal Employees Use?" *British Journal of Industrial Relations*, March 2003.

A. Bryman, "Leadership in Organizations," in *Handbook of Organization Studies,* ed. S.R. Clegg, C. Hardy, and W.R. Nord, Thousand Oaks, CA: Sage, 1996.

A.D. Galinsky, J. Stone, and J. Cooper, "The Reinstatement of Dissonance and Psychological Discomfort Following Failed Affirmation," *European Journal of Social Psychology*, 2000.

A.M. Eagly and S. Chaiken, *The Psychology of Attitudes*, Orlando, FL: Harcourt Brace Jovanovich, 1993.

A.P. Brief, *Attitudes in and around Organizations*, Thousand Oaks, CA: Sage, 1998.

A.R. Damasio, *Descartes 'Error: Emotion. Reason, and the Human Brain*, New York: Putnam Sons, 1994.

B. Miller, "Brann Baltimore Marketing Finn's Office Gets a Fun Make-over," *Daily Record,* October, 2002.

B. Motion, "Positive Work Environment Keeps Them Happy, Staffers Say," *Vancouver Sun,* October, 2004.

B.K. Hunnicutt, *Kellogg's Six-Hour Day*, Philadelphia: Temple University Press, 1996.

B.M. Bass, "From Transactional to Transformational Leadership," *Organizational Dynamics,* Winter 1990.

C.A. Higgins, T.A. Judge, and G.R. Ferns, "Influence Tactics and Work Outcomes: A Meta-Analysis," *Journal of Organizational Behavior*, 2003.

C.M. Falbe and G. Yukl, "Consequences for Managers of Using Single Influence Tactics and Combinations of Tactics," *Academy of Management Journal*, 1992.

Carter, "How a Hit Almost Failed Its Own Audition," *The New York Times,* April, 2006.

D. Hamilton, "Women to Watch: Susan Desmond-Hill-mann," *The Wall Street Journal,* October, 2005.

D. Rynecki, "Putting the Muscle Back into the Bull," *Fortune,* April, 2004.

D.C. McClelland, *Power: The Inner Experience*, New York: Irvington, 1975.

D.M. Rousseau et al., "Not So Different after All: A Cross-Discipline View of Trust," *Academy of Management Review*, 1998.

D.V Day and R.G. Lord, "Executive Leadership and Organizational Performance: Suggestions for a New Theory and Methodology," *Journal of Management*, 1988.

E.A. Locke, "Why Emotional Intelligence Is an Invalid Concept," *Journal of Organizational Behavior,* 2005.

E.J. Zajac and J.D. Westphal, "Director Reputation, CEO-Board Power, and the Dynamics of Board Interlocks," *Administrative Science Quarterly*, 1996.

E.M. Heffes, "Follow These Leaders," *Financial Executive,* April 2005.

E.W. Morrison and S.L. Robinson, "When Employees Feel Betrayed: A Model of How Psychological Contract Violation Develops," *Academy of Management Review,* 1997.

F.F. Reichheld, *The Loyalty Effect*, Boston: Harvard Business School Press, 1996.

G. Bethune, "From Worst to First," *Fortune,* May, 1998.

G. Morgan, *Images of Organization*, Beverley Hills: Sage, 1985.

G. Yukl and R. Lepsinger, "Why Integrating the Leading and Managing Roles Is Essential for Organizational Effectiveness," *Organizational Dynamics*, 2005.

G.D. Gottfredson and J.L. Holland, "A Longitudinal Test of the Influence of Congruence: Job Satisfaction, Competency Utilization, and Counter-productive Behavior," *Journal of Counseling Psychology*, 1990.

G.D. Gottfredson, "John L. Holland's Contributions to Vocational Psychology: A Review and Evaluation," *Journal of Vocational Behavior*, 1999.

G.N. Powell, "One More Time: Do Female and Male Managers Differ?" *Academy of Management Executive,* 1990.

G.R. Salancik, "Commitment and the Control of Organizational Behavior and Belief," in *New Directions in Organizational Behavior,* ed. B. M. Staw and G.R. Salancik, Chicago: St. Clair, 1977.

H. Mintzberg, "Managerial Work: Analysis from Observation," *Management Science*, 1971.

H. Mintzberg, *The Nature of Managerial Work*, New York: Harper & Row, 1973.

H. Selye, *Stress without Distress*, Philadelphia: J.B. Lippincott, 1974.

H.M. Weiss and R. Cropanzano, "Affective Events Theory: A Theoreti-cal Discussion of the Structure, Causes, and Consequences of Affective Experiences at Work," *Research in Organizational Behavior*, 1996.

J. Barling, T. Weber, and E.K. Kelloway, "Effects of Transformational Leadership Training on Attitudinal and Financial Outcomes: A Field Experiment," *Journal of Applied Psychology*, 1996.

J. Churchill, "To the Bitter End;" *Registered Rep.,* March, 2006.

J. Collins, *From Good to Great*, New York: Harper Collins, 2001.

J. Gleick, *Genius: The Life and Science of Richard Feynman*, New York: Vintage Books, 1992.

J. Kador, *Charles Schwab*, New York: Wiley, 2002.

J. Kotter, *The General Managers*, New York, Free Press, 1982.

J. Newman and D. Grigg, "Vancity's Robbery Intervention Program Wins Award," *Vancouver Sun,* October, 2004.

J. Porterfiled and B.H. Kleiner. "A New Era: Women and Leadership," *Equal Opportunities International*, 2005.

J. Rutenberg, "At Fox News, The Colonel Who Wasn't," *The New York Times,* April, 2002.

J. Thottam, "Reworking Work," *Time,* July 25, 2005.

J. Tupponce, "Listening to Those Inner Voices," *Richmond Times-Dispatch,* May, 2003.

J. Voight, "When Credit Is Not Due," *Adweek,* March, 2004.

J.A. Bargh and M.J. Ferguson, "Beyond Behaviorism: On the Automaticity of Higher Mental Processes," *Psychological Bulletin*, 2000.

J.A. Wall and R.R. Callister, "Conflict and Its Management," *Journal of Management*, 1995.

J.B. Rosener, "Ways Women Lead," *Harvard Business Review*, November-December 1990.

J.C. Quick et al., *Preventive Stress Management in Organizations*, Washington, DC: American Psychological Association, 1997.

J.J. Zhao, "The Chinese Approach to International Business Negotiation," *Journal of Business Communication,* July, 2000.

J.L. Holland, *Making Vocational Choices: A Theory of Careers*, Englewood Cliffs, NJ: Prentice-Hall, 1973.

J.L. Howard, "Workplace Violence in Organizations: An Exploratory-Study of Organizational Prevention Techniques," *Employee Responsi-bilities and Rights Journal*, June 2001.

J.M. Burns, *Leadership*, NewYork: Harper& Row, 1978.

J.P. Kotter, "Power, Dependence, and Effective Management," *Harvard Business Review,* July-August 1977.

J.P. Kotter, "What Leaders Really Do," *Harvard Business Review*, 1990.

J.P. Meyer et al., "Organizational Commitment and Job Performance: It's the Nature of the Commitment That Counts," *Journal of Applied Psychology*, 1989.

J.P. Meyer, "Organizational Commitment," *International Review of Industrial and Organizational Psychology*, 1997.

J.S. House, *Work Stress and Social Support*, Reading, MA: Addison-Wesley, 1981.

J.Z. Rubin and B.R. Brown, *The Social Psychology of Bargaining and Negotiation*, New York: Academic Press, 1976.

K. Danna and R.W. Griffin, "Health and Well-Being in the Workplace: A Review and Synthesis of the Literature," *Journal of Management,* Spring, 1999.

L. Festinger, *A Theory of Cognitive Dissonance*, Evanston, IL: Row, Peterson, 1957.

L. Hill, *Becoming a Manager: How New Managers Master the Challenges of Leadership*, Boston: Harvard Business School Press, 2003.

L. Thompson, *The Mind and Heart of the Negotiator*, Upper Saddle River, NJ: Prentice-Hall, 2000.

L.A. Hill, *Becoming a Manager*, Boston: Harvard Business School Press, 1992.

L.L. Thompson, "Information Exchange in Negotiation," *Journal of Experimental Social Psychology,* 1991.

M.J. Withey and W.H. Cooper, "Predicting Exit, Voice, Loyalty, and Neglect," *Administrative Science Quarterly*, 1989.

M.L. Loughry, "Coworkers Are Watching: Performance Implications of Peer Monitoring," *Academy of Management Proceedings,* 2002.

N. Rhodes and W. Wood, "Self-Esteem and Intelligence Affect Influenceability: The Mediating Role of Message Reception," *Psychological Bulletin*, 1992.

N., Wasserman, B. Anand, and N. Nohira, *When Does Leadership Mat-ter?* Harvard Business School Working Paper, 2001.

P. Guenzi and O. Pelloni, "The Impact of Interpersonal Relationships on Customer Satisfaction and Loyalty to the Service Provider," *International Journal of Service Industry Management*, 2004.

P. Salovey, and J. Mayer, "Emotional Intelligence," *Imagination, Cognition, and Personality*, 1990.

P. Szuchman, "The Job-Share Advantage," *Working Mother*, May, 2002.

P.O. Northouse, *Leadership: Theory and Practice,* 3rd ed., Thousand Oaks, CA: Sage, 2004.

P.P. Drucker, "The New Workforce," *The Economist,* November, 2001.

PH. Kirn, R.L. Pinkley, and A.R. Fragale, "Power Dynamics in Negotiation," *Academy of Management Review*, 2005.

Pollack, "She's Winning Her Drug War," *The New York Times,* May, 2005.

R,M. Stogdill. *Handbook of Leadership*, New York: The Free Press, 1974.

R. Basch, "Doing Well by Doing Good," *Searcher Magazine,* January, 2005.

R. Drago, D. Black, and M. Wooden, *The Persistence of Long Work Hours,* Melbourne Institute Working Paper Series, Melbourne: Melbourne Institute of Applied Economic and Social Research, University of Melbourne, August, 2005.

R. Jacobs, "Using Human Resource Functions to Enhance Emotional Intelligence," in *The Emotionally Intelligent Workplace,* ed. C. Cherniss and D. Goleman, San Francisco: Jossey-Bass, 2001.

R. Kanter, "Power Failure in Management Circuits," *Harvard Business Review*, July-August 1979.

R. Madell, "Ground Floor," *Pharmaceutical Executive (Women in Pharma Supplement),* June, 2000.

R. Vonk, "Self-Serving Interpretations of Flattery: Why Ingratiation Works," *Journal of Personality and Social Psychology*, 2002.

R.A. Caro, *The Path to Power: The Early Years of Lyndon Johnson*, New York: Alfred A. Knopf, 1982.

R.B. Cialdini and N.J. Goldstein, "Social Influence: Compliance and Conformity," *Annual Review of Psychology*, 2004.

R.B. Zajonc, "Emotions," in *Handbook of Social Psychology,* ed. D.T. Gilbert, S.T. Fiske, and L. Gardner, New York: Oxford University Press, 1998.

R.C. Ringer and R.W. Boss, "Hospital Professionals' Use of Upward Influence Tactics," *Journal of Managerial Issues*, 2000.

R.H. Fazio, "On the Automatic Activation of Associated Evaluations: An Overview," *Cognition and Emotion*, 2001.

R.J. House and R.N. Aditya, "The Social Scientific Study of Leadership: Quo Vadis?" *Journal of Management*, 1997.

R.J. House et al., "Personality and Charisma in the U.S. Presidency: A Psychological Theory of Leadership Effectiveness," *Administrative Science Quarterly*, 1991.

R.T. Mowday, L.W. Porter, and R.M. Steers, *Employee Organization Linkages: The Psychology of Commitment, Absenteeism, and Turnover*, New York: Academic Press, 1982.

S. Craig, "Merrill Brokers Fired in Scandal Win $ 14 Million," *The Wall Street Journal,* January, 2006.

S. Doctoroff, "Reengineering Negotiations," *Sloan Management Review*, March 1998.

S. Keer and J.M. Jermier, "Substitutes for Leadership: Their Meaning and Measurement," *Organizational Behavior and Human Performance*, 1978.

S. Lieberson and J.F. O'Conner, "Leadership and Organizational Per-formance: A Study of Large Corporations," *American Sociological Review*, 1972.

S. Pulliam and A. Latour, "Lost Connection," *The Wall Street Journal,* January, 2005.

S. Rosenbush, "Five Lessons of the World-Com Debacle," Business Week Online, March, 2005.

S. Schachter, *The Psychology of Affiliation*, Palo Alto, CA: Stanford University Press: 1959.

S.L. Bellar, M. Helms, and D.E. Arfken, "The Glacial Change: Women on Corporate Boards," *Business Perspectives*, 2004.

T.A. Judge et al., "The Job Satisfaction-Job Performance Relationship: A Qualitative and Quantitative Review," *Psychological Bulletin*, 2001.

T.A. Judge, E.A. Locke, and C.C. Durham, "The Dispositional Causes of Job Satisfaction: A Core Evaluations Approach," *Research in Organizational Behavior*, 1997.

T.S. Heffner and J.R. Rentsch, "Organizational Commitment and Social Interaction: A Multiple Constituencies Approach," *Journal of Vocational Behavior*, 2001.

V. Schultz, "Reconceptualizing Sexual Harassment," *Yale Law Journa,* April, 1998

VL. Goodwin, J.C. Wofford, and J.L. Whittington "A Theoretical and Empirical Extension to the Transformational Leadership Construct," *Journal of Organizational Behavior*, November, 2001.

W. Bennis, *Why Leaders Can't Lead*, San Francisco: Jossey-Bass, 1989.

W. Gouldner, "The Norm of Reciprocity: A Preliminary Statement," *American Sociological Review*, 1960.

W.C. Kim and Mauborgne, "Tipping Point Leadership," *Harvard Business Review*, 2003.

W.G. Bennis and R.J. Thomas, *Geeks and Geezers*, Boston: Harvard Business School Press, 2002.

W.M. Ensel and N. Lin, "Physical Fitness and the Stress Process," *Journal of Community Psychology*, January 2004.

Index

A

Action, 1, 55

Activity, 30, 38, 42, 49, 107, 168, 173

Applications, 95, 151

Arousal, 10

Attitudes, 107, 108, 158, 220, 221, 222, 224, 239, 286, 287, 289, 301

Attractiveness, 60

Awareness, 62

B

Behaviour, 1, 3, 16, 19, 20, 21, 23, 27, 29, 33, 40, 41, 43, 50, 73, 95, 121, 123, 125, 127, 129, 135, 141, 143, 164, 169, 172, 173, 175, 212, 221, 235, 237, 238, 241, 242

Broadening, 58

Buyer, 4, 29, 31, 140, 242

C

Categories, 91

Characteristics, 4, 34, 56, 69, 80, 88, 153

Cheap, 109

Choice, 61, 121, 126, 170, 235

Close Followers, 101

Cognitive, 10, 125, 304

Collection, 162

Colours, 48, 194

Commerce, 32, 122, 141, 142, 226, 291, 292

Communication, 47, 67, 83, 86, 87, 116, 118, 120, 121, 155, 304

Comprehension, 10

Concern, 146, 169

Conformity, 61, 306

Conspicuousness, 60

Consumer, 1, 2, 3, 4, 7, 9, 11, 13, 15, 16, 18, 19, 20, 21, 23, 24, 32, 33, 40, 41, 43, 44, 50, 53, 55, 61, 70, 75, 86, 87, 95, 104, 105, 121, 123, 126, 129, 130, 131, 133, 135, 136, 143, 145, 147, 148, 162, 164, 167, 168, 169, 172, 173, 176, 177, 201, 220, 235, 245, 246, 247, 269, 286

Consumerism, 95, 130, 131, 167

Credibility, 60, 164

Culture, 29, 33, 34, 35, 37, 40, 47, 187, 188, 189, 238, 257, 258

Customer, 129, 138, 155, 157, 158, 199, 225, 243, 267, 290, 305

Cycles, 69, 70

D

Decision, 2, 4, 15, 16, 17, 18, 21, 31, 32, 65, 73, 77, 78, 108, 123, 200, 203, 205, 235, 241, 268, 271, 272

Demographics, 106, 194, 263

Design, 163, 227

Deviant, 172

Diffusion, 79, 84, 85, 88, 92, 215, 282

Dimensions, 35, 190, 259

Disposable, 23

Disposers, 74

Domestic, 44

E

Early Adopters, 90

Early Majority, 90

Economic, 23, 32, 68, 305

Education, 34, 107, 141

Elaboration, 10, 213, 224, 280, 289

Electronic, 183, 225, 226, 292

Emotional, 3, 10, 68, 75, 302, 305, 306

Employment, 67, 71, 72, 77, 106, 168, 195, 264

Empty, 72

Enduring, 8, 9

Engine, 230

Enhancement, 92

Enigma, 140

Environmental, 33, 50

Ethics, 167, 169, 170, 171

Expensive, 225

Experience, 59, 80, 302

Exporter, 44

Extent, 10, 226, 291

F

Factors, 7, 8, 16, 56, 59, 208, 275

Family, 53, 65, 66, 68, 69, 73, 74, 76, 78, 87, 107, 203, 204, 205, 271, 272

Feeling, 12

Fraudulent, 173

Frequency, 82

Friendship, 48, 53

G

Gatekeepers, 74

Gender, 41, 42, 78, 106

Generation, 33, 142, 143, 174, 192, 238, 262

Global, 45, 46, 136

Government, 241, 248

Groups, 51, 52, 53, 54, 55, 57, 58, 61, 237, 238

H

Hierarchy, 11

Household, 41, 65, 66

Howard, 27, 29, 32, 33, 304

I

Illegal, 173, 177, 195, 225, 247, 264, 290

Image, 126

Implications, 19, 46, 305

Importance, 3, 29, 88, 120, 145

Importer, 44

Income, 23, 107

Individual, 4, 38, 73, 89, 205, 238, 242, 272

Influences, 33, 37, 41, 50, 65, 77, 78, 206, 273

Innovators, 81, 88, 90, 92, 216, 282

Intensification, 102

Interpersonal, 83, 305

Introduction, 33, 51, 65, 135, 145, 151, 175, 220

Involvement, 7, 8, 9, 11, 12, 13, 80, 236

Issues, 11, 12, 21, 40, 95, 96, 98, 118, 123, 133, 137, 167, 168, 169, 175, 179, 180, 182, 186, 188, 191, 194, 195, 202, 205, 213, 217, 227, 230, 245, 249, 250, 252, 255, 256, 257, 261, 263, 270, 272, 280, 283, 293, 295

J

Journey, 171

K

Kids, 71

L

Laggards, 90, 92

Language, 191, 261

Late Followers, 101

Leadership, 79, 83, 301, 302, 303, 304, 305, 306, 307

Learning, 11, 24, 26, 27, 32, 209, 212, 238, 276, 278

Life, 3, 7, 33, 34, 36, 38, 39, 40, 43, 69, 107, 131, 137, 141, 145, 170, 186, 201, 203, 215, 216, 237, 239, 255, 269, 271, 281, 282

Loyalty, 126, 129, 302, 305

Luxury, 61, 71, 72, 151

M

Maintainers, 74

Marketing, 1, 19, 20, 21, 26, 32, 45, 57, 83, 89, 97, 98, 105, 106, 110, 111, 112, 116, 120, 121, 123, 129, 151, 152, 154, 156, 164, 175, 301

Married, 70, 71

Marshallian, 23

Meaning, 33, 51, 66, 79, 104, 306

Model, 11, 13, 23, 24, 26, 27, 29, 30, 221, 224, 289, 302

Motive, 2

Motives, 2, 3, 27

N

Nationality, 35, 41, 107

Nature, 2, 39, 303, 304

Network, 16, 24, 79, 106, 120, 187, 256

Nicosia, 30, 32

Non-Profit, 21

Numbers, 49

O

Objectives, 43, 98

Occupation, 41, 107

Online, 182, 183, 225, 229, 252, 253, 290, 307

Opinion, 79, 80, 81, 82, 83, 84, 219, 285

Optimization, 228, 230, 231, 232, 294, 295, 297

Organizational, 4, 5, 32, 105, 233, 234, 241, 242, 298, 299, 301, 302, 303, 304, 306, 307

Overlap, 82

P

Pavlovian, 24

Perception, 27, 148, 160, 202, 208, 239, 240, 270, 275

Personality, 29, 42, 43, 108, 202, 270, 305, 306

Pertinence, 4

Pioneers, 101

Planning, 97, 156

Policies, 43

Positioning, 20, 32, 112, 113, 122, 195, 198, 215, 264, 266, 281

Processing, 10, 13

Product, 2, 3, 7, 13, 20, 26, 28, 31, 32, 44, 60, 61, 80, 86, 88, 101, 108, 109, 113, 133, 176, 246

Psychoanalytical, 26

Psychology, 24, 175, 245, 301, 302, 303, 304, 305, 306, 307

Purchase, 2, 16, 29, 87, 125

R

Regarding, 11, 17, 21, 32, 75, 78, 106, 149, 165, 168, 242, 299

Relevance, 169

Research, 20, 32, 59, 142, 151, 152, 153, 156, 177, 178, 186, 189, 230, 240, 247, 248, 255, 258, 295, 303, 305, 307

Rights, 131, 304

Risk, 39, 62, 148, 240

Roles, 73, 302

S

Sector, 147

Segmentation, 20, 32, 76, 105, 106, 108, 110, 195, 196, 264

Shopping, 53, 54, 121, 123, 171

Singles, 70, 71

Situational, 8, 9, 236

Social, 8, 27, 29, 36, 41, 43, 48, 51, 54, 56, 80, 87, 96, 140, 177, 195, 222, 237, 241, 242, 246, 264, 287, 301, 304, 305, 306, 307

Societal, 21

Society, 1, 4, 21, 26, 33, 34, 35, 36, 37, 38, 39, 41, 56, 69, 73, 83, 107, 123, 130, 136, 170, 175, 176, 188, 192, 195, 238, 241, 245, 246, 257, 258, 261, 264

Sociological, 26, 67, 307

Solitary, 72

Space, 47, 194, 263

Spacious, 109

Sporty, 109

Stage, 27, 28, 77

Strategies, 19, 45, 92, 98, 104, 110, 222, 287

Study, 3, 304, 306, 307

Subcultures, 40

Summary, 31, 133

Symbols, 48, 194, 263

T

Tailoring, 118

Tangible, 46

Teenagers, 76

Things, 48

Thinking, 11, 12

Time, 29, 47, 87, 88, 134, 141, 142, 204, 271, 303

Traffic, 228

Transmission, 10, 31

V

Variation, 38, 47

Versus, 2, 4, 13, 35, 36, 51, 52, 53, 76

Y

Young, 70